A SUMER-ARYAN DICTIONARY

AN ETYMOLOGICAL LEXICON OF THE ENGLISH &
OTHER ARYAN LANGUAGES ANCIENT & MODERN
& THE SUMERIAN ORIGIN OF EGYPTIAN
& ITS HIEROGLYPHS

BY

L. A. WADDELL

LL.D., C.B., C.I.E.

Fellow of the Royal Anthropological Institute
Linnean and Folk-Lore Societies, Honorary
Correspondt. Indian Archæological Survey,
Ex-Professor of Tibetan, London
University.

PART I. A—F

With 5 Plates

LONDON
LUZAC & CO.
46 GREAT RUSSELL STREET, W.C.
1927

**Kessinger Publishing's Rare Reprints
Thousands of Scarce and Hard-to-Find Books!**

We kindly invite you to view our extensive catalog list at:
http://www.kessinger.net

PLATE I. [Frontispiece.

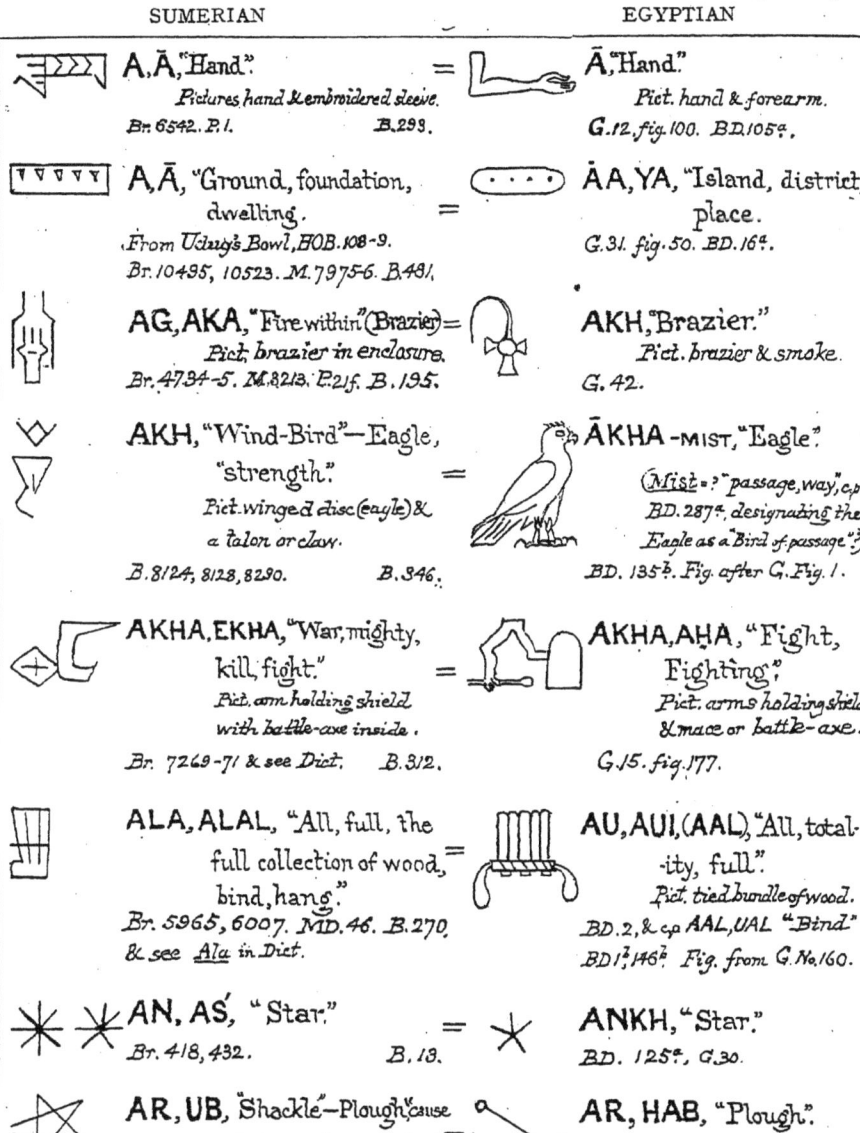

SUMERIAN ORIGIN OF EGYPTIAN HIEROGLYPHS.
(For continuation see Plates II-V.)

CONTENTS

	PAGE
INTRODUCTORY	ix
NEED FOR A COMPARATIVE SUMER-ARYAN DICTIONARY	xii
"ARYAN" ESSENTIALLY A RACIAL OR ETHNIC TERM	xiii
"SUMERIAN" AN ARBITRARY ETHNIC TERM OF ASSYRIOLOGISTS	xv
HOW THE SUMERIANS AND THEIR MONUMENTS WERE DISCOVERED AND THEIR WRITTEN LANGUAGE DECIPHERED	xv
THE SUMERIAN LANGUAGE IS ARYAN IN ITS STRUCTURE	xxvii
SUMERIAN SYLLABIC PICTURE-WRITING	xxviii
IDEOGRAPHS AND SYLLABIC WRITING	xxxi
HOMONYMS AND SYNONYMS	xxxii
SPELLING OF WORDS IN SUMERIAN AND IN LATER ARYAN LANGUAGES	xxxiii
THE WORD-LISTS IN THE DICTIONARY	xxxvi
EFFECTS OF THE DICTIONARY ON PHILOLOGY, ETYMOLOGY, ETHNOLOGY, FOLK-LORE AND HISTORY	xl
ABBREVIATIONS FOR REFERENCES	xlv

PLATES SHOWING SUMERIAN ORIGIN OF EGYPTIAN HIEROGLYPHS.

Pl. I. A-Ar	*Frontispiece*
Pl. II. Asaru-De	xxix
Pl. III. Er-Kha	xxxv
Pl. IV. Kha-Pad	xxxix
Pl. V. Pir-Ur	xliii

INTRODUCTORY

> "There was and is an *Aryan* Race, that is to say the characteristic modes of speech termed Aryan were developed among the Blond Longheads alone, however much some of these may have been modified by the importation of Non-Aryan elements."—HUXLEY.[1]

NOTHING has been known as to the racial and linguistic affinities of the Sumerians, the oldest of civilized peoples, whose monuments and vast city ruins in Mesopotamia began to be discovered some fifty years ago, but who seemed themselves after suddenly appearing there with a fully fledged higher civilization to have as suddenly disappeared after a comparatively brief existence as a nation and leaving no descendants to continue their culture and language. Study by leading Assyriologists and Sumerologists of their language and writing has tended rather to deepen than dispel the mystery surrounding them, for it has led to the conclusion, crystallized by continual repetition into a dogma that the language had no affinity with any recognized linguistic group, and that in particular it had no affinity whatever with the Aryan languages—the English and the continental languages of Europe and of India.

Thus the Sumerians with their marvellously high civilization, art, culture and language have hitherto been regarded as a sort of fossil curiosity, a remote and totally extinct alien race in no way related to any modern people nor to their civilization or language. The reverse is now found to be the fact.

In former works I have described the manner in which, in searching for clues to the lost origin of the early Aryans, our long lost racial ancestors of the "white race" to whom we owe our civilization and language, I was led by the facts to observe that the Sumerians were the Early Aryans;

---

[1] "The Aryan Question," *Nineteenth Century*, November 1890, 766.

that the portrait representations of the Sumerians on their own monuments and official and sacred seals are preponderatingly of the Aryan physical type;[1] that the "Sumerian" Language with its writing was the Early Aryan speech and script and the parent of the Aryan family of languages ancient and modern with their writing, and in particular the parent of the English, Anglo-Saxon, "Celtic," Gothic, Norse, Greek, Latin, Sanskrit and all unsuspectedly also, of the Ancient Egyptian languages and writing; that this Aryan speech with its writing was spread over the ancient world by the Phœnicians, who were not Semites, as hitherto supposed, but the leading seafaring branch of the Sumerians or Early Aryans.

Indeed, the arbitrariness of the Assyriologist dogma of the Non-Aryan nature of the Sumerian language was self-evident, in that it was admittedly not based upon any serious comparison of the languages themselves. Thus the leading Sumerologist in this country summarily dismisses the mere possibility of any such affinity with the words: " I am convinced that it [the Sumerian language] has no affinity with either the Caucasian, Aryan or Semitic groups. This side of the problem *has not occupied my attention as the futility of such efforts is at once apparent.*"[2] [*sic!*]

On the other hand, as the result of my actual detailed analysis and comparison of the Sumerian with the Aryan family of languages, I recorded that the Sumerian proved to be radically Aryan in its words, structure and script, and that " the whole family of Aryan languages with their written letters is derived from the Phœnician language and script and its parent the Sumerian, *and that about fifty per cent. of the commonest words in use in the English language to-day is discovered to be Sumerian in origin with the same word-form, sound and meaning.*"[3] And I gave many specific instances of the Sumerian origin of critical English

---

[1] The portrait statue of a chieftain of mongoloid racial type which has lately been unearthed by Sir J. Marshall in the excavations of the ancient city-site in the Indus Valley, which has yielded so many cultural objects and inscribed seals which I have termed " Indo-Sumerian " (WISD *passim*), in no way militates against the Aryan racial character of the Sumerians, for I have adduced the Indian Epic and Vedic evidence to show that that Sumerian colony traded with Tibet and conquered the mongoloid Sakas or Scyths of the Upper Indus Valley and incorporated them in the great Sumerian empire.

[2] LSG, 1911, ii.   [3] WPOB, xi.

and other Aryan and Egyptian words occurring incidentally in the texts of the Sumerian and Phœnician monuments and seals and on the prehistoric monuments of the Ancient Britons cited and translated therein. Further I adduced evidence for the Sumero-Phœnician origin of Egyptian civilization and its language and hieroglyphic writing, and found that Menes or *Aha* " the warrior," the First of the Pharaohs, and Sargon-the-Great were Aryan Sumero-Phœnicians—the former being clearly identified with the Mesopotamian emperor Manis-tusu or " Manis-the-warrior," the son of Sargon, and thus gaining for the first time a synchronism for Menes to fix his date, the most disputed of all critical dates in ancient history.

The present Dictionary, on the compilation of which I have been engaged more or less continuously for the past sixteen years, now gives the detailed results of my comparative analysis and exploration of the Sumerian and Aryan languages, and more especially in regard to the English language, which is disclosed as one of the chief branches of the Sumerian and Aryan Phœnician. It will be seen that where no Aryan affinity whatever has hitherto been found or even suspected by Assyriologists and Sumerologists as existing in Sumerian, practically all the Sumerian words are radically Aryan, and that over 75 per cent. of the current English words (numbering many thousands even from the radical word-signs and more common compound signs to which this Dictionary is limited) are derived from the Sumerian, and that the Ancient Egyptian language at present unsuspected of having any affinity with the Aryan is also with its system of hieroglyphic writing radically Aryan.

The Sumerian language, thus seen to have been evolved by our Aryan ancestors, has with the great spiritual and cultural current which it embodies flowed steadily down into our modern life, and so explains the remarkable fundamental unity of thought in the higher ancient civilizations which has endured down through the ages.

The vastly remote currency of Aryan words might indeed have been suspected from what we know of how poetic associations become attached and cling to words through long usage. And we may surmise that the rapid and enormous progress in literature with the revival of letters and the " word-magic " which characterizes the best poetry of both ancients and moderns—that of Homer and Virgil, of Dante, Shakespeare and Milton—have been due in a hitherto unsuspected degree to the long life and world-prevalence of the Aryan language which resulted from the enterprise of the Sumero-Phœnicians.

Need for a Comparative Sumer-Aryan Dictionary

In view of these discoveries, a comparative dictionary of the Sumer-Aryan family of words has now become a practical necessity, not only for expert philologists but also for the general educated public, English and other, in order to learn the original meaning, etymology and life-history of the Aryan words which they daily use. All the more so is this necessary, as etymology which is so essential for the right use of words is nevertheless sadly neglected nowadays in our schools and colleges, and the necessity voiced by Chaucer has not yet passed away:

> " And for there is so great diversite
> In English, and in writing of our tongue ;
> So pray I God that none mis-write thee." [1]

Until now, philologists and " purist " writers and speakers of the Aryan tongue, in seeking for the original meaning, etymology and pedigree of Aryan words, have been unable to go further back than the Greek and Sanskrit. Now, however, we go back some thousands of years farther to the common parent of all the Aryan languages. And we find that most of the common words in the English, " Anglo-Saxon " (now seen to be largely Briton), Gothic and Latin languages, supposed by classic scholars to be derived from the Greek, are now disclosed to be clearly derived independently of the latter from an earlier common parent, and often preserve purer forms than the Greek and Sanskrit.

As this work is written for the general educated reader, the following notes which seem called for by way of preliminary explanation have been rendered as free from technicalities as possible.

[1] *Troilus and Criseyde.*

SUMER-ARYAN DICTIONARY

"Aryan" essentially a Racial or Ethnic Term

The title "Aryan" is the Anglicized form of the Sanskrit *Arya*, "the noble or exalted," a term which is employed in Indian literature, ancient and modern, solely in a racial sense to designate the fair ruling and civilizing race as opposed to the dark aboriginal subject people, and India itself was called "the Land or Region of the Aryas (or Aryans)." It is also used in its proper racial sense by Huxley in the heading in designating the fair long-headed people, now mainly represented in Europe by the British and Norse or Scandinavians, the so-called "Nordics" of modern anthropologists.[1]

It is similarly used in a racial or ruling sense by the Sumerians, Akkads, Amorites and Hittites in its earlier form of *Ar*, *Ara*, *Ari*, *Har* or *Harri*, also meaning "exalted or noble" (see *Ar*, *Ara*, etc., in Dictionary), and similarly with a like meaning in Ancient Egypt (see *Hari*, *Heri* under *Ar* in Dictionary); and the ancient Greek name of *Aeria* or *Hariē* for Egypt, probably designated that country as "The Land of the *Ari* or Aryans." The Medes, as Herodotus records, were formerly called *Arii*; and "*Ariana*" or "Land of the *Ari*" was a title of Persia and the source of the modern name Iran for that land. The title *Harri* is used by the Mitani or the Early Medes, on their records of about 1400 B.C. Darius-the-Great calls himself on his tomb "an *Ariyo* of *Ariyo* descent." It is the *Her* title of the Ancient Goths, in their great epics, the Eddas, and the source of the modern *Herr* or "master" of Teutons and Scandinavians, of the Irish Celtic *Aira*, a "chief" or "nobleman," and of the *Ar* in aristocratic (see *Ari* "Aryan" in Dictionary).[2]

This title *Ar*, *Ari*, *Arya* or "Aryan," appears, as I have shown, to have originally designated the Early Aryans as "The ploughmen" from the Sumerian *Ar*, *Ara*, "plough," which is now disclosed as the source of the Old English *ear*, "to plough, to *ear* the ground" and of "ar-able," etc. (see *Ar*, "plough" in Dict.). The Aryans are now seen to have been the traditional inventors of the plough and of the Agricultural Era of the World;[3] and the sense of *Ara* or "the exalted ones" appears to

---

[1] See WPOB, 134 f.   [2] For further details see WPOB, 5 f, 132 f, 191 f, 257, 345 f.
[3] WOPB, 49, 170, 214, 338 f, 345 f, 354 f. This is supported by the ancient *Vedas*, the Psalms of the Hindus, which sometimes use the term "Cultivator" (*Krishna*) as the equivalent of *Arya* or "Aryan."

have been used for this title when this gifted race became the rulers of the various aboriginal tribes—the Sumerian also gives the plough sign the meaning of "raise up, exalt" as the secondary meaning of ploughing as "the uplifting" of the earth (see *Ara*, exalt, in the Dict.).

The present-day unwarranted restriction of this racial term "Aryan" to language was merely introduced about half a century ago by Germanic writers in order to support the "Teutonic" theory of the Teutonic origin of the English and Norse languages. Till then the Germans, largely owing to the writings and reputation of the English philologist Max Müller, were regarded as the leading European representatives of the Aryan race and language. In 1871, however, the eminent French anthropologist M. de Quatrefages conclusively demonstrated that the prevailing head-form of the Prussians, the dominant Germans, was *round*-headed and not *long*-headed, which is the Aryan type, thus proving that the Prussians (and with them the bulk of the German people) as a race were *not* Aryans at all. This was fully confirmed by subsequent observers and also in regard to the prevailing head-form throughout Germany. Forced in this way to abandon the *racial* use of "Aryan" for the Germans, Max Müller and the Germanic school still clung to the title of "Germanic or Teutonic" which they had gratuitously applied to the whole family of Aryan languages in Europe, and accordingly arbitrarily limited the use of "Aryan" to a linguistic sense. And by mere mechanical repetition, this nomenclature of "Germanic" or "Teutonic" as the equivalent of "Aryan language" in Europe is still used by docile English and continental philologists and grammar writers, excepting the French. The unfoundedness of this claim that the "German or Teutonic" language is the oldest and purest Aryan language in Europe is everywhere evidenced by the word-facts themselves throughout this comparative dictionary. It is there seen that the English, Briton, Anglo-Saxon, Eddic and Eastern Gothic, Norse, Celtic, French and Italian words generally all preserve relatively purer and older forms than the German, which moreover wants a considerable proportion of the most elementary Aryan words. Similarly in regard to the important Gothic groups, including the uniquely important famous ancient epic poems the Eddas, written in runes, and preserving a dialect of the Ancient Briton, to which the Teutons lay claim, it is significant, as the leading Runic scholar, Professor Stephens of Copenhagen has pointed out, that no runic monuments, so common in Britain, Norway, Sweden and Denmark, have ever been found in Germany.

"Sumerian" an arbitrary Ethnic Term of Assyriologists

The name "Sumerian" which is now applied by Assyriologists to this earliest civilized Non-Semitic people of Mesopotamia has never been found to have been used by these people themselves. It is coined by Assyriologists from the name "Sumer" which was applied to Lower Mesopotamia by the later Babylonians and Assyrians. The arbitrariness of this application is evidenced by the fact that this label was formerly attached by Assyriologists to the supposedly diametrically different race now called by them "Akkads" and whom they also arbitrarily term "Western Semites," but whom they previously called "Sumers," or "Sumerians." But latterly they arbitrarily reversed the labels with the result of adding still more to the confusion, as "Akkad" is a synonym for the Sumerian *Ari* (or Aryan) a title also of the Amorites who are admittedly non-Semites; and these "Akkads" from Sargon downwards I have shown are identical with leading early Aryan kings in the official king-lists recorded in the Indian Epics.

As this name "Sumerian" or "Sumer," however, has obtained currency for several decades as the title for these Early Non-Semitic civilized people in Mesopotamia, now found to be Aryans, and for their language, we are now forced to continue its use as such, despite its arbitrariness and misleading effects. Hence the present comparative Dictionary is styled "Sumer-Aryan."

How the Sumerians and their Monuments were Discovered and their Written Language Deciphered

The discovery of the "Sumerians" and their Language with the deciphering of the Sumerian writing is one of the greatest archæological romances of Science of the nineteenth century. It gains new and personal interest by the discovery that the Sumerians were our Early Aryan ancestors, and that their language with its writing was the parent of the

SUMER-ARYAN DICTIONARY

English and other Aryan languages with their alphabetic writing (see my *Aryan Origin of the Alphabet* now in the press). At the same time it illustrates the inveterate opposition of Semitic scholars to the discovery of the Truth regarding the racial authorship of Civilization and Writing.

The existence of the Sumerians and of their Non-Semitic language disclosing a remotely early civilized Non-Semitic ruling people of the ancient world wholly forgotten by Greek historians, was first elicited by the brilliant genius of Sir Henry Rawlinson in 1855. An officer of the East India Company's service, he had been sent as a lieutenant to Persia in 1833 to assist the Shah in the training of his army, and finding there in 1835 inscriptions in the as yet undeciphered cuneiform or "wedge" writing, he forthwith took up the task of intensive decipherment and became a leading pioneer explorer and in considerable part founder of the newly born science of Assyriology of his time.[1]

The key to the decipherment of the mysterious Babylonian and Assyrian writing and through it the Sumerian was eventually found in the cuneiform inscriptions of Persia of which Rawlinson was one of the pioneer decipherers, and of which large numbers had been brought to notice during the previous two centuries by travellers to Persepolis, the beautiful ancient Persian capital destroyed by Alexander, and as curiosities had been partially copied and published, but they remained undeciphered by orientalists.

The first observer to pave the way for the decipherment of these cryptic Persian cuneiform inscriptions was the Danish scientist Karsten Niebuhr. He was a member of an expedition sent by the Danish Government in 1761 to explore Arabia, where all the members of the ill-fated company perished except Niebuhr, who made his way under great privations to Bombay in 1764. Nothing daunted, after fourteen months stay at Bombay, he ventured forth to Mesopotamia and Persia to explore

---

[1] For fuller details see BRA, SAC, and JRAS X, 1846, 3 f. Latterly, Rawlinson, while consul-general at Bagdad, was Director-General of Excavations in Mesopotamia for the Trustees of the British Museum from 1846–1855, in which latter year he retired to devote himself entirely to cuneiform decipherment, and became Editor-in-chief for the publication of the vast body of cuneiform material then amassed in the British Museum, in the monumental five volumes of *Cuneiform Inscriptions of Western Asia* which, through its bilingual lists and Sumerian records continues to be a chief source of our knowledge of Babylonian and Sumerian words.

the famous ruins there. He spent three weeks at Persepolis making those complete and accurate copies of the inscriptions which together with his critical analysis of them made their decipherment possible. He observed that the inscriptions *always occurred in three distinct versions and in the same order*, and thus were presumably trilingual versions of the same record. He further noticed that the first version (afterwards discovered to be in Old Persian, an Aryan language) contained only forty-two signs usually separated by a dot, and he rightly inferred that this writing was *alphabetic;* and he actually drew up an alphabet of these signs, to which however he could not as yet assign letter-values which proved substantially correct, though it included punctuation marks and diphthongs. And he further observed rightly that this alphabetic writing was intended to be read from left to right as in European languages. Continuing these observations, another Danish scholar, Bishop F. Münter, in 1880, conjectured that a word which occurred near the beginning of each inscription in this first or alphabetic version signified " king," and this afterwards proved correct.

The first actual beginning of the decipherment of some words and letter-values in this first or alphabetic version of the Persian inscriptions was significantly made, not by an orientalist, but by an outsider, the Hanoverian schoolmaster G. F. Grotefend in 1802, using merely his common sense and scientific inductive methods. Adopting Niebuhr's suggestions that the inscriptions were trilingual and that the first version was alphabetic, he assumed that the first version would be in Old Persian, the language of the paramount ancient Persian kings, and that the other two versions were translations of the same record into the other two chief languages current in the old Persian empire, just as the later Persian kings were in the habit of translating their edicts into Turkish and Arabic for the information of the subjects who spoke those languages, and this ultimately proved correct. In analysing the first or " Persian " versions in the various inscriptions he accepted the recurrent word for " king " as suggested by Münter, and he read it provisionally as *Khsheh*, which was the Zend or ancient Persian word for " king " in the only Zend dictionary then known, instead of *Khshayathiya* as it afterwards proved to be—a name derived as we shall see from the Sumerian *Khat-ti* or

SUMER-ARYAN DICTIONARY

Xat-ti "a ruler" and the source of "*Satrap*" or subordinate ruler or governor. He then observed that the word in front of this word for "king," and which was presumably the personal name of the king, varied in different monuments, and that one of these front-names was peculiar to one set of monuments, whilst another of the front-names was peculiar to another set. Again other monuments gave both forms of these names, which he inferred represented the names of two ancient Persian kings in the relationship of son and father, with the latter in the genitive case, all of which proved to be correct. In this way he read, substantially correctly as it proved, the well-known classic names of Darius and Xerxes (the son of the former) and Hystaspes; and by the spelling thus elicited he succeeded in assigning correctly twelve letter-values to these hitherto wholly undeciphered Persian cuneiform signs. He presented his *Memoir* on 4th September 1802 to the Academy of Göttingen, but characteristically as he was an outsider and not an "established authority" they refused to print it.[1] As a result "for a whole generation the work of decipherment was allowed to sleep"!

Interest in Grotefend's discovery was partially revived in 1822 by the French orientalist Abbé Saint-Martin who adopted it and followed it up to some extent. This attracted the attention of the Sanskritists Emile Burnouf and the Norwegian Christian Lassen, both of whom published in 1836 almost simultaneously translations of the greater portions of the Persian alphabetic versions,[2] though they had correctly made out only about half of the Persian alphabet. Enough however was apparent to enable Lassen to show that the language was Aryan, and was Old Persian, a sister to the Zend and Sanskrit.

Meantime Rawlinson in Persia had taken up the task of decipherment in 1835 when, as military assistant to the governor of S.W. Persia, he visited Hamadan (Ecbatana) and copied the trilingual inscriptions there and at Behistun. Knowing only of the work of Grotefend, he detected the names of the three kings as described, *and independently made out his own working alphabet for the signs in the Persian version, and Rawlinson's alphabet proved to be the first practically complete alphabet of these*

---

[1] It was published elsewhere in 1815.
[2] Burnouf dealt specially with the Hamadan set.

signs. He was now the first to copy, decipher and translate the Persian version in the voluminous trilingual edict of Darius-the-Great carved on the great cliff at Behistun (and later of its other two versions), which through the extreme length of its text became a chief key to the decipherment of the Babylonian and through it of the Sumerian. In 1837 he sent to the Royal Asiatic Society a copy of the greater part of the Persian text of this edict with decipherment and translation of its opening passages and notes, which was a great advance on previous attempts on this script; but before it was published the articles of Lassen and Burnouf reached him, necessitating a revision of his work and the postponement of its publication. " By the beginning of 1839 he had deciphered and translated nearly all the 200 lines (of the Persian version), which he had copied from the Behistun text; and he says in his *Memoir* that in many cases Lassen had at that time understood neither the grammar nor the etymology of the texts he tried to translate. That same year he sent a supplementary paper to the Royal Asiatic Society containing a summary of the greater part of the Behistun text (Persian version). The translation which he made in 1839 is substantially the same as that published in his *Memoir* (received) in 1846, and modern scholars have succeeded in modifying it in a few details only. There is no doubt that before 1840 he had made himself the Father of the decipherment of the Persian cuneiform."[1]

But by far the greatest and most far-reaching problem still awaited solution, namely, the decipherment of the third version of the trilingual cuneiform,[2] which was early recognized to be Babylonian writing by the similarity and identity of its signs with those written on the clay tablets and monuments of Babylonia, and it still remained wholly undeciphered. The key to unlock the Babylonian writing had for long been recognized to be the Persian version of these trilingual cuneiform texts. But this key as it stood would not turn in the lock. The Babylonian writing was *not* in alphabetic characters, but by many hundreds of different signs of different shapes, though it was clear that the proper names of the first version when recognized in the Babylonian version would eventually furnish a key to the whole, and such proved to be the case.

[1] BRA, 52.
[2] The second version was found to be merely the dialect of Susa or Elam.

SUMER-ARYAN DICTIONARY

This trilingual key therefore to the decipherment of the Babylonian writing was analogous to the famous trilingual Rosetta Stone which formed the key to the decipherment of the Egyptian hieroglyphs through the proper names in its Greek version; and it was also analogous to the bilingual Phœnician inscription on the Newton Stone in the Don Valley in which, as I have shown,[1] the Ogamic confirmed the Aryan Phœnician version.

Urgent incitement to hasten the application of this potential key to the decipherment of the Babylonian writing ensued in 1843 from the sudden unearthing of immense masses of new specimens of Babylonian writing near Nineveh in Assyria in that year onwards. These profusely productive exploratory excavations resulted from the publication of the unique collection of Babylonian inscribed objects gathered by C. T. Rich, British Resident and Consul-General at Bagdad, and by his talented secretary Captain K. Bellins of the East India Company's service, and acquired by the British Museum in 1825. It comprised inscribed baked clay cylinders, clay tablets, stamped bricks and stone-monuments and fine copies of other inscriptions of the same class.

The publication in 1836 of this collection of Rich along with his *Narrative* showing where his specimens were found, with notes of other promising sites for excavation at Mosul (Nineveh), etc., created a profound impression on oriental scholars and archæologists with an urgently expressed desire for excavations at the sites indicated. The British archæologist and traveller Mr. (afterwards Sir) Austen Layard, incited by Rich's *Narrative*, visited the sites in 1840, and applied in 1842 for a permit to excavate the great mounds of ruins at Nimrūd (Calah) near Mosul (Nineveh); but it was refused. The French Government, more fortunate, and also led by Rich's results, succeeded in establishing in 1842 for this purpose a special vice-consulate at Mosul with M. Botta an Italian archæologist as vice-consul and excavator of that neighbourhood. In 1843 Botta at Khorsabad, about ten miles from Mosul, uncovered the magnificent palace of the well-known Assyrian king Sargon (721-705 B.C.), the same who had sent the Jews into captivity, with hundreds of yards of sculptured slabs with colossal winged man-headed bulls, etc., etc., and

---

[1] *Phœnician Origin of the Britons*, 26 f.

SUMER-ARYAN DICTIONARY

he returned to France in 1845 with a ship-load of magnificent sculptures, now in the Louvre, but with relatively few literary records.

The discovery of the first great mass of literary cuneiform material however was reserved for Layard after all. At Layard's repeated entreaties the British Ambassador at Constantinople, Sir Stratford Canning (afterwards Lord Stratford de Redcliffe), eventually procured in 1845 a *firman* from the Sultan for his own excavation of Nimrūd and Kuyunjik mounds to the north, with Layard as his agent, and he provided the very great expenses himself as no official British funds were forthcoming. Layard began his excavations in the winter of 1845 and the stupendous richness of his finds is a matter of history. He uncovered not only the magnificent palaces of several other Assyrian kings with even more colossal bulls, etc., and inscribed monuments, including "the black obelisk"; but most important of all his excavations unearthed the Royal and Temple Libraries with very many thousands of closely-written baked clay tablets, many of which proved afterwards to contain long lists of characters, dictionaries, bilingual lists and grammars.[1] These priceless finds, which Sir Stratford Canning with admirable public spirit gifted to the nation, now adorn the halls and galleries of the British Museum and fill a large proportion of its shelves with a profusion of cuneiform records, which have yearly been added to by subsequent excavations.

Yet all this vast collection of Babylonian and Assyrian writing amassed by Rich, Layard and Botta still remained undeciphered and its contents sealed.

The first application of the Persian key scientifically and successfully to the decipherment of Babylonian writing was made by the Irish scholar and Egyptologist, Dr. E. Hincks, rector of Killyleagh, who had never been in Mesopotamia himself. In 1846 he published[2] his long article "On the Three Kinds of Persepolitan Writing." In this he showed through his knowledge of Egyptian that the multitudinous characters in the second and third versions were *syllabic* and not alphabetic. And by the phonetic values of the proper names obtained through their Persian

---

[1] His productive excavations were continued by his assistant, Mr. Hormuzd Rassam after his departure.

[2] *Trans. Royal Irish Academy*, XXI, 240 f.

SUMER-ARYAN DICTIONARY

key, he was able to read many of the other words, and thus found that the language of the Babylonian versions was Semitic, and allied to the Hebrew. And by the decipherment and analysis of some of the Assyrian texts he laid the first solid foundations of Assyrian grammar. One of the first fruits of his discovery was his recognition in the Assyrian inscriptions of the well-known names of Hazael of Damascus and Jehu of Israel, and later Nebuchadrezzar, Sennacherib, Hezekiah and Jerusalem; and a French savant had found the name of Sargon, the late notorious Assyrian.

Many Semitic scholars were now attracted by the task of trying to decipher the Semitic, Babylonian and "Assyrian" texts, dictionaries and grammars and to extend the word-signs lists, and the new science "Assyriology" took shape.

Rawlinson, now Consul-General at Bagdad and Director of the British Museum excavations in Babylonia and Assyria, took a leading part in advancing the work of Babylonian or "Assyrian" decipherment. In 1850 [1] he communicated his independent analysis and decipherment of the long Babylonian text of the Behistun edict with translations, grammar, commentary and list of the majority of the signs with their phonetic values. This long Behistun text proved to be a uniquely fertile source for the decipherment of the Babylonian through its Persian version, as the edict bristled with the proper names of the many lands and peoples whom Darius had conquered and with names of kings and chieftains. He also contributed in the same year his *Memoir* on the Babylonian and Assyrian inscriptions.[2]

In the former article he announced the discovery of two fundamental facts of Babylonian writing, namely, that the signs besides their phonetic (or "syllabic") values were also used *ideographically* to denote objects and ideas—a fact which had meantime, unknown to Rawlinson, just been recognized in Europe—and secondly, the important fact, which no one had previously noticed, that most of the signs were "polyphonous," each character possessing more than one phonetic value. This latter fact was contemptuously rejected by Semitic scholars as being contrary to all established notions. But it was accepted by the sage Dr. Hincks.

Hincks, as an Egyptologist, appears to have been the first to recognize

[1] SAC, 24.   [2] *Ib.*

that the ideographic feature of the signs implied that the latter were originally pictorial as in Egyptian, notwithstanding that the pictorial feature was scarcely if at all recognizable in the conventional cuneiform shapes of the signs hitherto unearthed (the Sumerian pictograph hieroglyphs not having yet been found to any extent). He also explained the "polyphony" on the same basis. Thus the pictograph word for "foot" he showed would denote not only "foot" but also "go," "run," "walk," etc., each of which names would become a phonetic value of the sign. And this fact of "polyphony" was fully confirmed by further research, and is now universally accepted, even by the Semitic scholars who had formerly rejected it.

Now comes the great epoch-making discovery of the "Sumerians" and their Non-Semitic language and race, a discovery which proved to be of more overwhelming importance than all the others. This discovery was announced by Rawlinson in 1855.[1] He noticed that the language in many of the texts from Nineveh and in a tablet from Larsa in Lower Babylonia was written in a Non-Semitic language, that the Non-Semitic texts, which were mostly of a religious kind identical with the Assyrian, were furnished with interlinear Assyrian translations, and that many of these Non-Semitic words were found in other tablets containing bilingual lists (or "syllabaries") of these words to which Semitic Assyrian equivalents or translations were attached, showing that these bilingual lists were used as dictionaries to this earlier Non-Semitic language. Further, he found several actual contemporary inscriptions in this early writing in the date-records, building inscriptions, bricks and votive texts unearthed in Southern Babylonia and Susa by W. K. Loftus, a scientific geologist, and J. E. Taylor in their excavations, in 1852-54, *beneath* the Babylonian period foundations.

From these facts Rawlinson, with rare insight, concluded that this Non-Semitic early language was spoken by the early civilized inhabitants of Mesopotamia, who were Non-Semites in race and had given the Semitic Babylonians and Assyrians their civilization, religion, and writing—for this latter also was now seen to be obviously derived from the writing of

[1] "Notes on Early History of Babylonia," JRAS, XV, 1855, 221 and f.n.; XVI, 1856, vii.; N.S. XIX, 1887, 664.

these early peoples who appear to have been the first inventors of linear writing. He considered that these early people were "Akkadians," as he had observed that the "Semitic" Babylonian and Assyrian kings styled themselves in their historical inscriptions "King of Sumer and Akkad," and "Akkad" was the name of a city founded by Nimrod along with Babel according to the Old Testament. And their language he called "The Hamitic language of Babylonia,"[1] as it was Non-Semitic.

The Semitic scholars protested; but Hincks confirmed and adopted these discoveries of Rawlinson, and he called this early Non-Semitic language as well as its authors "Akkadian." He showed by further evidence that they were the founders of Babylonian Civilization, Religion and Writing, and that the language was agglutinative like that of the Turks and Finns.

Again the Semitic scholars protested. It was impossible, they urged, that the Semites had borrowed their civilization, religion and writing from any other race, for the mere suggestion of such a thing was contrary to all established authority!

The facts, however, as published by Rawlinson and Hincks were fully confirmed and extended in 1863 by the brilliant French professor of Assyrian, Jules Oppert, who conducted an exploring and excavating mission in Mesopotamia for three years for the French Government. He called these early people by the alternative title "Sumerian"; and he showed in more detail that a large proportion of the tablets in the temple library of Nineveh consisted in translations, mostly religious, from this older Non-Semitic language with Assyrian translations, comparative grammars, vocabularies and reading-books in the two languages.[2] And his title of "Sumerian" for these people was eventually adopted by English Assyriologists after 1887[3] in place of "Akkad," which latter title they transferred to the "Semitic" people and their language.

Semitic scholars still refused to admit the facts, and declared that the Sumerians and their non-Semitic race and language were non-existent

[1] He also provisionally called the language "Chaldean," as that was the name in use for the ancient people of Babylonia; but this name, I have shown, belonged more especially to the Pre-Sumerian aborigines and their descendants.
[2] *Expédition scientifique en Mésopotamie*, 2 vols, 1863 f.
[3] Sayce, *Hibbert Lects.*, 1887, *passim*.

and were merely " the folly of a few ' untrained amateurs ' who could be safely disregarded ! "[1]

Nevertheless the little band of pioneer scientific Sumerologists, Rawlinson, Hincks and Oppert, patiently continued their researches unmoved by these sneers, amassing further details regarding the Sumerians and their texts and records, and gained to their ranks such noted Sumerian scholars as Lenormant, Haupt, Sayce, Schrader, Hommel and others.

Suddenly, in 1877, the massive structural remains of a mighty Sumerian city and seaport of " about 3100 B.C." was unearthed at Tello (or " The mound ") in the delta of Lower Babylonia by the French Expedition under M. de Sarzec. The city was so large and rich in sculptures, inscriptions, etc., that M. de Sarzec continued without intermission the work of its excavation for twenty-three years, until 1900 ; and its treasures now adorn the Louvre. It had been destroyed by fire about 2300 B.C and ever since, except for a superficial occupation of its mounds of ruins by Parthians in the second century B.C., it had lain deserted and undisturbed by Babylonians and Assyrians, awaiting the spade of the scientific modern excavator to bring to the light of day its wealth of archaic monuments and records to tell their own story at first hand.

This old Sumerian city covered an area of about two and a half miles by a quarter of a mile in breadth, and contained great buildings, palaces, temples, granaries and other public buildings built of good kiln-made bricks, the lower portions of the walls in many cases still standing intact over ten to fifteen feet high. It teemed with stone sculptures, mostly bas-reliefs, covered with inscriptions in the old pictographic linear writing occasionally merging into early cuneiform, with rich stores of votive records, foundation tablets, edicts, inscribed clay cones and tablets, sacred and official cylinder-seals engraved with marvellous art and technique, carved and inscribed stone mace-heads, alabaster and other vases inscribed, jewellery enamelled and worked in gold and silver, embossed silver-ware, copper weapons, decorated earthenware, and a host of other cultural objects of a great civilized and literate people.

The city was revealed by its inscriptions to have been a capital of the great " Sumerian " king Uruash-the-Khād (the so-called " Ur-Nina " of

[1] SAC, 25.

Assyriologists), whom I have proved elsewhere to have been an Aryan Phœnician and the founder of The First Phœnician Dynasty, and a famous Aryan priest-king in the Indian Vedas and Epics. It yielded multitudes of inscribed monuments of himself, his sons and descendants in the dynasty for about two centuries, in several of which monuments they are portrayed of Aryan and non-Semitic physical type, and his descendants also are famous Aryan kings and priest-kings in the Indian Vedas and Epics. Their monuments contained records of great public works, and of temples built or repaired by them, and of their wars against revolting and other city-states, codes of laws and regulations, etc. Numerous and more finely executed inscribed monuments, statues, seals, etc., were also found of the priest-king Gudea of the later "Sumerian" dynasty, and he too was a famous Aryan priest-king in the Indian Epics.

Besides these discoveries at Tello, the deeper excavations at other ancient sites all over Babylonia, below the foundations of the "Semitic" Babylonian period have yielded similar Sumerian records of these and many other early Sumerian kings and governors. And nearly every year has added to the number of Sumerian sites found with monuments and inscriptions and kings' names. Amongst the later notable excavations of Sumerian sites, not to mention those which have lately yielded the Indo-Sumerian seals, etc., in the Indus Valley, are those at Susa begun by Loftus and continued by the French Expedition under M. de Morgan, the American exploration of Adab by the Chicago Expedition under Banks, and of Nippur by the University of Pennsylvania, and of Kish by Professor Langdon. The Nippur Expedition unearthed the temple library of that great Sun-temple there, recovering amongst other things over 50,000 inscribed clay-tablets many of which are not yet deciphered, and from beneath the foundation of its temple tower was unearthed the oldest historical Sumerian record yet known, the inscribed votive "Bowl of Udug."

These Tello Sumerian texts and records disclosed unequivocally that the Semitic Babylonians and Assyrians had borrowed their system of government, laws, literature and writing and art from the "Sumerians." Haupt in his *Sumerian Family Laws* in 1879, in which he begins the scientific analysis of Sumerian etymology, discloses Sumerian family customs which are now seen to be essentially similar to those of the Early Aryans, and this is confirmed by the later and more detailed finds. The Sumerian law-codes were seen to be the basis of Hammurabi's code of Babylon which is now universally regarded as the basis of the Mosaic code and legislature. The leading elements of the Babylonian and Assyrian or Chaldean religion in regard to the Father-god, which so strongly influenced the Hebrew religion and gave the latter its God-name *Jah*, were disclosed to be derived from the Sumerians. And the practice of the Semitic Babylonians and Assyrians in mechanically repeating the old Sumerian religious texts was seen to be analogous to the repetition of the old " dead " Latin language in the rituals of medieval and modern Roman churches.

In former works I have shown that the reason why so many of the Babylonian inscriptions are in the Semitic language is because great numbers, perhaps a majority of the subjects of the Empire, spoke Semitic languages and understood no other; and in a monograph now passing through the press I give in detail the proofs that Sargon-the-Great and his Akkads were Aryan in race and speech. That others besides myself are awaking to the truth in these matters is indicated by the steady diminution in the number of scholars who think that the Babylonian civilization was derived from the Semites, that the Sumerian was an invention of Semitic Babylonian priests, that cuneiform writing was Semitic and not Sumerian in origin, that the Hammurabi Law Code was the invention of Semites, and that the Muru or Amorites were Semites.

THE SUMERIAN LANGUAGE IS ARYAN IN STRUCTURE

Sumerian is a written language, in which the writing is a practical and ingenious attempt to represent scientifically by pictographs the living speech of a highly civilized people. This Sumerian writing has its interest greatly enhanced by the discovery I previously announced and which is detailed in my forthcoming work on " The Aryan Origin of the Alphabet " that it is the hitherto unknown source of our modern alphabetic letters and writing. And significantly it is ordinarily written

SUMER-ARYAN DICTIONARY

in the *Aryan* direction of writing, that is from the left hand towards the right, the direction of the apparent movement of the Sun, as in English writing, in contradistinction to the retrograde or reversed " Semitic " direction in the path of the Moon—a distinction presumably based upon the Sun-worship of the Aryans as opposed to the inveterate Moon-worship of Darkness and demons requiring bloody sacrifices, characteristic of the Semites, Chaldees and primitive tribes.

As the present work deals only with the individual *words* of the language, it is unnecessary to describe here the structure of that speech which is already detailed in its special grammars. It need only be mentioned that, like the more primitive languages, Early Sumerian is largely " agglutinative," that is to say it forms compound words and sentences by strings of root-words arranged in a definite order according to the sense intended, either alone or with suffixes to the qualifying words ; but even in Early Sumerian there is already a certain amount of inflection. What appear to be vestiges of this early agglutinative stage are the survivals in Indian Pali and Sanskrit of frequent compound words and strings of such, and in English the not infrequent use of compound words, and of occasional uninflected sentences, such as " No work no pay." In its later and more developed stage, however, the Sumerian introduces a considerable number of inflections by prefixes and suffixes, gunification or the addition of several strokes, and alterations in the consonants and vowels for vowel-harmony, which are generally in phonetic series with the chief inflections, prefixes and suffixes in the later and more highly developed Aryan languages such as English which is practically non-inflective. And after all inflections are so little essential that even in modern grammars they are called " accidence " i.e., " non-essentials."

THE SUMERIAN SYLLABIC PICTURE WRITING

The writing in Sumerian is not by alphabetic letters, which were a later adaptation of the Sumerian writing, but by picture-signs or pictographic word-signs. Such signs occurring in Egypt were called by the Greeks " hiero-glyphs " or " sacred writing," as these ancient scripts were especially used by the priests for sacred writing long after they had become

PLATE II.

SUMERIAN ORIGIN OF EGYPTIAN HIEROGLYPHS (*and see Plates I, III-V*).

SUMER-ARYAN DICTIONARY

more or less obsolete. This term "hieroglyph" is also applicable to the Sumerian writing which I show to be the parent of the Egyptian hieroglyph system, see plates I-V and text.

These hieroglyph word-signs number about six hundred. The older signs are pictures mostly of well-known natural and artificial objects, which were self-interpreting in their earlier fuller forms. Those signs represent [1] heads and other principal parts of the bodies of men, women, children and animals, figures of birds, reptiles, fishes and insects, trees, plants, fruit, grain, etc.; the heavenly bodies, sun, moon, stars, sky, etc., earth, mountains and water, fire and lighting, etc., weapons, tools, domestic and other utensils and furniture; buildings, forts, towers; carriages, ships, etc., articles of clothing, crowns, jewellery; food, drink, etc., etc.; and many of the signs are not yet identified as to the object they represent, even when their phonetic value is known. In the earlier writing the pictures are drawn more elaborately and naturalistically than in the later period when the signs were made with as few strokes as possible for rapid writing, curved lines tending to be written by straight strokes, and circles diamond shaped, so as to become almost diagrams, yet still retaining characteristic features, see plates I-V.

Each of these pictographs possessed the phonetic value or name of the object pictured which became the primary meaning of the word-sign thus written.

In the accompanying plates I-V, are given some of these simple Sumerian pictographs with their word-values, most of which it will be seen possess essentially the same word-form and meaning as in English. And alongside are placed the corresponding Egyptian hieroglyph with its word-value, showing the radical identity of the hieroglyph, as well as of its phonetic value and meaning with the Sumerian.[2] The more detailed and realistic drawing in the Egyptian hieroglyphs is seen to be merely a neo-archaism or pseudo-archaism, as the earliest known hieroglyphs in Egypt for continuous writing on the ebony label of Menes, are of the simple Sumerian type and approximate to the Sumerian forms.

[1] As shown in the classic work of Professor Barton, see BW, Part I.

[2] The Sumer signs are taken from BW (see Abbreviation List), and the phonetic values and meanings from the same, supplemented by PSL. The Egyptian signs and values and meanings are from GH.

SUMER-ARYAN DICTIONARY

IDEOGRAPHS AND SYLLABIC WRITING

Besides the primary word-sound and meanings expressed by these pictorial signs employed for writing the spoken name of the object pictured, the Sumerians adapted these syllabic pictographs to the fuller expression of speech and abstract ideas by making the signs express also the various ideas connected with the objects pictured. Thus the pictograph of the Sun stands not only for the Sun itself and its name, but also for shine, light, bright, glow, warm, heat, day; the pictograph of the Moon for shine, month, thirty (days), wax, wane, dark, death and fate; the picture of a Club or Bat for bat, baton, beat, fatal, etc., and so on, the particular meaning being indicated by the position of the sign in the sentence or by the context or prefixes or affixes, etc. In this usage the signs are called " ideograms " or " ideographs."

A further stage was the use of these ideographs merely for their sound as phonograms, without any ideographic sense, for spelling words of more than one syllable. This usage is termed " syllabic " as opposed to the later " alphabetic " spelling; and it continued in Sumerian and Babylonian down till the latest period.

Many of these signs when used to express more complicated abstract ideas are compounded or " *gun*-ified " by the introduction within them of strokes or other signs. And here it is significant of the essential identity of the Sumerian and Sanskrit to find that this Sumerian term *Gun* used by the Sumerians for their compounding sign, from *Gun*, " a collection, totality,"[1] is identical with the Sanskrit *Guna*, " a multiplier, a co-efficient "[2] which Sanskrit grammarians use as " gun-ate " in an analogous sense; and this Sumerian *Gun* is disclosed as the source of the old Latin ' Con ' " together with," i.e., ' a similar sense ' (see *Gun* in the Dict.).

These various ideographic words in the Sumerian vocabulary are catalogued and their respective meanings defined in the copious bilingual glossaries in Sumerian and Babylonian of the Assyrian and Babylonian grammatical tablets to the number of many thousands of words. They give us a vivid insight into the scientific psychology of our ancestral Aryans in regard to the workings of their fertile mind and imagination in exploring the realms of Thought and in coining for us abstract words.

[1] Br., 3220–2.   [2] MWD, 357.

SUMER-ARYAN DICTIONARY

Homonyms and Synonyms

As in English and other Aryan languages, the Sumerian possesses a considerable number of words of the same sound but differing in their meaning, the so-called "homonyms." Just as in English, for example, *Air* = variously "atmosphere," "haughtiness," "mien" or "manner" and "a tune"; and *Bear* = "carry," "suffer" and "an animal"; and *Can* = "able" and "a vessel," or the contents of vessel, *e.g.*, "no comfort but a hearty can" (Burns's *Jolly Beggars*); *Dam* = "mother" and "embankment"; *Jar* = "a vessel," "quarrel," "discordant sound," "a shaking," etc., etc., so in Sumerian we have this same feature. Thus *As'* means in Sumerian "a star" (aster), the number "one" (ace), the number "six" and "an arm," etc. (see Dict.); *Bar*, means in Sumerian "a bar," "brother," "bright," "barrack," etc. (see Dict.) and so on. This feature is also particularly conspicuous in Sanskrit. In Sumerian, however, such homonyms are usually distinguished by different pictographs or hieroglyphs which indicate the different meanings. And it is supposed that as in Chinese, which also possesses homonyms, and which I find contains several Sumerian words written by practically the same hieroglyphs, the different meanings were distinguished in the spoken speech by different tones or pitch.

Moreover, as in English and other Aryan languages, the Sumerian possesses a large number of synonymous words, i.e., different words expressing the same meaning. This synonymy in Sumerian has been called "polyphony," and treated as if it were a peculiarity of the Sumerian. These synonyms are grouped together under their respective Sumerian syllabic pictograph or word-sign in the Babylonian and Assyrian bilingual glossaries. They are apparently in the main dialectic words of different tribes for the same sign, or for different shades of meaning.

As example of these synonyms, the word-sign for "water" picturing a wavelet has besides its common word-value of *A* or *Ā* (i.e., the source of the *Aa, Ae, Awe, Eye*, etc., river-names, see Dict.) also the synonym of *Bur* (i.e. the source of the English Bore a tidal surge, Brook and Burn, a stream, see Dict.), also the synonym of *Dur* or *Duru* (i.e., the *Dara* of Sanskrit, *Darya* of Indo-Persian, *Dwr* of Cymric, *U-Dor*, water, of Greek and cognate with the Sumerian *Badur* and Hittite "*Waa-tar*"

SUMER-ARYAN DICTIONARY

and English "Water"); and *Me* probably a contraction for Sumerian *Mer* a marsh, sea, disclosed as the source of English *Mere, Marsh, Marine*, Latin *Mare* and French *Mer*.

These synonyms are exceptionally numerous in Sumerian, most words having two or three or more, and several having a dozen or more. As a consequence, Sumerian proper names, which are written by a string of such ambiguous synonymous syllabic signs are exceptionally difficult and generally impossible to "restore" with certainty into their true form in "Roman" alphabetic letters, without a key to the traditional forms of the names. Assyriologists have hitherto possessed no key whatever to the traditional form of the names of the Sumerian and Akkad kings (excepting the solitary Sargon and doubtfully "Gilgamesh") and of their cities. Yet they are in the habit of reading or "restoring" these names by pure conjecture, selecting haphazard one or other of the various synonyms of the signs according to their individual fancy with the result that the readings or "restorations" of the names by different scholars not only differ more or less widely from one another, but few are strictly correct and many of them are entirely distorted and fictitious. Now, an unique key to the traditional form of these ancient "Sumerian" kings' names exists, as I have shown, in the official systematic and detailed lists of the Early Aryan kings which are fortunately preserved in the Indian Epics of the Ancient Aryan kings. And in previous works I have demonstrated the use of this key in recovering the proper forms of the names of the kings in entire dynasties of the Early Sumerians.

Spelling of Words in Sumerian and in Later Aryan Languages

The spelling of words in Sumerian writing is remarkably fixed and uniform in the different texts and documents. The usual dialectic differences however occur through the phonetic interchange of consonants of the same class as in other Aryan languages, such as between the labials *B, P, F, M* and *W*, the dentals *D* and *T*, gutturals *H, K* and *Q* and the cerebrals *L* and *R*, as is partly expressed in "Grimm's Law." And the vowels are almost always freely interchangeable, which is possibly a reason for the notorious vagaries in the pronunciation of the vowels in English.

SUMER-ARYAN DICTIONARY

The spelling of the Sumerian words is obtained from the numerous Babylonian and Assyrian bilingual glossaries. These glossaries, written in "cuneiform" or "wedge-headed" writing, a later form of writing the Sumerian pictographs by dabs with a wedge-shaped style on wet clay-tablets afterwards baked, are classified for easy reference in the standard dictionaries of Brünnow, Meissner, Prince, Barton and Muss-Arnolt. In the latter three, and also in the partial lists of Delitzsch, Pinches and others, the words are transliterated into "Roman" letters by the universally recognized system of Assyriologists and other oriental scholars. The elementary vowel and consonantal letter signs thus comprised in these Sumerian words is detailed in the companion work on "The Aryan Origin of the Alphabet," wherein is disclosed for the first time the origin of our Alphabetic letters from the pictographic word-signs in Sumerian writing.

The changes in the forms and spellings of Aryan words in the course of "wear and tear" down through the ages are now seen to be very much less than has hitherto been supposed. When a literary language, such as Greek, Latin, Sanskrit, French and English, is examined at different periods or stages in its development or currency, it is seen to have undergone great changes. But these changes relate more to the grammatical construction of the sentences and their idioms than to changes in the form or meaning of the actual words themselves. And colloquial, as opposed to "book," language often preserves archaic forms of the words practically unchanged. Thus we shall find from this comparative dictionary how remarkably little alteration has occurred in the spelling of radical Sumerian words in the various modern Aryan languages. Indeed common essential words appear to be amongst the most imperishable of human things.

This relative fixity of Sumerian words was doubtless due in considerable part to the syllabic writing and spelling which is mainly etymological and self-explaining. It is all the more remarkable in view of the notorious vagaries in medieval and modern spelling, e.g., in Anglo-Saxon and Early and Middle English down to the invention of the printing-press which tended to stereotype writing; though even Shakespeare some centuries after the printing-press is said to have spelt his own name in over half a dozen different ways on the same document.

PLATE III.　　SUMERIAN　　　　　　　　　EGYPTIAN

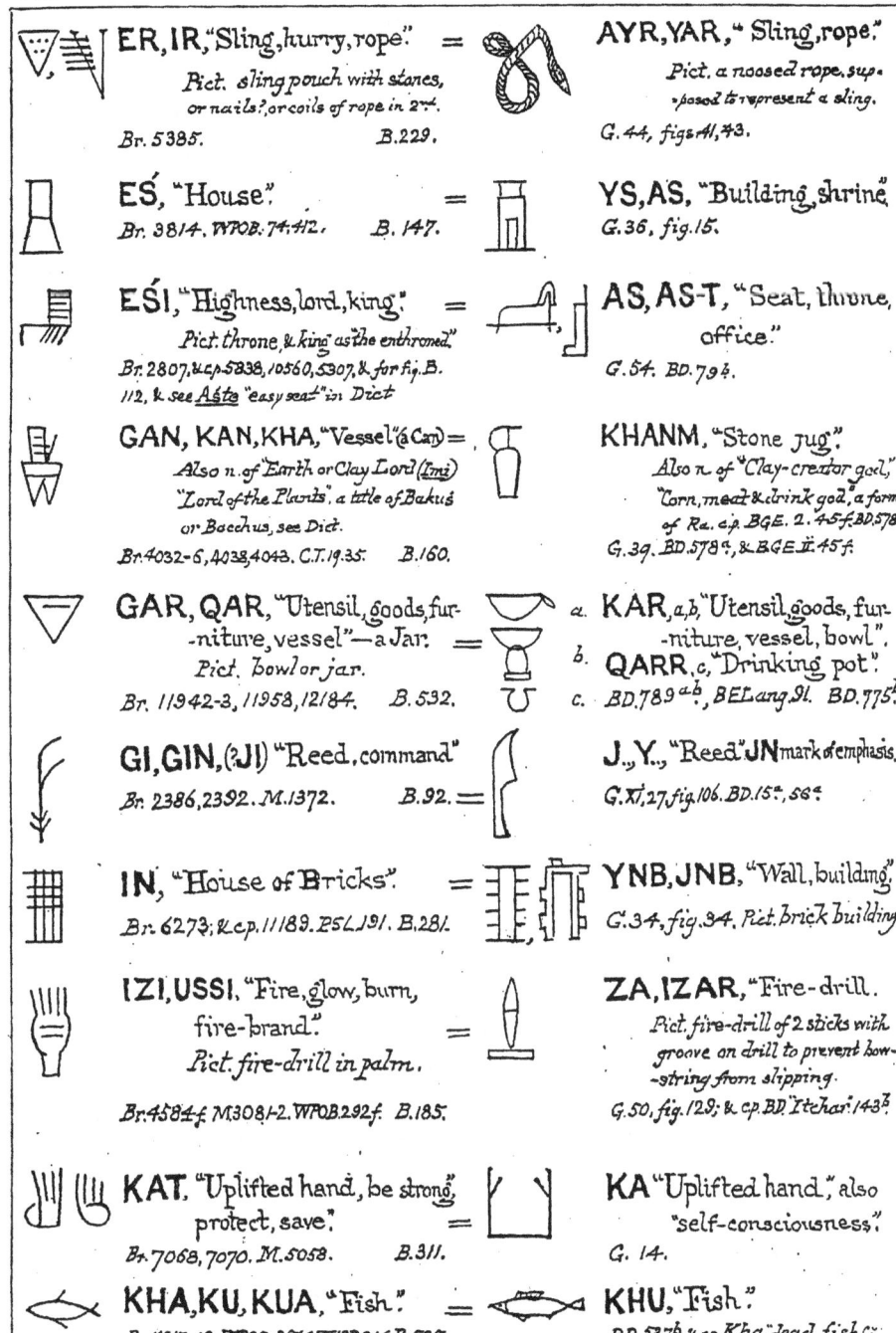

Sumerian	Egyptian
ER, IR, "Sling, hurry, rope." Pict. sling pouch with stones, or nails?, or coils of rope in 2nd. Br. 5385.　B.229.	AYR, YAR, "Sling, rope." Pict. a noosed rope, supposed to represent a sling. G.44, figs A1, 43.
ES, "House." Br. 3814. WPOB.74,412.　B.147.	YS, AS, "Building, shrine." G.36, fig.15.
ESI, "Highness, lord, king." Pict. throne, & king as the enthroned." Br. 2807, & cp.5338, 10560, 5307, & for fig. B. 112, & see Asta "easy seat" in Dict	AS, AS-T, "Seat, throne, office." G.54. BD.794.
GAN, KAN, KHA, "Vessel"(a Can) Also n. of Earth or Clay Lord (Imi) "Lord of the Plants", a title of Bakus or Bacchus, see Dict. Br.4032-6, 4038, 4043. C.T.19.35.　B.160.	KHANM, "Stone jug." Also n. of "Clay-creator god," "Corn, meat & drink god," a form of Ra. c.p. BGE. 2. 45 f BD.578. G.39. BD.578 a, & BGE.II.45 f.
GAR, QAR, "Utensil, goods, furniture, vessel"—a Jar. Pict. bowl or jar. Br. 11942-3, 11953, 12184.　B.532.	a. KAR, a,b, "Utensil, goods, furniture, vessel, bowl". b. QARR, c, "Drinking pot". c. BD.789 a,b, BELang.91. BD.775 b.
GI, GIN, (JI) "Reed, command" Br. 2386, 2392. M.1372.　B.92.	J., Y., "Reed". JN mark of emphasis. G.XI,27, fig.106. BD.15 a, 56 a.
IN, "House of Bricks". Br. 6273; & cp.11189. P5LJ91. B.281.	YNB, JNB, "Wall, building." G.34, fig.34. Pict. brick building.
IZI, USSI, "Fire, glow, burn, fire-brand." Pict. fire-drill in palm. Br.4584f. M308 f-2. WPOB.292 f. B.185.	ZA, IZAR, "Fire-drill. Pict. fire-drill of 2 sticks with groove on drill to prevent bowstring from slipping. G.50, fig.129; & cp. BD. Itchar,143 b.
KAT. "Uplifted hand, be strong, protect, save". Br. 7068, 7070. M.5058.　B.311.	KA "Uplifted hand," also "self-consciousness". G. 14.
KHA, KU, KUA, "Fish." Br.11817-19. WPOB.? S7EWISD.31f. B.525.	KHU, "Fish." BD.537 b & cp Kha "dead fish" L.A.W. del

SUMERIAN ORIGIN OF EGYPTIAN HIEROGLYPHS (and see Plates I-II, IV-V.)

SUMER-ARYAN DICTIONARY

Writing tends to preserve the more archaic and truer pronunciation which is evidently indicated by the earliest written or spelled forms of words. The later varying ephemeral fashions in pronunciation which have crept into English and the other Aryan languages by clipping and eliding consonants and introducing *r* so as to emasculate the language and make it differ considerably from the spelling, a custom or usage more in vogue in cities than in the provinces where the older and truer forms tend more to linger on, in the living speech or colloquialisms and " provincialisms "—the country life being always a truer index of the people than the town—have led to the popular notion that the spelling is wrong and should be amended by " reformed spelling " and by an universal " fonetik " language " Esperanto." But this is now seen, more clearly than before, to be an entirely mistaken view, and mischievous in that it would effectually destroy the keys to the etymological meanings of the self-explaining words which have been so faithfully conserved by our ancestors down through the ages by what has been supposed to be " peculiar " spelling, but which has generally preserved the earlier and truer forms of the words.

The Word-Lists in the Dictionary

In this pioneer comparative Dictionary of the Sumero-Aryan languages the radical words only in the Sumerian or Proto-Aryan are chiefly dealt with, as these have been most fully analysed and studied by Assyriologists and their various shades of meaning well ascertained. They are largely verbal roots, which by their compounds form the great majority of the words in common use in Aryan languages, ancient and modern. Of the compound Sumerian words existing in the vast Sumerian vocabularies preserved in the bilingual glossary tablets of the Babylonians and Assyrians, and numbering along with the relatively few radical words 14,487 in Brünnow's *Classified List*, to which Meissner's List makes many thousands of additions, only a few have been included here, as the great mass of these compound words have not yet been critically examined by scholars and still await study by the new Aryan keys in the hands of the younger Sumerologists. Of the compound Sumerian words included in this dictionary several are hitherto unrecognized critically important

SUMER-ARYAN DICTIONARY

historical and mythological Aryan proper names, see next section on Historical Effects.

The Dictionary is arranged in alphabetic order—the Sumerian origin of the signs and phonetic values of our Alphabetic Letters being disclosed in detail in the companion volume on " The Aryan Origin of the Alphabet," now in the press.

Under each alphabetic letter are grouped the Sumerian root-words beginning with that letter, in their transliteration into " Roman " characters. These are mostly simple roots without their phonetic complements, rendered into modern alphabetic spelling according to the universally accepted system of transliteration of the word-signs by Assyriologists, in which the vowels have generally their continental values—the English vowel pronunciation varying so greatly—and the authority for the spelling of the word is invariably cited. Following the Sumerian word is given its dialectic variants in spelling where such exist, also the chief synonyms of the word ; and thereafter the literal definition of the Sumerian word-sign from the bilingual glossaries, all duly vouched for. The authorities chiefly cited are the great standard *Classified List* of signs by Brünnow, the uniquely full and standard book of the Sumerian signs and their definitions by Barton, supplemented by Meissner's List and Prince's invaluable Sumerian Lexicon. And a description of the object represented by the pictorial word-sign is given when the pictograph is recognizable.

In the second paragraph under each word are given the Babylonian or Assyrian equivalents of the Sumerian word, which define the meanings of that word, from the bilingual glossaries, each with its English translations, chiefly from the great standard Assyrian Dictionary of Muss-Arnolt, which is specifically cited for reference. And here are included some of the few known words of the late " Semitic " Phœnician from Carthage, etc.[1]

In the third paragraph, the Egyptian derivations from the Sumerian

[1] The Semitic Phœnician inscriptions occurring in Phœnicia, Carthage, Sardinia, Marseilles, Cyprus and Egypt are mostly of a formal votive character with not a very great variety of critical words ; and similarly those on the tombstones in Sardinia and Mediterranean sites (see WPOB, 53). A few short bilingual inscriptions occur in Semitic Phœnician, and Cuneiform, or in Greek, on weights, seals, coins, etc. Vernacular Phœnician bilingual with Latin in the Carthage dialect of the third century B.C. is found in the Pœnulus play of the dramatist, T. M. Plautus, the translation of which has been attempted by Schröder (SP, 285 f) and others, but these words have not yet been identified with certainty.

are given, in their various dialectic spellings from the great monumental dictionary of Sir Wallis Budge—a rich mine of Egyptology—supplemented by Mr. Griffith's *Hieroglyphs*, and this discloses for the first time the radically Aryan nature of the Ancient Egyptian language and its derivation along with its hieroglyph system from the Sumerians.

In the remaining paragraphs are given the equivalents in the leading languages of the Aryan Family, ancient and modern, namely Sanskrit and Pali, with Ancient Persian or Zend, Greek, Latin and the chief Latin languages, French and Italian; Gothic of the great Edda epics which I have found is essentially a dialect of the Ancient Briton,[1] the " Western " Gothic of Ulfilas (*c.* A.D. 350), and the kindred Norse including Danish and Swedish, the German or Teutonic; Cornish, which is especially rich in Sumerian words as was to be expected from the long association of the Amorites and Phœnicians with the tin-mines there, also the " Celtic " including Breton, followed by the Anglo-Saxon and Old English.

In the last paragraph is given the current English form of the Sumerian word, with a cluster of the chief English derivatives from that Sumerian word or root in question as a nucleus. Many more such derivative English and other words will be apparent to the reader.

These Sumerian radical words, it will be seen, equate substantially and often absolutely both in sound and in meaning with the corresponding words in English and the other Aryan languages, ancient and modern, including Egyptian. And it will be found that these radical words or word-stems form in English and the other Aryan languages by their compounds the great bulk of the words in those languages, as contained in their respective dictionaries, the majority of the words therein being coined from such relatively few radical words. When the Sumerian compound words have been more fully studied this word-list may be largely extended.

For comparative purposes, in Egyptian the final *t*, a feminine or abstract suffix, is usually placed within brackets, as the Sumerian made no distinction in gender. And similarly in the Gothic the nominative suffix *r*, which is a grammatical accretion, is omitted.

[1] WPOB, 178 f.

PLATE IV. SUMERIAN   EGYPTIAN

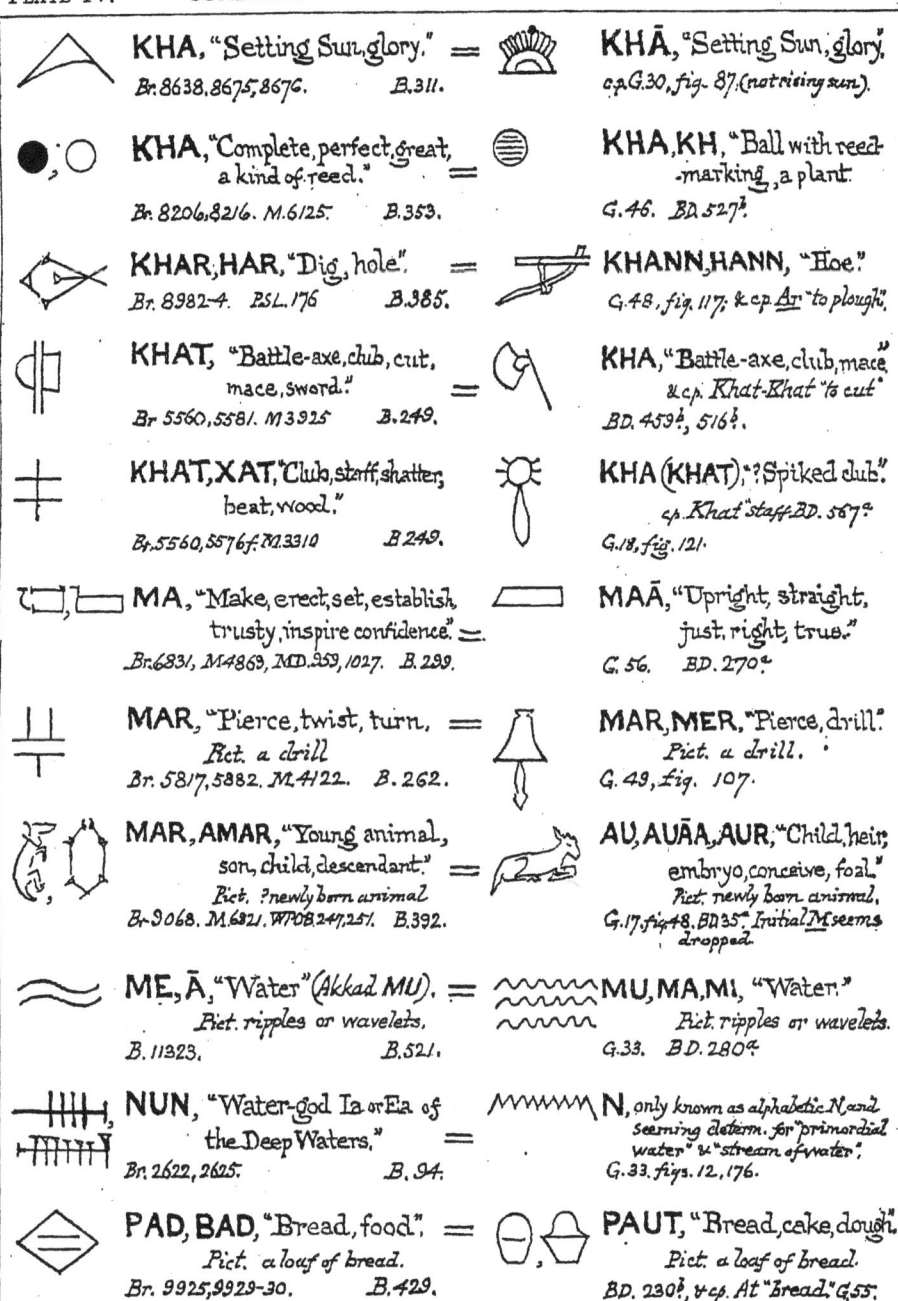

Sumerian		Egyptian	
⌒	KHA, "Setting Sun, glory." Br. 8638, 8675, 8676. B.311.	◠	KHĀ, "Setting Sun, glory," c.p. G.30, fig. 87. (not rising sun).
●, ○	KHA, "Complete, perfect, great, a kind of reed." Br. 8206, 8216. M.6125. B.353.	⊜	KHA, KH, "Ball with reed-marking, a plant." G.46. BD 527ª.
◇	KHAR, HAR, "Dig, hole." Br. 8982-4. P.S.L. 176. B.385.	𓌢	KHANN, HANN, "Hoe." G.48, fig. 117; & cp. Ar "to plough".
⊄	KHAT, "Battle-axe, club, cut, mace, sword." Br 5560, 5581. M 3925. B.249.	◐	KHA, "Battle-axe, club, mace," & c.p. Khat-Khat "to cut" BD. 459½, 516½.
✚	KHAT, XAT, "Club, staff, shatter, beat, wood." Br. 5560, 5576f. M.3310 B.249.	⚘	KHA (KHAT), "?Spiked club." cp. Khat "staff." BD. 567ª. G.18, fig. 121.
⌒,▭	MA, "Make, erect, set, establish, trusty, inspire confidence." Br. 6831, M.4869, M.D. 959, 1027. B.299.	▭	MAĀ, "Upright, straight, just, right, true." G. 56. BD. 270ª.
⊥⊥	MAR, "Pierce, twist, turn." Pict. a drill Br. 5817, 5882. M.4122. B.262.	⧖	MAR, MER, "Pierce, drill." Pict. a drill. G. 49, fig. 107.
🐂	MAR, AMAR, "Young animal, son, child, descendant." Pict. ?newly born animal Br.9068. M.6321. W.P.O.B. 247, 251. B.392.	🐃	AU, AUĀA, AUR, "Child, heir, embryo, conceive, foal." Pict. newly born animal. G.17, fig 48. BD 35ª. Initial M seems dropped.
≈	ME, Ā, "Water" (Akkad MU). Pict. ripples or wavelets. B.11323. B.521.	≋	MU, MA, MI, "Water." Pict. ripples or wavelets. G.33. BD. 280ª.
⫲⫲	NUN, "Water-god Ia or Ea of the Deep Waters." Br. 2622, 2625. B. 94.	⋀⋀⋀	N, only known as alphabetic N and seeming determ. for "primordial water" & "stream of water". G.33. figs. 12, 176.
◇	PAD, BAD, "Bread, food." Pict. a loaf of bread. Br. 9925, 9929-30. B.429.	⌒,⊔	PAUT, "Bread, cake, dough." Pict. a loaf of bread. BD. 230⅔, & cp. At "Bread." G.55.

L.A.W. del.

SUMERIAN ORIGIN OF EGYPTIAN HIEROGLYPHS (*and see Plates I-III, and V.*)

SUMER-ARYAN DICTIONARY

Effects of the Dictionary on Philology, Etymology, Ethnology, Folk-lore and History

On Philology and Ethnology the effect of the discoveries embodied in this Dictionary must necessarily be of far-reaching fundamental importance. The science of philology, and especially its branch etymology, has fallen into considerable disrepute by its fantastic abuse by so many scholars and popular writers, whose wild guesswork and transparently false etymologies justify the sarcasm of Voltaire that " Etymology is a science in which the vowels signify nothing at all and the consonants very little." But rightly used philology and etymology are invaluable scientific branches of history and ethnology, as well as aids to literature, and they are now placed upon a much more solid basis than before by the discovery of the hitherto unknown parent of the Aryan languages.

Availing ourselves of the treasure of written words with graphic details of original meanings and pronunciations going far behind all previously known sources, which the restored Sumerian puts at our disposal, we can hear the voices of our Early Aryan forbears with almost gramophonic fidelity repeating the current words and language in our everyday modern speech.

English etymology is especially illumined by these discoveries. Of scientific works on this subject the most outstanding are the great classic dictionary of Professor W. W. Skeat—which has been specially helpful in compiling the later columns in this work—and the Oxford English Dictionary of Dr. J. A. H. Murray. These two treatises are now materially supplemented and their sources for most of the chief words greatly extended by the new evidence. This also discloses the Sumerian or Sumero-Phœnician origin of a considerable number of obscure roots and in their original forms, the existence of which in supposititious forms had been merely inferred or marked " unknown "; and not a few of the supposed derivations are found to be no longer tenable.

The English language significantly is seen to preserve to an especial degree the older and purer word-forms of the Sumerian or Sumero-Phœnician or Early Aryan speech with also a good many of its structural features. It thus preserves along with the Eddic Gothic a considerable number of purer Sumerian word-forms with their original meanings than the Greek, Latin, Sanskrit, German and Anglo-Saxon, from which latter two nevertheless the English has hitherto been supposed to be derived although neither of them contain many of the elementary Aryan Gothic words present in English. Moreover its words approach more nearly to the Eddic Gothic than do any of the other European Aryan languages, owing apparently to its having been derived, as I have already indicated, from the Ancient Briton or " Catti " language or British Gothic,[1] of which literary specimens appear to survive in the older Gothic Eddas, which epics have been shown by Bugge and others to have been evidently composed in Britain. Whilst Anglo-Saxon and German, on the other hand, appear to have been merely local dialects of the Briton resulting from the former colonizing conquests of Germany and Denmark and Jutland, by the Britons or Phœnician " Catti," " Chatti " or Goths.[2]

The indigenous origin of the English language is confirmed by a large series of Phœnician inscriptions in the Ancient Briton language dating from 1100 B.C. onwards recently found on a prehistoric tomb in Ireland, and forming the subject of my special memoir which is now in the press. And it now appears that most of the words in " Anglo-Saxon " are neither continental Angle nor Germanic Saxon, but Briton.

The intimate affinity of the Eddic or Northern Gothic Language with the Sumerian or Sumero-Phœnician is also seen from the occurrence in Sumerian literature of the same personal and names, titles and exploits for the Early Sumerian kings and heroes as in the Gothic Eddas. Thus we now find through the Dictionary that the leading early Sumerian hero, who was afterwards deified, Lord or King *Dar*, *Dur* or *Tur*, is in the same relative position, with the same titles, and with the same exploits as *Thor* or *Dor* of the Eddas with his titles of Bur, Fiorgyni, Miot, Ottar, Sig, Uko and Ygg. The queen of Dar or Tur is *Sib*, the lady of the magic divining bowl, in series with Thor's queen *Sif* and the magic bowl of the Well of Urd, of which *Sif* was a vestal priestess. As contemporaries of King Dar or Tur in the Sumerian we find *Frigg*, *Idun* of the apples of Life, *Thiazi*, *Bauge* and others as in the Eddas. The generic title of *Asa* or " Lord " or " lady " for Thor and his royal Goths is now found to have its origin in the Sumerian *As'*, " lord " or " lady " which is also

---

[1] WPOB, 167 f, 179 f, 370.   [2] Ib., 135, 157, 186.

applied to these personages in the Sumerian. And the Eddic name of "*Ginnunga Gap*" or "Gulf or Gape of *Ginnunga*" for the name of the plain conquered by Thor is now disclosed as the Sumerian *Kan-in-gi*, the ancient Sumerian name for the deltaic plain of Chaldean Mesopotamia on the Persian Gulf. Most of these identities are established in the present part of the Dictionary, and fuller details are given in my new literal translation of the Gothic Eddas as a historical epic of human Early Gothic kings—a translation made many years ago, but the publication of which has been long delayed.

The Sumerian origin of the Egyptian hieroglyphs with their word-forms and meanings, hitherto wholly unsuspected is disclosed. This is illustrated in the plates in regard to 48 chief radical signs, and many others are given in the companion work on the Aryan Origin of the Alphabet. The radically Aryan source of the Egyptian Language and Civilization is also freely evidenced in the text, despite the infiltration of Semitic forms and idioms from the Semitic of Akkad and the Land of Ham.

On History and Ethnology, some of the effects of the new evidence in recovering remote history are indicated in the above paragraph—the detailed evidence for the date of King Dar is given in the work now in the press. Amongst other legendary heroes and demigods and people who have their *Sumerian* and human basis and identity thus recovered, are the Homeric Dar-danus, the Achaians, Dardanians, Dorians, Trojans and Phrygians, all of whom seem to be found also in the Egyptian. Mythologically, the gods Bacchus, Ouranos, and the goddesses Athene and Diana are also disclosed as Sumerian in origin and also appear to occur in Egyptian. Osiris, Isis, Ra and Ammon are found to be Sumerian and the original Sumerian forms of their names are recovered. Iron, under its Sumerian name of *Bar* or *Bir*, is seen the Sumerian source of the Latin Fer-rum, and the French *Fer*, and the English "Iron," and indicates the remote acquaintance of the Sumerians or Early Aryans with that metal. Whilst the identification of Menes, the founder of the First Dynasty of Egypt with Manis-tusu, the son of Sargon-the-Great, a Sumero-Phœnician, supplies for the first time the criterion for fixing that most disputed yet critically important of all dates in ancient history—the date of Menes.

PLATE V.   SUMERIAN   EGYPTIAN

Sumerian	Egyptian
PJR, PIUR. "Base, foundation, floor, platform." —(?Pier) = Br. 5480, 5489, M.D. 415. B. 234. On Pi value cp. Br. 7506.	**P.** "Base, stand, block of wood or stone." (word unknown in Egypt, only initial known.) G. 47, fig. 95. BD. 229ᵃ
RA, "Sun, bright, Sun-god." Pict. winged disc or circle. M. 5741, 5785, 5807. WPOB 242f. B. 337.	**RĀ,** "Sun, Sun-god." G. 30, fig. 10.
SAT, "Land, country, mountain." Pict. of three hills. Br. 7392, 7396. B. 322.	**SAT, SAMT,** "Foreign land, hilly desert. Pict. 3 hills.—M in neighbourhood of S seems negligible. G. 31.
SAB, "Heart, interior, midst". Pict. diag. of heart with valves. B. 7988. B. 340.	**AB,** "Heart, interior, middle." Pict. heart with vessels & valves. G. 18, fig. 46.
SAR, "Garden, plantation, park, grove, marshland, green." = Pict. garden with plants. Br. 4237, 4303, 4315f. M. 1865. B. 170	**SA,** "Garden, plants, orchard, grove, meadow, green." Pict. pool with lotuses. G. 28. BD. 721ᵃ The final R is ? dropped.
SIR, ṢIR, "Serpent." Pict. serpent with coils. Br. 7638-39. B. 328. And see Ar "serpent" & Fi "Viper" in Dict.	**YĀR, AĀR,** "Serpent (uræus)" a. **ZE-T, SYA-T,** "Snake (cerastes)" b. BD. 29ᵃ, 593ᵃ, 641ᵃ; G. 24, figs 16, 173. a. b. S initial seems dropped out in a.
-U, "Go, come, bring." Pict. a pair of feet & legs. Br. 4933-34. M. 3369. B. 208.	**AU,** "Go, come, visit, return." Pict. a pair of feet & legs. G. 16, fig. 156. BD. 30ᵃ-31ᵃ
KI, GI, QI, "Earth, land, ground." = Pict. a mound of earth. Br. 9621, 9636. B. 419.	**QAY, KHI, KHUI,** "Earth, land, high ground". G. 32; BD. 537ᵇ
NA, "Stone." Pict. a stone with strokes for solidity. Br. 1632. B. 71; & cp. Na "jewel", PSL 149.	**NA,** "A kind of Stone, a gem, determinative of stones." BD. 344³ & cxxvi, 69.
UR, URU, "Dog." Diagram of dog's head & neck. Br. 11260. M. 8642. B. 516.	**UHR,** "Dog". Pict. of mastiff. BD. 147²; 177²

L.A.W. del.

SUMERIAN ORIGIN OF EGYPTIAN HIEROGLYPHS (and see Plates I-IV.)

SUMER-ARYAN DICTIONARY

On Folk-lore, it is seen that the early Hitto-Sumerians, or Hitto-Phœnicians brought with them to Britain as part of their most treasured possessions, their body of traditional romance and nursery tales, now seen to be epic and infantile versions of great historical events in the rise of the Aryans. Thus the Arthur and Thor legends with their Holy Grail are based upon historical Sumerian heroic achievements. And similarly Jack-the-Giant-Killer, Jack-and-the-Bean-Stalk, Old Mother Hubbard, Old Mother Goose, Little Red Riding Hood and so on.

In such a pioneer work dealing with so many details and compiled from so many diverse sources and languages, although great pains have been taken to avoid errors, it is too much to hope that none have crept in. But, like the author of a famous dictionary, the writer would say, that the number of mistakes that critics may find will be a source of satisfaction rather than annoyance, as bringing us nearer to the absolute Truth.

Here it is a pleasure to acknowledge the kind assistance of my friend Dr. Islay B. Muirhead for several suggestions for clarifying expressions in this preface; the ever-ready help extended by Prof. T. G. Pinches in solving Assyrian knotty points; and the courtesy of Sir Wallis Budge for several additional references to the pioneer work of Sir Henry Rawlinson. My thanks are also due to the Edinburgh Press for their special care in printing the detailed references.

The present volume, forming Part I, gives the Sumerian words with their Aryan derivatives from A to F. In the concluding part it is hoped to supply as an appendix an index to the English words derived from the Sumerian or Early Aryan for facility of reference.

In conclusion, it only remains to add that not only as preserving the language, but as reflecting the mind and temperament of the parents of our Civilization as expressed in their art, science and religion, the Sumerian or Early Aryan has in these days a unique and growing interest; and it may be hoped that the younger generation of philologists, for whom this work is written, may be led to devote time and attention to its sympathetic study in the light shed upon it through the newly found Aryan keys.

L. A. WADDELL.

December 1926.

LIST OF ABBREVIATIONS

B.	The Origin and Development of Babylonian Writing. G. A. Barton, Leipzig, 1913.
BAD.	Anglo-Saxon and English Dictionary. J. Bosworth, 1901.
BB.	Bismya: The Lost City of Adab. E. J. Banks, New York, 1912.
BC.	Antiquities, Historical and Monumental, of the County of Cornwall. W. Borlase, 2nd Ed., 1769.
BD.	An Egyptian Hieroglyphic Dictionary. E. A. W. Budge, 1920.
BGE.	Gods of the Egyptians. E. A. W. Budge, 1904.
BP.	Phœnicischen Glossar. A Bloch, Berlin, 1891.
Br.	Classified List of Cuneiform Ideographs. R. E. Brünnow, Leyden, 1889.
BRA.	Rise and Progress of Assyriology. E. A. W. Budge, 1925.
CD.	Pali Dictionary. R. C. Childers, 1875.
CIS.	Corpus Inscript. Semiticarum : Inscript. Phœnicias. Paris, 1883 f.
CIWA.	Cuneiform Inscripts. of Western Asia. H. C. Rawlinson.
CT.	Cuneiform Texts from Babylonian Tablets, etc., in the British Museum.
EB.	Encyclopedia Biblica. T. K. Cheyne, 1902.
Edda.	Codex Regius af den Ældre Edda. L. F. A. Wimmer and F. Jönsson, Copenhagen, 1891 (WJ.) ; Edda Text, ed. G. Neckel, Heidelberg, 1914 (N).
FN.	River Names of Europe. R. Ferguson, 1862.
GD.	Dictionnaire Celto-Breton. J. F. M. A. le Gonidec, Angoulême, 1821.
GH.	Hieroglyphs. F. L. Griffith, 1898.
GSP.	Scripturae Linguasque Phœniciae. G. Gesenius, Leipsiae, 1837.
GTM.	Teutonic Mythology. J. Grimm, 1880.
H.	Herodoti Historiarum, Lib. IX, ed. Kallenberg, Leipsiae, 1890.
HOB.	Old Babylonian Inscriptions. H. V. Hilprecht, 1896.
IA.	Indian Antiquary. Bombay.
ID.	Dictionary of the English and Italian Languages. J. E. Wessely.
JRAS.	Journal of Royal Asiatic Society.
JSD.	Dictionary of the Scottish Language. J. Jamieson, ed. W. M. Metcalfe, 1912.
KD.	Inscriptions of Darius the Great at Behistun. L. W. King, 1907.
LD.	Latin Dictionary. C. T. Lewis and C. Short, 1879.
LSD.	Greek-English Lexicon. Liddell and Scott, 1897.
LSG.	Sumerian Grammar. S. Langdon, Paris, 1911.
M.	Seltene assyrische Ideogramme. Meissner, Leipzig, 1906.
MD.	Dictionary of the Assyrian Language. W. Muss-Arnolt, Berlin, 1905.
MGD.	Etymological Gaelic Dictionary. A. Macbain, 1911.
MKI.	Vedic Index of Names and Subjects. A. A. Macdonell and A. B. Keith, 1912.
MTG.	Dictionnaire comparatif des Langues Teuto-Gothiques. H. Meidinger, Francfort, 1836.
MWD.	Sanskrit-English Dictionary. M. Monier-Williams, 1899.

SUMER-ARYAN DICTIONARY

MWG.	Grammar of the Sanskrit Language. M. Monier-Williams, 1864.
PL.	Sign-List of Babylonian Wedge-Writing. T. G. Pinches, 1882.
PRE.	Religion of Ancient Egypt. Wm. Flinders Petrie, 1908.
PSL.	Sumerian Lexicon, J. D. Prince, Leipzig, 1908.
PV.	Vocabulaire Hiéroglyphique. P. Pierret, Paris, 1875.
RP.	History of Phœnicia. G. Rawlinson, 1889.
RV.	Rig Veda.
SAC.	Archæology of the Cuneiform Inscriptions. A. H. Sayce, 1908.
SD.	Etymological Dictionary of the English Language. W. W. Skeat, 1898.
SG.	Gothisches Glossar. E. Schulze, Magdeburg, 1847.
SMG.	Moeso-Gothic Glossary. W. W. Skeat, 1868.
SP.	Die Phœnizische Sprache. P. Schröder, Halle, 1869.
St.	Strabo.
TIS.	Les Inscriptions de Sumer et d'Akkad. F. Thureau-Dangin, Paris, 1905.
TWP.	Words and Places. I. Taylor, 1864.
VD.	Icelandic-English Dictionary. G. Vigfusson, 1874.
WBT.	The Buddhism of Tibet. L. A. Waddell, 1895.
WDD.	English Dialect Dictionary. J. Wright, 1898.
WISD.	Indo-Sumerian Seals Deciphered. L. A. Waddell, 1925.
WPOB.	Phœnician Origin of the Britons, Scots and Anglo-Saxons. L. A. Waddell, 1924, 2nd Ed., 1925.

ABBREVIATIONS

(For other Abbreviations see fuller "List of Abbreviations," p. xlv.)

Su.=Sumerian. Numbers in Br. B =BW. M.=M. P.=PSL.
Ak.=Akkad, including Semitic Phœnician. Numbers in MD. P=Semitic Phœnician.
Eg.=Egyptian. Numbers in BD. G.=GH.
Sk.=Sanskrit. IP.=Indo-Persian. P.=Pali. Z.=Zend.
Gr.=Greek.
Lat.=Latin. F.=French. I.=Italian. S.=Spanish.
Goth. & Anc. Br.=Gothic, including Ancient Briton. E.=Edda. I.=Iceland. U.=Ulfilas.
Nor.=Norse Group. D.=Danish. L.=Lithuan. N.=Norse. S.=Swede.
Ger.=German. O.=Old High German.
Co. & Celt.=Cornish & "Celtic." Br.=Breton. Co.=Cornish. Cy.=Cymric. G.=Gaelic. I.=Irish. S.=Scots.
A-S.=Anglo-Saxon. N.=Northumbrian.
O.E.=Old English.
E.=English.

A

Changing dialectically and inflectively to E, I and U

A

Su.—**A,** intensive, augment or abstract prefix to verbs and other roots. P.6. LSG.95.
Eg.—*A,* intensive prefix. 105*b.*
Sk.—*A,* augment prefix.
Gr.—*A,* intensive prefix.
Lat.—*A,* intensive prefix.
Goth. & Anc. Br.—*A,* intensive prefix to verbs sometimes. EI.
A-S.—*A,* intensive prefix to verbs sometimes.
E.—A, intensive prefix to verbs, with sense of "out, out from, in, or up," e.g., *A*rise, *A*bide, *A*base, *A*go, *A*maze, *A*rouse; or the sense of "very" in *A*ghast, etc.

A

Su.—**A,** first personal pronoun I; also Thou, he, and she. 11,327 f. B.521(6). And see *Aqu, Egi,* I.
Ak.—*Anak,* I. P (BP. 14). *Anāku,* I, 70.
Eg.—*A or J,* first pers. pr. I. 15*a.*
Sk.—*Ah(am),* first pers. pr. I.
Gr.—'*E,* him-, her-, or it-self.
Co. & Celt.—*A,* my, his, hers. Co. *Aff* I, me. Co. *A* his, her. I.
E.—A, for pers. pron. I, He, and She in provincial dialects.

A

Su.—**A,** preposition To, unto, for, upon, in, into, near, by; also ablative suffix At, with, by, from, 6651, 11,365, M.4681, 8696, B.293,521.
Ak.—*Ana,* prefix To, unto, for, etc., 64. *Ina,* prefix, In, into, upon, near, by, from, 66. *Itti,* suffix, At, with, from, 127.
Eg.—*A,* prep. Before, in the presence of. 105*a.*
Sk.—*A,* prep. To, from, towards, near to, in, at, on.
Lat.—*A,* prep. To, from, out of. *Ā,* to, with, etc. F. *A,* to, for, on, by, in. I.
Goth. & Anc. Br.—*A,* prep. To, on, upon, in, with, by, from. EI.
Co. & Celt.—*A,* of, by, from, out of. Co. *A,* in, from, out of. GI.
A-S.—*A,* prefix From, out, away.
E.—A- prepositional prefix in many words, e.g., A-bed, A-board, A-breast, A-broad, A-field, A-float, etc., etc.

A

Su.—**Ā,** interjection Ah! O! M.8694, B.521.
Ak.—*Ūa,* Ah! Oh! Alas! 1.
Eg.—*Ā,* Oh! Alas! 106*b.* *Aa, Ha,* Glory! O! hail. 15*a,* 438*a.* *Au,* cry out, wail. 7*b.*
Sk.—*A, Ā,* Ah! Oh! *Ahve,* call, invoke.

I

Gr.—*A*, Ah! O!
Lat.—*A, Ah,* Ah! Ha! *Ave,* hail!
Goth. & Anc. Br.—*Á, Ai, Æ,* Ah! O! EI.
Nor.—*A,* Ah! DNL.
Ger.—*Ah ! Ach.* Ah!
Co. & Celt.—*A, O,* Ah! O! Co.GI.
A-S.—(absent).
O.E.—*A !* interject.
E. Ah ! an interjection of surprise, joy, pain, etc. Ave ! hail !

A, Ā

Su.—**A, Ā,** Water, flood, flowing water. Word-sign pictured by a Wavelet essentially similar to the Egyptian hieroglyph Water sign. See *Me, A,* pl. IV. 11,331, 11,341 f. B.521. And see *Ab, Agià, Ara,* to hurry or flow, *Bur, Dur, E, Ege,* Ocean and *Me,* Water.
Ak.—*Mu,* water, 503. *Ea,* king of the ocean, 2.
Eg.—*Au, Auh,* river, stream, to flow. 31*b*, 35*b*. *Aur,* river. 35*b*. *Ar,* river. The Nile (as the Hurrying One, see *Ara,* to hurry). 69*a. Mu,* water, G.33 [from Akkad, *Mu,* water] with hieroglyph as in Sumerian. See pl. IV., *Me.*
Sk.—*Ahi,* water. *Ha,* water.
Lat.—*Eau,* water, river. F.
Goth. & Anc. Br.—*Á,* river. EI.
Nor.—*A, Aa,* river, rivulet. DN.
Co. & Celt.—*Awy,* river. Co. *Aw,* river. Cy. *A, Au, Ow,* river, sea. S(JD.).
A-S.—*Æ, Eā, Ie,* water, river, running water.
E.—*Aa, Ae, Awe, Eye, Yeo,* etc., river names, e.g., Ae in Dumfriessh., Awe in Argylesh., the 5 Yeo rivulets in Devon, Eye in Berwicksh., Aa rivers in France, Holland and Russia. And see *E* variant of *A* water, and *Ar* as the Hurrying Water under *Ara,* Hurry.

A

Su.—**A,** Father, mother, abbreviation for *Abu, Ad,* father, q.v. Pictured by the foregoing Water sign. 11,324, B.521.
Ak.—*Ab,* father. P. *Abu,* father, 4.
Eg.—*A,* an old man. 15*a*.
Sk.—*Ā,* grandfather.
Gr.—(*Iō,* traditional ancestress of Cadmus and the Phœnicians and Egyptians).
Lat.—*Aio,* governor, preceptor. I. *Aïeux,* forefathers, ancestors. F.
Goth. & Anc. Br.—*Ai,* great-grandfather, ancestor. EI.
Co. & Celt.—*Aho,* pedigree (paternity). Co.

Ā

Su.—**Ā,** Arm, hand, side, the right hand. Pictured by a Right Hand with Forearm as in Egyptian hieroglyph *A*, arm, hand, see *Ā,* pl. I. 6542, 6548-9. B.293, and see *As', Id,* Hand, Arm, Side.

Ak.—*Aenonu,* right hand. 58 cp. M.1822. *Ida,* side, 17.
Eg.—*Ā,* hand, arm. 105*a*, G.12, with. Fig. 100, with same hieroglyph as in Sumerian *Ā,* see pl. I., and cp. Ramen (Armen) arm. 425*a*.
Gr.—('*Armos* a joint, the shoulder).
Lat.—*Armus,* the shoulder. .
Goth. & Anc. Br.—*Arm,* an arm. EI.
Nor.—*Arm,* an arm. DNS.
Ger.—*Arm,* an arm.
A-S.—*Earm,* arm.
O.E.—*Arm, Ærm,* arm.
E.—Arm, ? from Akkad, *Amenu* or Eg. *Armen*: Arm-chair, Arm-ful, Arm-less, Arm-let, Armpit.

A, Ā

Su.—**A, Ā,** Ground, foundation, dwelling, rise up, be high ——— ? Island. Pictured by an oblong enclosure with dots or short transverse strokes (in its earliest form on Udug's Bowl, HOB.108-9) which is substantially identical with the Egyptian hieroglyph for Island, *Aa.* 10,495, 10,521,10,523,M.7,975-6, B.481. See pl. I.
Ak.—*Ae, Ai,* island P(BP.12). *Aśāśu,* ground, foundation, dwelling, 122. *Iśdu,* ground, foundation, 113. *Naśu,* rise up, be high, lift up, 732 f.
Eg.—*Aa, Aa-t, Yat,* an island. 16*a* and G. 31, Fig. 50, with hieroglyph as in Sumerian. See pl. I. *Aaa,* ground, earth, 16*b*.
Gr.—*Aia,* land, earth. *Eion,* sea-shore, bank, beach. (*Nēsos,* an island. ? from Akkad, Nas'u.)
Goth. & Anc. Br.—*Ey,* island of the sea. EI.
Nor.—*Öy,* island, N. *Oe,* D. *Ö,* S.
Ger.—*Aue,* meadow pasture ground.
Co. & Celt.—*Aut,* sea-shore, bank of a river. Co.
A-S.—*Æg, Ig, Icg,* island.
O.E.—*Ait, Eyght,* islet.
E.—Ait or Eyot, a little island, *-ay, -ea, -ey,* suffixes for islands and place-names, e.g., Aldern-ey, Bermonds-ey, Cherts-ey, Guernsey, Jers-ey, Orkn-ey, Putn-ey, Sels-ey, Shepp-ey, Stepn-ey, Thorn-ey, Far-oe, Cumbr-ae, Batters-ea, Chels-ea, Colons-ay, Ronalds-ay, Rothes-ay, etc. And see WPOB.43.

AB, AP

Su.—**AB, AP,** House. Pictured by a House. 3815, B.147. And see *Bid,* Abode and *Eś,* House.
Ak.—*Aptu,* house, 83.
Eg.—*Ap-t, Apa,* house, dwelling, palace, 41*b*, 42*a*. *Ab-t,* abode, building, 37*b*, 38*a*.
Sk.—*Āvasa,* abide in.
Lat.—*Abbatia,* abbey.
Goth. & Anc. Br.—*Hof,* temple, hall, court. EI.(*Hafa,* hold. EI.)

Nor.—*Hof*, court. DN.
Ger.—*Hof*, court, farm.
Co. & Celt.—*Havodry*, cottage. Co. *Haft*, a dwelling. S.
A-S.—*Hōf*, house, palace. (*Habban*, to hold).
O.E.—*Abbēye*, religious house.
E.—Abbey, a religious house. Haven, a harbour, see *Ab*, Sea, as "House of Waters."

AB, AP, ABBA

Su.—AB, AP, ABBA, Father, old man, leader, also a title of the Father-god Bel. Pictured by the House sign, with the idea of the Father as the master of the house. 3816, 3819, 3821, etc. M.2486, etc., B.147. And see *A*, Father, and *Ad, Adda*, Father.
Ak.—*Ab*, father. P(BP.9). *Abū*, father, 4. *Babu*, father, 142.
Eg.—*Ab*, father. 5*a*. *Aba*, captain. 117*b*. *Abu(t)*, forefathers, grandparents. 4*b*. *Papa*, father. 233*b*. *Uāb*, holy man, a priest, pourer of Water. 155*a*. *Abb*, title of Father-god Osiris. 118*a*.
Sk.—*Av*, to protect. *Pa, Papa*, protector. *Bāp*, father. I.P. *Bābu*, master, Hindi.
Gr.—*Abba*, father. *Aba*, manhood. *Pappa*, father. (Homer Od., 6.57.)
Lat.—*Abbas*, father. *Avs, Avus*, grandfather, ancestor. *Abbas*, an abbot. *Abbé*, an abbot, priest. F. *Papa*, spiritual father, bishop. *Papa*, father. F. *Babbo*, father. I.
Goth. & Anc. Br.—*Aba, Avo, Afi*, grandfather. E.I. *Aba*, husband. U. *Awo*, grandmother. U.
Nor.—*Afi*, grandfather. DN.
Ger.—*Abt*, abbot. *Haupt*, chieftain.
Co. & Celt.—*Abat*, abbot. Co. *Abod*, abbot. Cy. *Aba*, an abbot. GI.
A-S.—*Abot, Abod*, abbot.
O.E.—*Abbot, Abbod*, abbot. *Pope*, the Pope.
E.—Abbot, the father of an abbey: Abbé. Pa, Papa, father, by reduplication of *Ap, Abba* and dropping of initial *A*, see WPOB. 318. Pope, the father of a church, the bishop of Rome: Pope-dom, Pope-ry, Pop-ish, Pap-acy, Pap-al, Pap-ist, Pap-ism. *Bābu, Baboo*, master, a gentleman (Ind.).

AB, AP, ABBA

Su.—AB, AP, ABBA, Sea, ocean, the Deep. Pictured by the same House sign with the idea of the Sea as "The House of the Waters." 3822, M.2492, B.147. And see *A, Badur*, water, *Abzu*, Abyss, *Agia, Ega. Durabba*, Ocean, and *Dur, Me* or *We*, water.
Ak.—*Tāmtu*, the ocean, the sea. 1173.
Eg.—*Ab*, purification by washing with water, 38*b*, 177*a*. cp. G.40. *Hapi*, Water-god of Nile, 475*b*. *Apap*, Serpent of the Deep. 111*a*.
Sk.—*Ap*, water, the Waters. *Apo*, waters. *Apas*, watery.
Gr.—*Aphros*, a river.
Lat.—? *Abas*, a shower (bath). F. ? *Abée* a mill-dam. F. ? *Abîme*, unfathomable depth. F.
Goth. & Anc. Br.—*Haf*, the ocean. EI. *Hōfn*, haven. EI. *Ahva*, river. U.
Nor.—*Hav*, the sea. DN. *Affa*, river. DN. *Uppe*, river. L. *Havn, Hafn*, haven. DN.
Ger.—*Hafen*, haven.
Co. & Celt.—*Awy*, river. Co. *Afon*, river. Cy. *Abhainn, Abhann*, river. GI.
A-S.—*Ap-flod*, overflowing sea. *Hæfene*, haven.
O.E.—*Haven*, haven.
E.—Haven, a harbour, port (? in Sumerian sense of "House of the Waters"): in place-names, New-haven, Stone-haven, etc. *Avon, Evan, Owen, Ive*, etc., as proper names of rivers: Avon of Stratford, Avon of Bath, Avon or Evan in Gloucester, Hants, Devon, Monmouth, Glamorgan, Lanark, Stirling, Banff, Ross, Kincardine, Dumfries. *Ive* and *Ehen* in Cumberland, etc. *Aune* in Devon; and in Ireland *Aven*-banna in Wexford, *Aven*-bui in Cork, *Aven*-gorm in Sligo, *Aven*-more in Mayo, see TWP.205 f. And note the *Abana* river of Damascus, a city of the Phoenicians. And see *Abzu*, Abyss.

AB, AP

Su.—AB, AP, Beget of animals and things, be born, cattle, create for one's self. Pictured by a sign of two bracketed confluent lines and supposed to signify pairing or doubling. 8869-71. M.6648-9. P.13. B.373.
Ak.—*Banū*, beget of animals, etc., create for one's self. 173. *Arhu*, ox. 98. *Littu*, cow. 500. *Miru*, colt, young of animals. PSL.13. (*Aplu*), son).
Eg.—*Ab*, a calf. 37*b*. *Ābu*, cattle (for sacrifice). 116*b*. *Abb*, sheep, goats. 39*b*. *Hap*, "Apis" Bull. 487*a*. *Api(t)*, nursing Mother-goddess. 41*b*.
Sk.—*Ap-nas*, progeny, property, wealth.
Gr.—*Aph-nos*, wealth.
Lat.—*Ops*, abundance, wealth, riches. *Opulens*, wealthy. (*Copia*, plenty). *Ops*, earth goddess of abundance and agriculture. *Habere*, to have.
Goth. & Anc. Br.—*Ap-li*, an ox, or horse. EI. *Afla*, farming. I. *Afla, Afli, Ave*, produce, gain, acquisition. EI. *Hafa*, to have. EI. *Hafan*, to have. U.
Nor.—*Af-la*, beget, breed stock. S. *Avling*, farming. DN. *Hafva*, to have. S. *Have*, have. DN.
Ger.—*Far, Pfar*, ox (Old G.). *Haben*, have.
A-S.—*Afaran*, children. *Eafora*, progeny, offspring. *Heahfore*, heifer. *Habban*, to have.

O.E.—*Far*, an ox (Northumb.). *Hayfare*, heifer. *Hauen*, to have.

E.—Op-ulence, wealth (? originally wealth in cattle): Op-ulency, Op-ulent. Heifer, a young cow (as breeder). Have, to possess (seems to come here); see *Buz*, possess. The *Apis* Bull of the Egyptians is disclosed as deriving its name from the Sumerian, *Ap*, ox. *Ops*, the Roman Earth goddess of abundance and tender of young children, is seen to be obviously cognate with the Egyptian Nursing Mother-goddess *Api(t)*.

AB, AP

Su.—**AB, AP**, Operate, work, do, make, construct, build, erect. Pictured by the sign as the foregoing (Opulence) with which the idea of Work was related by the Sumerians. M.6649. B.373.

Ak.—*Banū*, do make, construct, build, erect. 174.

Eg.—*Aabu*, an official. 19b. *Uba*, work, toil. workman, artisan, servant. 158a. *Upi*, work, business, affairs, workers, 160b. *Āb*, strength. 115b.

Sk.—*Ap* work. *Apas*, work, action.

Lat.—*Ops*, might, power. *Opus*, work, labour. *Officium*, service, duty, dutiful, action. *Officier*, an officer, one who performs service.

Goth. & Anc. Br.—*Afl*, might, power, strength, to cause, help, aid, to earn. EI. *Afli, Eflu*, to make strong, build, to perform. EI.

A-S.—*Eafoth*, strength, valour.

O.E.—*Able*, having power. *Offiz*, office.

E.—Able, skilful, having power, strength, Able-bodied—A.B. seaman, Ab-lest, Ab-ility, Ab-ly. Off-ice, work, employment, duty, service: Office-bearer, Offic-er, Offic-ial, Offic-ialism, Offic-iant, Offic-iate, Offic-iator, Offic-inal, Offic-ious, Offic-iously, Offic-iousness. Oper-ate, to work, to exert strength, to produce an effect: Op-erant, Op-eration, Op-erating, Op-erator. Opus, work, a work.

ABA

Su.—**ABA**, Off, after, behind, thereupon, thereon, 11,367-8.

Ak.—*Arku*, after, behind, thereupon, thereon, backward. 100. *Arkatu*, back, backwards, after. 101.

Eg.—*Ăb*, to drop back, to ebb (of Nile). 116a. *Au, Haa*; behind. 30b, 457b. *Ăb*, resist, oppose. 116a. *Ub*, opposite. 158a.

Sk.—*Apa, Ava*, back, down, away from. *Upa*, under, down, and used as prefix as "son" in personal names. *Apara*, posterior, after.

Gr.—*Apo*, from, off. *Epi*, upon, over, after. *Upo, Hypo*, below, under. *Opse*, after a long time, late, the evening.

Lat.—*Ab*, from. *Ob*, out of, over, near, against, etc.

Goth. & Anc. Br.—*Aptr, Eftir*, after, behind, back, backwards. EI. *Af*, from, of. EI. *Efri*, the latter part, last, upper. EI. *Afar*, after. U. *Aftra*, back. U. *Aftan, Aptan*, the evening, behind, or late. EI.

Nor.—*Efter*, after. DN. *Af*, former of. DN. *Ebbe*, ebb. DN. *Ebb*, ebb. S. *Aften, Afton*, evening. DNG.

Ger.—*Ab*, off, from. *Auf*, on, upon, up, after. *Abend*, evening.

Co. & Celt.—*Ap*, son, as prefix in surnames in Br. and Cy.

A-S.—*Æft, Efter*, after, behind, afterwards. *Ebba*, ebb. *Æfen, Efen*, evening.

O.E.—*Aft*, after, back, behind. *Ebbe*, ebb. *Eue, Euen*, evening.

E.—Aft, After, behind in place, later in time: After-crop, After-damp, After-glow, After-guard, After-hands, After-image, After-ings, After-math, After-most, After-noon, After-piece, After-supper, After-thought, After-ward, After-wards, Ab-aft. *Ab-*, prefix in words, for "from, away from." Ab-breviate, Ab-dicate, Ab-erration, Ab-hor, Ab-ject, Ab-jure, Ab-lution, Ab-negate, Ab-rade, Ab-rogate, Ab-rupt, Ab-scess, Ab-scind, Ab-sent, Ab-solve, Ab-sorb, Ab-stract, Ab-surd. *Ap-* and *Up-*, prefix for "son" in Welsh personal names, e.g.: Ap-John, Up-John or son or descendant of John. Similarly in Breton, *Ab* or *Ap*; Ab-Jann, son of John, Ab-Ivin, son of Evan. *Apo-*, prefix in words from the Greek for, from, off. Apo-calypse, Apo-crypha, Apo-gee, Apo-logue, Apo-logy, Apo-thegm, Apo-plexy, Apo-stacy, Apo-state, Apo-stle, Apo-strophe, Apo-thecary, Apo-theosis. Ebb, the backward going of the tide: Ebb-tide, Low ebb. Eve, evening, the latter part of the day: Ev-en-fall, Ev-ening-dress, Ev-ening star, Ev-en-song, Ev-en-tide. *Epi-*, prefix in words for "upon, after": Epi-demic, Epi-dermis, Epi-gastrium, Epi-gram, Epi-graph, Epi-lepsy, Epi-logue, Epi-phany, Epi-sode, Epi-stle, Epi-taph, Epi-thelium, Epi-thet, Epi-tome, Ep-och, Eponym. *Hypo-*, prefix in words from the Greek for "below, under": Hyp-hen, Hypo-chondria, Hypo-crisy, Hypo-gastric, Hypo-tenuse, Hypo-thec, Hypo-thesis. *Ob-, Of-, Op-*, prefix in words from the Latin for "over, near, against," etc.: Ob-durate, Ob-edient, Ob-eisance, Ob-fuscate, Ob-ject, Ob-late, Ob-lige, Ob-lique, Ob-literate, Ob-livion, Ob-long, Ob-loquy, Ob-noxious, Ob-scure, Ob-sequies, Ob-serve, Ob-solete, Ob-stacle, Ob-stetric, Ob-stinate, Ob-streperous, Ob-struct, Ob-tain, Ob-trude, Ob-tuse, Ob-verse, Ob-viate, Ob-vious. Off, away from: Off-al, Off-ing, Off-scouring, Off-set, Off-shoot, Off-spring.

ABNI

Su.—**ABNI**, Oven, furnace, defined as "The place of Fire." 9688, P.15.
Ak.—*Masādu*, a furnace. PSL.15.
Eg.—*Aabes*, fire-brazier. 110b.
Gr.—*'Ipnos*, oven, furnace.
Goth. & Anc. Br.—*Ofn, Own*, oven. EI. *Auhns.* U.
Nor.—*Ovn*, oven. DN.
Ger.—*Ofen*, oven.
Co. & Celt.—*O'on*, oven. S.
A-S.—*Ofn, Ofen*, oven.
O.E.—*Ouen*, oven.
E.—Oven, a furnace, a heated cavity for baking bread, etc. Dutch oven.

ABZU

Su.—**ABZU**, Deep, the ocean, the sea—Abyss. Also the name of the font or basin of water or "sea" for Purification in Early Sumerian temples, see WPOB.273.
Ak.—*Apsū*, deep, the ocean, also the name of a font or basin—"the Sea" for purification in Babylonian temples. 80.
Sk.—*Apas*, the Waters.
Gr.—*Abussos*, bottomless, deep gulf.
Lat.—*Abyssus*, bottomless, deep gulf.
Co. & Celt.—*Isav*, the bottom. Co. *Aibheis*, sea, the deep. GI.
E.—Abyss, a deep gulf: Abys-m, Abys-mal. "Abyss" was also the name for the font or "sea" of water for purification in Sumerian Sun-temples, and the obvious source of "the Sea" basin in Solomon's temple, and of the *Piscina* (or "Fish-pond") beside the altar in old Christian churches. See details in WPOB.273 f.

AD, AT, ADDA

Su.—**AD, AT, ADDA**, Father, also Mother. Pictured by a sign variously interpreted: (1) as a house containing the sign for Protection and thus designating the Father as "Protector of the House" or "Hus-band," or (2) a Nest with the sign for "Build or Beget." The sign also means "Mother" and this may be as P. suggests, a vestige of the early matriarchal period when the mother was the head of the gens or family. In this regard it is noteworthy that the mother is often mentioned before the father, e.g., "Mother and father" the reverse of the Semitic usage. This, however, may be owing to the well-known chivalry of the Early Aryans and their treatment of women as equals. *Adda kur-Martu* or "Father of the Western Land" was a Sumerian title as supreme ruler and emperor. 4165-7, 4186. P.15, B.162.
Ak.—*Ad-n*, lord. P(BP.10). *Abū*, father. 4. *Ummu*, mother. 54.
Eg.—*At*, father. 96b. *Ata, Ati*, king. 97a, G.13. *Aut*, family. 105b. *Hat*, ancestor. 460. *Ahti*, Father-god, Osiris. 77a. *At*, a house. 106a.
Sk.—(*Adi, Adya*, first, head-personage). (*Adhiraja*, head king or emperor). (*Adhi-kāra*, supreme rule).
Gr.—*Atta*, father.
Lat.—*Ata-vus*, father of forefathers. *Atta*, father. *Ædes*, a house, a building.
Goth. & Anc. Br.—*Ått, Ætt*, lineage, family, race. EI. *At-la*, grandfather. EI.
Co. & Celt.—*Ath-air*, father. GI. *Tad*, father. Br.Co.Cy. *Adail*, a house. Co. *Aidha*, a house. I.
E.—Dad, a common term for a father: by duplication of *Ad* and dropping of the initial *A*, as in *Papa* for *Ap*, see *Ab, Ap*, father, in series with Cornish and Welsh *Tad*. Ata-vism, reappearance of ancestral characters (not immediately parental) in an individual: Ata-vism. Hat-man, Het-man, title of the headman or chief of the Cossacks, and cp. the Sumerian title of *Adda*, "Father" for supreme ruler in the West, see para. 1.

AD, AT

Su.—**AD, AT**, Snake, serpent, as "The piercer." (-Adder.) This snake meaning is inferred from this *Ad* or Dagger-sign, which is a determinative of the Serpent-name *Sir*, and also means Scorpion. 303, 309 and cp. 7642 where the Serpent-name seems to read in Akkad, *Sir-ad*. M.172 and 179, B.10, 328. And see *Fi*, Viper, Serpent.
Ak.—(*Siru*, a snake, a serpent. 891). *Zuqaqi*, a scorpion. 291. *Aru*, enemy. 91.
Eg.—*At*, the snake Cerastes or horned Viper, is used as a determinative of *At* (father) which is inexplicable in G.25, but is presumably because it has itself the value, *At*. *Aārt*, a snake. 29a. *At*, to hate. 140a. *Nāu*, a serpent, viper. 346b. *Nait*, serpent goddess. 346b, cp. *Nadr* of Gothic.
Sk.—*Ahi*, great serpent. *Ati*, knife for bloodletting.
Gr.—*Atē*, a pest, blind ruin. (*Atē*, avenging goddess of ruin and blindness).
Lat.—*Atrox*, fierce. *Odi*, I hate. *Od-ium*, hatred. *Od-ieux*, odious. F.
Goth. & Anc. Br.—*Nadr*, adder. EI. *Æda*, rage, fury, fear. EI. *Hat*, hate, spite. EI. *Atall*, fierce, loathsome. EI. *Audh*, fate, die. EI. *Hatis*, hate. U.
Nor.—*Nadr*, adder. DN. *Had*, hate. DN. *Hat*, hate. S.
Ger.—*Natter*, adder.
Co. & Celt.—*Naddyr*, adder. Co. *Ate*, spite. Co.
A-S.—*Attor*, a snake in Attor-lic = snake-like.

Nædre, adder. *Attor, Ator*, poison. *Hĕte*, hate.

O.E.—*Addere*, adder. *Hate*, hate. *Odious*, hateful.

E.—Adder, the common viper : Adder's-tongue, Adder's-wort. Hate, intense dislike, to detest : Hate-able, Hate-ful, Hate-fully, Hate-fulness, Hate-r, Hate-red. Odious, hateful : Od-ium, Od-iously, Od-ious-ness.

ADUENI, ATUENI, IDDUENI

Su.—ADUENI, ATUENI, IDDUENI (*Aś*-), The Lady (*Aś*) *Atueni* or *Iddueni*, defined as " The Lady Queen-Seer Woman " and " Lady of the Magic Jar or Bowl," and " of the Bronze Vessel." 11,553-8. On *Id* value for *A*, see 11,322, and for *-ni* syllable, 4574. And see *Aś*, Isis and *Dur*, Magic Bowl.

Ak.—*Il Nin-dar* (or *-ib*), *aśtu*=Lady Queen-Seer Woman. The "*Adar*" read by Br. is purely arbitrary and the " Woman " *aśtu* is omitted. On *dar* as " seer " see Br.10,482.

Eg.—*Āāt*, a title of Isis, *As* or *As-t*, the Mother-goddess. " The Great Enchantress," " Lady of Life," " Lady of Bread and Beer," " Maker of kings," " The placer of enemies under foot." BGE.2, 205-14. Isis or *As* (or *Āāt*) was often called by the Egyptians *Athēne* says Plutarch (De Iside et Osir, c. lxii.)

Gr.—*Athēne*, keeper of the keys of Zeus' chamber of the thunderbolts, protectress of the heroes who fought with Zeus against the Titans.

Goth. & Anc. Br.—*Idunn, Idwyn*, The lady *Asa* of the vessel of the rejuvenating apples for Thor or Sig, the first king of the Goths and his lords the *Asas*, in the Gothic " Edda " epics.

E.—*Idun* or *Idwyn* the Lady Asa in the Gothic Edda epics who carried the " basket " of rejuvenating apples for King Thor, the first traditional king of the Goths, and his Asa lords. Her Magic Bowl is frequently referred to in Sumerian records. See *Aś*, Lady, *Dur*, Magic Bowl and *Edin*, the oracle shrine of the Sun-priestess of the Sumerians. *Athene*, tutelary and war-goddess of the Greeks, is disclosed to have had her human original in the Sumerian priestess-queen Atueni or Idun, whose historicity is detailed in my following work on the Eddas.

AG, AK, AGGA

Su.—AG, AK, AGGA, Act, do, make, command, order. Pictured by a sign supposed to be a tool or drill, see representations in WISD.57, etc. 2772, 2778 and cp. 4744. M.1826. B 110.

Ak.—*Epeśu*, act, do, make, practise, build. 82. *Tertu*, order, command. 1197.

Eg.—*Aakh*, to set, or place. 22a. *Akha*, an auxiliary verb. 133a. *Akh*, to go, 74a. *Aaq*, to rule or govern. 25b. *Haq, Heq*, to rule, direct, command. 512b.

Sk.—*Aj*, to move, drive or throw. *Ac*, to go, make round. *Ajna*, command. *Huqm*, order, command. IP.

Gr.—*Agŏ*, drive, lead.

Lat.—*Ago*, act, drive, etc. *Act-um*, act, a thing done. *Agir*, to act. F. *Acte*, act. F. *Axione*, action. I.

Goth. & Anc. Br.—*Aka*, to move, drive. EI. *Eigia*, to egg, urge or incite, impel. EI.

Nor.—*Akt*, act. DN. *Jag*, hurry, hunt, drive. DN.

Ger.—*Acte*, act. *Jag*, run, hunt.

Co. & Celt.—*Aige, Ect*, act, deed. I. *Eagar*, order. I. *Eg-ni*, activity. Cy. *Aigne*, swift, agile. GI.

O.E.—*Act*, act.

E.—Act, to perform, to exert force or influence, something done : Act-ing, Act-ion, Act-ionable, Act-ive, Act-ivity, Act-or, Act-ress, Act-ual, Act-uality, Act-uary, Act-uate, Ex-act, Re-act, Re-act-ion, Re-act-ionary, etc. Act, a law or legislative command : Acta, Act of Parliament. Uk-ase imperial Russian order. En-act, En-act-ment. Agent, one that acts : Ag-ency. Agile, active : Ag-ility, Ag-ileness. Agitate, to keep moving : Ag-itation, Ag-itator. Agog, astir, eager. Egg, to incite to action : Egg on. Hack, over-worked, a drudge : Hack-ery, a native bullock-cart. Hack-ney carriage, Hack-neyed words. Hack-work, Jack-of-all-trades. Jog, to stir up, Jog-ging, jog-trot.

AG, AKA, ANG

Su.—AG, AKA, ANG, Flame, fire, anger. Pictured by a Fire-torch within an enclosure, which is essentially similar to the Egyptian hieroglyph for *Akh* flame. See pl. I. 4734-5. B.195. On nasalized *Ang*, see P.22.

Ak.—*Akku*, a firepan. 28. *La'abu*, flame. 465.

Eg.—*Aga*, be hot, burn. 140a. *Akh*, fire-brazier, flame. 125a and G.42, with hiero-glyph essentially similar to the Sumerian, see pl. I. *Aakhu*, fire. 22b. *Aug*, heat. 115b. *Ukha(t)*, brazier. 178a.

Sk.—*Ag, Agni*, fire. *Aggi*, P. *Ukha*, oven ash, shine. *Akra*, a kiln. I.P. *Angi-ras*, fire-worshippers.

Gr.—*Augē*, a bright light. *Aig-lē*, bright light, gleam.

Lat.—*Ig-nis*, fire. *Ig-nire*, to set on fire. *Ig-neus*, fiery.

Goth. & Anc. Br.—*Azgo*, cinder-ash. U. *Angr*, anger, grief. EI.

Nor.—*Asz, Ugni*, fire. L.

Co. & Celt.—*Aingeal*, fire. G. *Ingel*, ingle, fire. S. *Lowe*, flame, S. from Akkad, *La'abu*.

O.E.—*Ingle*, fire. *Ig-nition*, a setting on fire.
E.—Igneous, pertaining to fire : Ig-nescent, Ig-niferous, Ig-neous. Ignite, to set on fire : Ig-nitible, Ig-nition, Ingle, fire : Ingle-nook ? Ingot, a mass of metal moulded by fire. Anger, a burning emotion excited by a sense of injury : Ang-rily, Ang-riness, Ang-ry. Lowe, flame (Scot.), from Akkad *La'abu*, flame.

AG, AGGA

Su.—AG, AGGA, Spirits (? Fiery) of the Deep, Evil Spirits. Pictured by same Flame sign as foregoing. 4738, and cp. P.35. B.195.
Ak.—*An-āk*, *Anun-aki*, water-spirits, evil spirits. 71.
Eg.—*Akhu*, *Iaku*, *Yaku*, spirits of Light. 9a, 77b.
Sk.—*Yākka*, P., *Yāxa*, Skt., shining genii of earth, trees and water. *Jāk*, genii. IP.
Gr.—*Aiakos*, a judge of Hades.
Lat.—*Æacus*, a judge of Hades.
Goth. & Anc. Br.—*Ægis*, a spirit of the Deep. EI.
Co. & Celt.—*Acr*, vile, base. Br.
E.—*Jack*-o'-lantern or *Ignis fatuus*, a light seen over marshy places, misleading travellers—also called " Will-o'-the-wisp."

AG, AK

Su.—AG, AK, Hedge in, fence, edge. 2791. P.19. B.110.
Ak.—*Rapaqu*, a fence. 976.
Eg.—*Akhau*, boundaries, delimitation posts. 133b.
Sk.—*Açri*, an edge.
Gr.—*Akē*, a point.
Lat.—*Acies*, an edge.
Goth. & Anc. Br.—*Egg*, an edge. EI. *Hagi*, hedge, a fence. EI. *Ecke*, edge. U.
Nor.—*Æg*, *Eg*, edge. DN. *Hegen*, a hedge. DN.
Co. & Celt.—*Ach-less*, defence, protection. Co.
A-S.—*Ecg*, edge. *Haga*, *Hege*, hedge.
O.E.—*Egge*, edge. *Hegge*, hedge.
E.—Edge, the border of a thing : Edge-d, Edge-less, Edge-tool, Edge-ways, Edge-wise, Edg-ing, Edg-y, Set-on-edge. Hedge, a fence round a field, a boundary, protection : Hedge-bill, Hedge-hog, Hedg-er, Hedge-row, Hedge-sparrow, Hegde-ing.

AG, AKA

Su.—AG, AKA, Grow, Grow up, Land Treasure, property, Harvest. *Ag*, 5946, pict. by " a net + fill." 270. PSL.21. *Ag = Haru*, " dig and harvest " and *Su*, " growth," 5974, and Akkad, *Bassū*, " possessions, treasure," MD 200. *Aka—Busū*, 4742. M.3211-12. B.196. And see *Agar*, " field " and *Buz*, veg-etation.

Ak.—*Sihū*, grow, grow up. 1018. *Busū*, possession, treasure, etc. 200.
Eg.—*Uakh*, grow, increase, be green, flourish. 148a-b. *Uaz*, flourish, be green, fertile. 150a. *Akhs*, harvest. 8b.
Sk.—*Aksh*, pass through, pervade. *Upaci*, grow.
Gr.—*Auxō*, *Aexō*, make, grow, increase, multiply. ? *Agora*, a market-place.
Lat.—*Augeo*, *Uegeo*, increase, make grow. ? *Agora*, a market-place. F.
Goth. & Anc. Br.—*Aexa*, wax or increase. EI. *Aigin*, property, goods. U. *Auka*, to increase, produce of the earth. EIU. *Auka*, increase. U.
Co. & Celt.—*Ach*, issue off, spring, root of a tree. Co. *Achta*, possession, inheritance. Co. *Iz*. corn. Co.
A-S.—*Eac*, eke, increase.
O.E.—*Eche*, *Eke*, increase.
E.—Eke, to increase : Ek-ing, Eke out. Aug-ment, to increase, add to : Aug-mentable, Aug-mentation, Aug-menter. August, majestic, Aug-ustly. Wax, increase, see *Buz*, grow, increase.

AG, AKA, ZAG

Su.—AG, AKA, ZAG, Lord *Ag* (or *Zag*) of Growth (*Aś-śu*, 5974, 10,842)—a title of Bakuś or Bacchus. Also called " *Ag* or *Zag*, the Lord Harvester of Abundance " (*Aś haru-walu śar*, 5974, 8227) ; and " *Ag* or *Zag*, the Lord of the Granary Jar," or *Pišan* (5978, 5967), or " *Aka*, The Lord Digger," 122. And see *Azag*, *Bakuś* (Bacchus), *Buz*, *Buzur*, *Haru* and *Zag*, the harvester.
Ak.—*Sihū*, grow, grow up. 1018. *Busū*, possessions. property, treasure. 200.
Eg.—*Akhkhu*, god of Vegetation. 9a. *Uazet*, Green goddess of Vegetation. 151b. PRE.26.
Sk.—*Yākka*, *Yāxa*, genii of trees, water and earth produce. *Jāk*, genii of trees. IP.
Gr.—*Iakchos*, n. of Bacchus.
Lat.—*Iacchus*, n. of Bacchus.
Goth. & Anc. Br.—*Ægis*, lord of agriculture in E. ; also called *Osk*.
E.—*Iacchus*, a name of Bacchus. *Jack*-and-the-Bean-stalk of nursery tales.

AGA

Su.—AGA, Crown, a headgear. 6949. Pictured by a crown.
Ak.—*Agū*, a crown, or diadem, a headgear. 12.
Eg.—*Aakhu-(t)*, a crown, Pharaoh's crown, with fiery—Uræus, serpent. 23.
Sk.—*Agra*, the top, the crown of the head.
Gr.—*Ak-ra*, top, highest point. *Ak-mē*, literally a point, also the highest point.
E.—Ac-me, the top or highest point.

AGAR

Su.—AGAR, Field (lit. " fettered earth "), Acre MD.15 ; P.24 and see *Gar*, fetter or garter.
Ak.— *Ugaru*, a field. 15.
Eg.—*Aākh-t*, field. 30a, 75a. *Akha-(t)*, field. 8b and cxli.
Sk.—*Ajra*, field.
Gr.—*Agros*, a field.
Lat.—*Ager*, a field. *Acre*, acre. F.
Goth. & Anc. Br.—*Akr*, *Ekra*, acre, field. EI.
Nor.—*Aker*, field. DN.
Ger.—*Acker*, field.
Co. & Celt.—*Agh*, field. I. *Auch*, field. S.
A-S.—*Æcer*, *Acvr*, field.
O.E.—*Aker*, field.
E.—Acre, a field, a measure of land : Acre-age, Acre-d, God's acre. Agr-arian, relating to fields, acres or land. Agriculture, the cultivation of acres, fields or land : Agri-cultural, Agri-culturalist, Agri-culturalism.

AGIA, EGA, EGURA

Su.—AGIA, EGA, EGURA, Ocean, flood, black water. 11,593, 6105. P.8. And see *Ab*, *Dur*, *Durabba*, Ocean and *Ega*, flood-water.
Ak.—*Agu*, flood, high tide, current. 13.
Eg.—*Ag*, *Aug*, stream, flood. 95b, 115b. *Aaki*, flood. 22a. *Aukh*, flood. 31b. *Uazur*, ocean. 151a, equating with Sumerian *Egura* and English *Eager*.
Sk.—*Ogha*, flood, stream. *Ashu*, quickly. 90. *Kāla pāni* or " Black water," the Ocean. IP.
Gr.—*Ōkus*, fleet going. *Oke-anos*, ocean. *Axenos*, the Euxine or Black Sea. ? *Isca*, river-name.
Lat.—*Aqua*, water, sea. *Eux-ine*, Black Sea. *Isca*, *Issura*, river-names. *Acqua*, water. I.
Goth. & Anc. Br.—*Ægir*, the ocean. EI.
Nor.—*Ukana*, water. L.
Co. & Celt.—*Eigian*, ocean. Cy. *Isge*, water. Co. *Egian*, the bottom, deep. Co. *Uisge*, water. I. *Aigen*, ocean. GI.
A-S.—*Æg*, *Eg*, *Eegor*, *Eagor*, ocean, the sea, sea-stream, water.
O.E.—*Eagre*, *Egear*, flood-tide.
E.—Aqua, water : Aqua-fortis, Aqua-rium, Aqua-rius, Aqua-tic, Aqua-tint, Aque-duct, Aque-ous, Aqui-ferous, Aqui-form. Eager or Eagre, a tidal bore. Euxine, the Black Sea, preserving the original Sumerian meaning. Ocean, the main sea : Ocean-ia, Ocean-ic, Ocean-ography, Ocean-ology. ? Azure, blue colour of water or sky. Whisky, a distilled spirit, or named through the Irish for " Water." *Axe*, *Exa*, *Esk*, *Iska*, Ouse, etc. River-names.

AGU

Su.—AGU, I, 1st pers. pronoun. 4766, B.195. And see *A*, *Egi*, *Iggi*, I and *Ma*, *Me*, Me and I.
Ak.—*Anak*, I, P(BP.14). *Anāku*, I. 70.
Eg.—*J.Y.A.*, I. 15a. *Anuk*, I. 60a from the Phœnician or Akkad.
Sk.—*Aha(m)*, I.
Gr.—*Egō*, I.
Lat.—*Ego*, I. *Je*, I. F. *Io*, I. I.
Goth. & Anc. Br.—*Ek*, I. EI. *Ik*, I. U.
Nor.—*Jeg*, I. DN.
Ger.—*Ich*, I.
Co. & Celt.—*Agan*, ours. Co.
A-S.—*Ic*, I.
O.E.—*Ik*, *Uch*, I, I.
E.—Ego, the " I " which is conscious and thinks : Ego-ism, Ego-ist, Ego-istic, Ego-istical, Ego-tise, Ego-tism, Ego-tist, Ego-tistic, Ego-tistical.

AIAR, AAAR

Su.—AIAR, AAAR, Silver, as " the shining." 9896, 9907, 9901, P.26. The same sign is used for Gold with the Akkad value of *Khurasu* (9898), now seen to be the Akkad source of the Great *Chrysos* " Gold." And see *Ara* " shining " *Ara*, copper-bronze, and *Azag*.
Ak.—*Sibu*, grey, white. 1081. *Ellu*, shining. 40. (*Sarpu*, silver. 894).
Eg.—*Arqur*, silver. 131b. *Har*, silver and gold. 492b.
Sk.—*Arc*, to shine. *Arka*, copper (? silver). *Har-ita*, gold. *Hiranya*, gold.
Gr.—*Argyros*, silver. (*Chrusos*, *Chrysos*, gold, derived from the Akkad, *Khurasu*).
Lat.—*Arg-entum*, silver. (*Aur-um*, gold). *Argent* silver. F.
Co. & Celt.—*Arhans*, *Argan*, silver. Co. *Airgiod*, silver. GI.
E.—Argent, silver, silvery, white in heraldry. Argent-al, Argent-iferous, Argent-ine. Silver ? from the Akkad *Sarpu* Silver (*l* for *r*) or from the Akkad *Sibu*, white or grey. Aur-eate, golden, from the same Sumerian word: Aur-eole, Aur-ic, Aur-iferous.

AKA, ANG

Su.—AKA, ANG, Cry, howl, lament, be excited, Ache. Pictured by the Flame sign of a fire within an enclosure. 4746, B.195. And *Akkil*, cry of woe. 2710. And see *Ag*, Flame, *Aka*, Augury.
Ak.—*Ramāmu*, cry, howl. 973. *Sarāhu*, be excited, cry, howl, lament.
Eg.—*Aka*, *Akk*, cry out. 94a-b. *Ak*, feel pain. 11b. *Ak(t)*, pain. 94a. *Aasha*, " the howler," the jackal, a form of Set as Typhon. 25b.
Sk.—*Agha*, pain.
Gr.—*Iachē*, cry of woe. *Achos*, ache, pain, distress. *Agchō*, strangle. *Acherōn*, lower world of torment.

Lat.—*Angor*, anguish. *Angore*, anguish, grief. I.
Goth. & Anc. Br.—*Agi, Ang(r)*, uproar, grief, terror. EI. *Agis*, awe. EIU. *Agi*, fear. EI. *Ag-lo*, anguish. U.
Co. & Celt.—*Anken*, grief. Co. *Acaid*, pain. G. *Eagal, Eagle*, fear. GI.
A-S.—*Æce*, pain. *Ange*, sad. *Ege*, fear.
O.E.—*Ake*, pain, ache.
E.—Ache, pain, continued pain or distress: Ach-ing. Agony, a violent painful struggle, see *Akh*, to fight. Anguish, excessive pain of body or mind. Ang-uishment, Ang-ina pectoris. Awe, fear, dread: Awe-less, Awesome, Awe-struck, Aw-ful, Aw-fully, Aw-fulness, and see *Aka*. Augury. *Acheron*, the lower world of torment of the Greeks: Hades, the river, Ach-eron, the Styx.

AKA

Su.—**AKA**, Augury, revelation, omen, divine command. 4750. B.195. And see *Buz*, Voice.
Ak.—*Tertu*, revelation, omen, divine command, etc. 1197.
Eg.—*Haka, Heke*, to utter spells and incantation. 514a, 515b. *Hakai, Hekai*, a sorcerer, enchanter or magician. 514a.
Sk.—*Aj, Ajā*, illusion, omen. *Ajnya*, an augur.
Gr.—*Acha, Achō*, a sound. *Echō*, to be possessed by. *Agos*, curse, religious awe, expiatory sacrifice. *Hagios*, devoted to the gods, sacred.
Lat.—*Augur*, a foretelling priest of Rome. *Echo*, a sound.
Co. & Celt.—*Aegix*, one who frightens. I.
A-S.—(*Hux, Husc*, a taunt).
O.E.—*Augerie*, an augury. *Ecco*, echo.
E.—Augury, a soothsaying or divination by the cries of birds, etc.: Aug-ur, Aug-ural, Augurship, In-aug-urate. Echo, a repeated sound, probably comes here. Hagi-ography, a name adopted through the Greek for the last of the 3 Jewish divisions of the Old Testament: Hagi-ology, Hagi-ologist, see *Azu*, Wiseman, augur. Hoax, to trick or cheat, probably is derived here, when the trickery of augury and soothsaying was exposed. Hoc-us, Hoc-us-pocus.

ĀKAIA

Su.—**ĀKAIA** (Uku-), The Ākaia people—Achaians. They are defined as "The host of the nation or people of the city of *Dura*" (or Troy, see *Dura*). This important historical record of the Achaians, not hitherto recognised, occurs in CIWA. IV. 28, 23a. It confirms my previous evidence that the Achaians and Trojans were Sumero-Phœnicians (WPOB.117, 238 f., 246, 325, 331, 411 f., WISD.77 f.), and that the Trojan war in Homer's *Iliad* romance was an internecine feud between the rival sections of the same Aryan Sumerian people. The date of this tablet may help to fix the actual date of the "Trojan War," or reconquest of Troy by the Western Achaians of Greece. 5915. And see *Dura*, Troy.
Ak.—*Tirit kiššat niši*. The host of the nation of *Tiri* (or Troy)—a city spelt in the Sumerian *Dura*, q.v., and cp. on "host and nation." 453,737.
Eg.—*Aqau*-asha, a Mediterranean people. 93a. *Aqa*-bat (or ? *Aqa*- people), a foreign (to Egypt) people. 11a. (*Akaru*, earth-god ancestors of Rā. 11b). (*Aaku*, a group of warriors in the Lower World (Tuat)). 26a.
Sk.—? *Yaksu* or *Yadu*, the oldest and leading one of the five tribes of the Aryans, in the Vedas and Epics of which the others were *Turvasa, Druyu, Puru* and *Anu* (? Ionian).
Gr.—*Achai-oi*, the Ancient Aryans of Greece who conquered Troy in the Trojan war of Homer's *Iliad*.
Lat.—*Achaei*, the Achaians of Ancient Greece.
Goth. & Anc. Br.—*Öku, Uku*, title of Thor or Dor, in the Snorri Edda, wherein he is styled *Öku-Thor*, or ? "Thor the *Oku-*ain or Achaian."
E.—Achaian, a Sumerian title for the Trojans or Dardanians or Dorians. On the identity of King Thor, Dor or Dur, the first traditional king of the Goths with Dar-danus, first king of Troy, see *Dar*, King Dar.

AKH, UKH

Su.—**AKH, UKH**, Eagle or "Bird of the Wind." Pictured by a Winged Disc above an object which appears to be a talon or claw, see pl. I., and cp. Egyptian hiero. 8124, 8130, 8290. B.346. And see *Ari*, Eagle and *Bak*, Hawk.
Ak.—*Issur šari*, bird of the wind. 1106.
Eg.—*Akha*-mist, the Eagle. 135b., and cp. Figs. 1, 75 in G. which distinctly picture an Eagle. See hiero. in pl. I. *Akhai*, a soaring bird. 135a. *Agbu*, the wind. 96a.
Sk.—*Aksha*, the great sky-bird of prey. *Ag*, the wind.
Lat.—*Aquila*, the eagle. *Aquilo*, the stormy wind. *Aigle*, eagle. F.
A-S.—*Egle*, troublesome, hateful.
O.E.—*Egle*, an eagle. *Aquilon*, the north wind (Shakespeare).
E.—Eagle, the king of birds; of the Falconidæ family: Eagle-eyed, Eagle-sighted, Eagle-hawk, Eagle-owl, Eagle-t, Eagle-winged, Spread-eagle. Aquil-ine, relating to the eagle, curved or hooked like an eagle's beak.

AKHA, AHA, EKHA

Su.—**AKHA, AHA, EKHA**, Strike down, kill, destroy, draw the sword—Fight. Pictured by an arm holding a shield with battle-axe, substantially identical with the corresponding Egyptian hieroglyph *Aha* or *Akha*, Fight: see signs in plate I. 7265, 7269-71, 7274, M.5259. B.312. On the *Akha* or *Aha*, revised value of this sign, see *Akha* reading of 7265 and cp. 5448, where the sign spells *A-kha* (-*du*). The "Lulu" conjecturally read in 7265 appears to be not a phonetic value, but a definition of *Akha*, "seize, go or advance, take hold, capture" (by the Akkad definitions *Alāku, Kamū, Sabatu*, etc., 10,674, 10,727 and MD.45, 392, 860, etc.). The rest of the definition in 7265 thus reads *Akhala=Akhula* or "cut down" (or reap in the agricultural sense of "cut down," MD.29, as also in the Egyptian). And this sense of "cut down" or fight is confirmed by its further definition of "draw the sword." Akkad, *Śilipu*. 7283 and MD.1046. And see, *Aka*, ache, *Nar* and *Pakh*, Fight and *Tuś* or *Tussu*, Tussle, strife.

Ak.— *Nāru* (*awelu*), strike down, kill, destroy (+man). 721. *Kuru*, scourge. 432. *Sarru*, rebellion. 782. *Il Ea awelu*, Man of god *Ea*. Br. 7270. (*Akhu*, hostile enemy. 28). (*Tuśśu*, strife, tussle. 1199 and cp. Br.10,515 and M.7999).

Eg.—*Akha, Aha*, fight, fighting. 132a, G.15. It is pictured by a similar hieroglyph to the Sumerian: hands holding a shield and battle-axe, see plate I.* N.B.—This is the well-known title of Menes, the founder of the First Dynasty in Egypt. *Ahi*, strike, fight. 76a. *Haki*, to fight. 515b. *Aghu*, an axe. 11a. *Aāka*, a hewer. 26a. *Ukha*, to hew or cut stone, to reap corn, to prune, to harvest. 178a.

Sk.—*Ahva*, battle, war. *Aji*, contest, prize-fight.
Gr.—*Agōn*, contest, fight.
Lat.—*Agon*, contest.
Goth. & Anc. Br.—*Agg*, strife, brawl. EI. *Aga*, chastise. EI. *Haga*, devour. I. *Hacke*, hew, cleave. U.
Nor.—*Agg*, strife. DN. *Hakke*, to hack. DN. *Hacka*, to hack or chop. S.
Ger.—*Hacken*, to hack.
Co. & Celt.—*Agary*, enemy. Co. *Ag*, battle. I.
A-S.—*Haccan*, to hack.
O.E.—*Hakken*, to hack, to hew.
E.—Hack, to cut down, chop, mangle: Hacking of things, and a cough, Hack-log. Agony, violent struggle: Agon-ise, Agon-ising, Agon-y column, Agon-ist, one who contests for a prize, Agon-istic, Ant-agon-ist, Ant-agon-istic, Ant-agony, Prot-agon-ist. Axe or hatchet, see *Xat*, an axe. Haggle, to cut down awkwardly, to cut down prices in a bargain, Hag-gler. Haggis ?—the Scottish dish of meat chopped up. Hash, to hack, to chop up: Hash-er, Hash-y. Hatch, to cut or engrave cross-lines in shading: Hatch-ing, Cross-hatching. Hew, to cut down, cut in pieces, to shape: Hew-er. Tussle, a contest, a struggle, from the Sumerian synonym, *Tuś*, battle. *Aha* or *Akha*, title of King Menes, the founder of the First Dynasty in Egypt, who I show was a Sumerian Akkad and identical with king Manis-tusu, or Manis-the-Warrior, the son of Sargon the Great.

AL

Su.—**AL**, Strength, might (of men, animals and gods). Pictured by a sign suggesting a Stag's Head and horns. 5746. B.260. And see *Bal*, Bold, valour.
Ak.—*Allu*, strength. 39. *Ālu, A'alu*, a stag. 39.
Eg.—*Aul, Aur*, strength, violence. 4a. *Au, Āa*, strong, violent. 3a. *Ail*, a stag. 2b.
Sk.—*Al*, be able, competent, prevent.
Lat.—*Ual-eo*, be strong, valiant. *Uiol-are*, to violate. *Valor*. F.
Goth. & Anc. Br.—*Hal*, a hero, a man. EI. *Elg*, a stag, an elk.
Nor.—*Helt*, a hero. DN. *Hel*, to pull. DN. *Elg*, an elk. *Olene*, a stag (Russ.).
Ger.—*Held*, a hero, a man. *Eland*, an elk (Dutch).
Co. & Celt.—*Hylly*, might. Co. *Hyll*, fierce. Co. *Halle*, pull. Co. *Allaidh Alltu*, fierce. GI.
A-S.—*Hæleth*, a brave man, a hero. *Eolh*, an elk.
O.E.— *Valid*, strong.
E.—Hale, Haul, to drag with force: Haul-age, Haul-er, Hal-yard. Hale, strong, healthy, well, whole, see *Al*, whole. Valour, bravery, see *Bal*, Bold. Violent, acting with physical force or strength: Viol-ence, Viol-ently. Elk, a kind of stag or deer.

AL

Su.—**AL**, High and lofty—Hill. 5749, B.260. And see *Ar*, lofty, *El, Ili*, a hill.
Ak.—*Elu*, high, rise, mount. 41. *Sēru*, high lofty. 889.
Eg.—*Ala, Ara*, to ascend. 29a. *Hal, Hel, Her*, lofty. 450a.
Lat.—*Altus*, high. *Altare*, a high place, altar. ? *Ala*, a wing. *Alto*, high, tall, deep. I.
Goth. & Anc. Br.—*Hall*, a hill, a slope. EI. *All*, exceeding high, capital. EI.
Co. & Celt.—*Ehual*, high. Co. *Hal*, a hill. Co. *Als, Aules*, a cliff. Co. *Ail*, a rock. I. *Alt*, height. I. *Alp*, high mount. G.
A-S.—*Hyll*, a hill. *Heallie*, high.
O.E.—*Altere, Auter*, an altar. *Hil, Hul*, a hill.
E.—Altar, a high place, a place for sacrifices. Altitude, height: Alti-tudinal, Alti-tudinarian, Alt-issimo, Alti-meter. Hill, a mount or

small mountain : Hill-folk, Hill-fort, Hill-iness, Hill-men, Hill-ock, Hill-ocky, Hill-side, Hill-top, Hill-y.

AL

Su.—AL, Guard, keep, protect, preserve. 5748. B.260. *Alala*, a bucket. P.27. See *Bal*, a pail.
Ak.—*Naṣāru*, guard, keep, preserve. 714.
Eg.—*Ali*, *ari*, a keeper. 69*b*.
Sk.—*Alaya*, a receptacle, a house.
Lat.—? *Alo*, support, nourish. *Val-ise*, a wallet. F.
Goth. & Anc. Br.—*Halda*, to hold. EI. *Haldan*, to hold. U.
Nor.—*Holde*, hold. DN. *Halla*, hold. S.
Ger.—*Halt-en*, to hold.
Co. & Celt.—*Alek*, a key. Co. *Alwed*, an enclosure. Co.
A-S.—*Hald-en*, *Healden*, to hold.
O.E.—*Hold-en*, to hold. *Walet*, a bag.
E.—Hold, to keep, preserve, support, retain, contain : Hold-all, Hold-back, Hold-er, Hold-fast, Hold-ing, Hold-hard, Be-hold-en, etc. Valise, a travelling-bag, a small portmanteau. Value ? worth : Valu-able. Wallet, a small bag or pouch, a knapsack.

AL

Su.—AL, Bind, yoke, chain, fetter. 5746. P.27
Ak.—*Allu*, yoke, chain, fetter, bind. 39.
Eg.—*Aal*, *Aar*, bind, tie, restrain. 1*b*.
Lat.—? *Balteus*, a belt. *Allis*, an ally. F. *Allier*, to combine, join, unite, mix. F. *Aloi*, alloy. F.
Goth. & Anc. Br.—*Al*, a strap, a bridle. EI. *Belti*, belt. EI. ? *Halt*, halt, lame. EI. *Halts*, lame. U.
Nor.—*Halt*, lame. DNS.
Ger.—*Hale*, a band. Dutch. *Halfter*, a halter.
Co. & Celt.—*Balt*, a belt. GI. *Gwald*, a hem. Cy.
A-S.—*Heald*, fast, secure, supported, bent, bowed. *Healt*, lame. *Healfter*, a halter.
O.E.—*Alied*, allied. *Halt*, lame. *Halter*, a halter. *Belt*, a belt. *Welter*, a binding or hem in garments.
E.—Ally, to bind together : All-ied, All-ies, Alliance. Alloy ? a mixture of metals. Belt, a band, a girdle : Belt-ed, Belt-ing. Halt ? lame : Halting, Halt-ingly. Halter, a rope for binding a horse, a yoke, noose. Welt, a binding or hem in a garment, or edging round a shoe, to flog : Welt-ed, Welt-ing.

ALA, ALAL

Su.—ALA, ALAL, All, full, totality—Whole. Literally defined as "The full collection of wood," "The weighed wood," and "Whole of the balance." Pictured by a tied Bundle of wood which is essentially identical with corresponding Egyptian hieroglyph, see plate I. 5947, 5965. B.270. And see *Meś*, Measure.

Ak.—*Alalu*, bind, hang, suspend, yoke. 46. And definitions cited above.
Eg.—*Alau*, all, entirely. 414*a*. Its hieroglyph sign is essentially identical with the Sumerian, see plate I.* *Ābāl*, to complete. 129*b*. *Ab*, to complete, to finish. 129*b*. *Au*, *Aau*, all, totality, full, length. 2*b*. *Ual*, *Uar*, measuring cords. Cp. G.44.
Sk.—*Āli*, a row, range, swarm.
Gr.—*Olos*, all, whole.
Goth. & Anc. Br.—*Al*, *All*, all. EIU. *Heill*, whole. EI. *Alls*, all. U. *Hails*, whole. U.
Nor.—*Al*, *Alle*, all. DN. *All*, *Alle*. S. *Hal*, whole. DN.
Ger.—*Alle*, all. *Heil*, whole. *All*, the universe.
Co. & Celt.—*Ol*, all. Co. *Oll*, all. Cy. *Uile*, all, whole. GI. *All*, great. I. *Aw*, all. S.
A-S.—*Eal*, all. *Hāl*, *Hael*, whole. *Haelu*, *Hel*, health.
O.E.—*Al*, all. *Hol*, *Hool*, whole. Ful.
E.—All, the whole of, every one of : All but, All in all, All over, All over with, All right, After all, For good and all, Once for all. Al-mighty, All Father, all-hallow, All Saints, All-fool's day, Al-most, Al-one, Al-so, Although, Al-ways, With-al, etc. Hale, Whole, Well and their compounds are probably from the same root.

AM

Su.—AM, Amity, love, compassion, possession, fire-place—? Home, literally, "Fire within." Pictured by the Fire-torch within an enclosure. 4736, 4739, 4745, M.3211-3, P.2129, cp. B.195.
Ak.—*Rāmu*, to love, belove, favour, conciliate, compassionate, be gracious. 966 f. *Bisitu*, treasure, possession. *Aśru*, place. ? *Libbutu*, flame. 465 f.
Eg.—*Am*, *Amm*, *Uam*, burn, fire. 6*a*, 49*a*, 146*b*. *Ami*, *Um*, "that which is *in*," "devouring flame." G.37. Pictured by the Wooden Fire-cross. *Amirab*, one who is within the heart—a darling, a friend, a trusted one. 44*b*. *Amer*, to love. 54*b*. *Amam*, a house. 50*a*.
Sk.—*Oma*, friend. *Amā*, at home. (*Kām*, love).
Gr.—? *Kōmē*, a village, a ward.
Lat.—*Amo*, I love. *Amicus*, a friend. *Amour*, love. F. *Amabilis*, amiable. F. *Ami*, friend. F.
Goth. & Anc. Br.—*Im*, embers. EI. *Eimyria*, embers. I. *Heima*, *Heim*, house, abode. EI. *Haims*, a village. U.
Nor.—*Emmer*, embers. DN. *Hiem*, home. DN. *Hem*, home. S. *Kemas*, a village. L.
Ger.—*Eimurja*, embers. OG. *Heim*, home.
Co. & Celt.—*Ameris*, embers. I. *Amana*, kiss. Co.
A-S.—*Amyrian*, embers. *Ham*, home.

AMA—AMANA SUMER-ARYAN DICTIONARY

O.E.— *Ymber*, ember. *Amitie*, amity. *Aimiable*, amiable. *Hoom*, home.

E.—Amity, friendship. Amiable, friendly, lovable, worthy of love: Ami-ability, Ami-ableness. Amicable, friendly: Amic-ability, Amic-ableness, Amic-ably. Amorous, full of love: Amor-ously, Amor-ousness, Am-ative, Am-ativeness, Am-atory, Am-atorial. Ember, a live firewood or piece of charcoal or coal in flame, red-hot ashes: Ember-days, Ember-week. Home, one's house, place of residence: Home-born, Home-bound, Home-bred, Home-brewed, Home-grown, Home-keeping, Home-less, Home-lessness, Home-liness, Home-ly, Home-made, Hom-er, Home-sick, Home-sickness, Home-spun, Home-stead, Home-ward, Home-ward-bound, Hom-ing, Home-circuit, Home-counties, Home Office, Home Secretary, Home Rule, Long Home.

AMA, EME

Su.—**AMA, EME**, Mother, love, grace. Pictured by a Star within a house. 5445, 5454-5, 5457. B.231. And see *Am*, love, *Madur*, *Mudru* and *Umu*, Mother.

Ak.—*Ama*, mother. P(BP.13). *Amū*, *Ummu*, mother. 52. *Rīmu*, grace. *Rāmu*, love. 966.

Eg.—*Ham(t)*, wife, woman. 481a. *Ames*, give birth. 55b. *Āmā*, to nurse. 122a.

Sk.—*Ambā*, a mother, a good woman, a title of respect *Am*, honour. *Āma*, n. of the cow. *Āma*, a nurse. IP.

Gr.—*Mammu*, mother, breast.

Lat.—*Mamma*, mother, breast. *Mamma*, infantile for mother. F. *Mamma*. I. *Mama*. S.

Goth. & Anc. Br.—*Amma*, grandmother. EI. ? *Ahma*, spirit, The Holy Ghost. U.

Ger.—*Amme*, a nurse. *Mama*, infantile for mother.

Co. & Celt.—*Mam*, mother. Cy.

E.—Ma, Mamma, infantile term for Mother: Mammy. Mammalia, a class of animals that suckle their young: Mamm-alian, Mamm-illary.

AMA

Su.—**AMA**, Womb, wide, hold. 5452, 5455. M.3757. B.231.

Ak.—*Ummu*, womb. 54. *Kālu*, hold. *Rapśu*, wide.

Eg.—*Am*, within. 44a. *Am*, to swallow. 6a. *Amen*, secret, hidden, concealed. 57a.

Sk.—*Amb-ara*, circumference, compass.

Gr.—*Eima*, a cover. *Amphi*, around. *Amphoreus*, a jar.

Lat.—*Amb*, around. *Amplus*, spacious. *Amphora*, a jar. *Ampis*, spacious. I.

Goth. & Anc. Br.—*Vōmb*, belly. EI. *Ama*, tub. EI. *Ampli*, a jug. E. *Wamba*, belly. U.

Nor.—*Vom*, belly. DN. *Vāmm*, belly. S.

Ger.—*Wamme*, belly.

Co. & Celt.—*Wm*, hollow. Cy. *Vaimh*, belly G. *Wame*, belly. S. *Weem*, a cave. S.

A-S.—*Wamb*, *Womb*, belly. *Hom*, a covering. *Amber*, a jug or vessel.

O.E.—*Wombe*, belly. *Awme*, a tub.

E.—Womb, the womb, the belly, the paunch: In the Womb of the Future. Weem, Weems, Weemys, cave, caves, place-names: Wemyss Bay, East Weemys, etc. Ample, large, spacious: Amp-lify, Amp-lifier, Amp-lification, Amplitude, Amp-leness, Amp-ly.

AMA

Su.—**AMA**, Wild Ox, strong, warrior leader, lord. Pictured by the head and horns of the Wild Ox. See representation in WISD.40, etc. 4543-5, M.3059, B.183.

Ak.—*Rīmu*, wild ox. *Emēqu*, strong. *Bēlu*, lord. *Qarādu*, warrior.

Eg.—*Āam*, sacred cattle. 111b. *Am*, *Amm*, seize. 6a. *Amen*, a Bull-god. 53a.

Sk.—*Ama*, strength, violence. *Āma*, raw (? wild). *Yama*, god of Death who rides on a Buffalo or Bull.

Gr.—*Ōmos*, savage, cruel, raw. (*Amazōn*, female manlike warriors of Scythia).

Lat.—*Vehemens*, vehement, violent. *Vehement*, passionate. F. ? *Amer*, harsh, galling. F. ? *Amaro*, cruel, grievous, bitter. I.

Goth. & Anc. Br.—*Ama*, molest, vex. EI. *Emia*, *Ymia*, to roar, echo, howl. I. *Ōmi*, n. of Wodan.

Co. & Celt.—*Amhas*, beast-man, wild man. G.

E.—Vehem-ent ? (usually supposed to be derived as "passionate of the mind," but the Greek is against this). Vehem-ence, Vehem-ently. Amazon ? fierce female manlike warriors of Scythia: Ama-zonian.

AMANA, MAN

Su.—**AMANA, MAN**, A name of the Sun as the dual or twin (day and night or antipodal sun) Pictured by two Suns. See for representation and description, WPOB. 242 f. 246 f., WISD. 51 f. 9942, 9960. M.5807. B.431. See *Man*.

Ak.—*Samaś*, the Sun-god. 1063.

Eg.—*Aman*, *Amen*, *Amianu*, title of Sun-god Amen-Ra, figured with Ram's horns, cp. 46a. f. and 51b. *Amenui*, dual Sun-god. 51b.

Sk.—? *Yama*, or "The twin," title of the Son of the Sun. ? *Zima*, solar patriarch of the Zoroastrians.

Gr.—*Ammōn*, Sun-god of the Egyptians, and made a form of Zeus.

Lat.—*Ammon*, title of Jupiter as Jupiter-Ammon. *Ammon*, ammonite, sermon-stone. F.

Goth. & Anc. Br.—? *Imi*, *Ymi(r)*, n. of a giant. EI.

O.E.—*Ammon* (Jupiter-).

E.—Ammonia, the volatile alkali of Sal Volatile

first manufactured from Sal Ammoniac, obtained from the camel caravansery of the great Egyptian temple of Ammon or Jupiter-Ammon, from which it derived its name: Ammon-iac, Ammon-iacal, Ammon-iated. Ammonite, the fossil shell of an extinct giant mollusc, named from the resemblance to the ram's horns of Jupiter-Ammon, the *Bel Haman* solar deity of Phœnicians.

AN

Su.—**AN**, High, Heaven, Star, God, King, Lord, Lady. Pictured by a Star, pl. I. 418,429. B.13. And see *Anu*, God and *Bar* and *Imin*, Heaven.

Ak.—*Anu*, the god of heaven. 65. *Bēlu*, lord. *Bēltu*, *Antu*, lady. *Elū*, be high. *Kakkabu*, a star. *Samū*, heaven. *Sarru*, king.

Eg.—*An*, *Ani*, a n. of the Father-god Osiris. 59a. *Aauna*, god of the Sky. 18a. *Anit*, female Osiris. 123b. *Ankh*, star. See pl. I.

Sk.—*Anu*, n. of god Shiva. *Anāhitu*, Zoroastrian goddess of Fertility, probably derived from Ak. *Antu*, see col. 2.

Gr.—*Ana! Ō Ana! Ōna!*, invocation to gods, wherein *Ana* is supposed to be a contraction for *Anax*, king.

Goth. & Anc. Br.—*Oinn*, n. of the father of King Thor as *Andvari* in the E.

E.—*On*, mystic title for God, presumably based on the Greek *Ōna*. "The most *High*," title of God.

ANA

Su.—**ANA**, One. Pictured by a straight stroke or bar as in Egyptian and Aryan numeral scripts. Also written in early lapidary script as a circular depression or "cup" or semi-circle. For representation in Mesopotamia, Ancient Britain, etc, see WPOB.241 f. 10,058, B.439, WPOB.240 f. And see *A* and *As*, One.

Ak.—*Isten*, one. 124.

Eg.—*A*, *Ua*, one. 105a, 153a, G.37 and 52. Figured by a straight bar as in Sumerian. *An*, a pillar. 58b.

Sk.—*Ani*, a pin, a stake. *Anu*, an atom. ? *Anna*, unit of Indian currency.

Gr.—*Oinōs*, one.

Lat.—*Unus*, one. *Un*, one. F. ? *An-ulus*, a ring. ? *Anneau*, a ring. F.

Goth. & Anc. Br.—*Eia*, one, only. EI. *Ains*, one. U.

Nor.—*En*, *Een*, one. DNS.

Ger.—*Ein*, one.

Co. & Celt.—*Un*, one. Cy. *Euin*, a nail. Co. *Aon*, one. GI. *Ane*, one. S. *Aince*, once. S.

A.-S.—*Ān*, *Æn*, one, an, only, sole.

O.E.—*Oon*, *On*, one.

E.—An, one, the indefinite article before vowels. One, single, undivided, whole (the modern pronunciation *Won* seems cognate with *Ua* of the Egyptian): One-eyed, One-handed, One-horse, One-idea'd, One-r, One-self, One-sided, One-sidedness, One-by-one, Al-one, L-one. Once, one time a single time. Only, single in number and kind. Unit, one, a single thing or person, the least whole number: Unit-arian, Unit-arianism, Unit-ary. Unite, to make one: Uni-ted, Uni-tedly, Uni-ter, Uni-ted States, Uni-ted Free Church, Uni-ty. Union, making one: Uni-onist, Uni-on-Jack, Uni-verse, Uni-versal, Uni-versalism, Uni-versally, Uni-versity.

ANA

Su.—**ANA**, God as Unity, totality, title of Ia (or Jah). 10,067-8, 10,072, B.439, WPOB. 241 f., with representations. And see *As*, *Dis*, *Sar*, God.

Ak.—*Anu*, head of the triad godhead. 65. *Ea*, Lord of the shining countenance. 2. *Sar*, *Saru*, totality, the number 3600 as an æon.

Eg.—*An*, n. of Osiris. 59a, BGE.2, 20, 154. *Aun*, a god. 115b. *Uā*, the One god. 153a. *An*, totality, full. 2b.

Sk.—*Anu*, n. of god Shiva.

Gr.—*Ana?* invocation to the gods. *Aiōn-ios*, eternal.

E.—"The One" title of God. *Æon*, eternity, *Æon-ian*, eternal. Tri-une God: Trinity in Unity: Uni-ty, Uni-tarian.

ANA, ANNA

Su.—**ANA, ANNA**, On, unto, upon, along with, during. 10,066. B.439. And see *En*, and, unto.

Ak.—*Ana*, unto, to, along with, and, for, during, in, etc. 64. *Elis*, up, upon, above. 50.

Eg.—*An*, to, in, for, by. 56a.

Sk.—*Anu*, to, over, near, etc. *Anah*, bind to.

Gr.—*Ana*, unto, on, upon, along, thereon, towards, all over.

Lat.—*In*, in, to, for, towards. *A*, to. F.

Goth. & Anc. Br.—*An*, *Ana*, on, to, upon. EIU. *Ana*, upon, on, over, in. U.

Nor.—*An*, *Ana*, on. DN.

Ger.—*An*, on, by, near, up, about.

Co. & Celt.—*Yn*, to. Co. *An*, *Ann*, on. GI. *Yn*, in. Cy. *Enogoz*, near. Co. *Eneudh*, also. Co.

O.E.—*On*, upon; *Unto*, unto.

E.—On, Upon, Unto, even to. Until. Ana-prefix, up to, upon, thereon, towards, through the Greeks: Ana-gram, Ana-logy, Ana-lyse, Ana-tomy, An-eurism, etc.

AN-DARA, ANDARĀ, AN-INDURU, AN-DUR

Su.—**AN-DARA, ANDARĀ, AN-INDURU, AN-DUR**, Andara or Andur, title of Lord (or *As*), Dara, Dur, the Father-god of the

Sumerians, or Thor, the Asa, the deified first king of the Goths in the Eddas, see below. 2948, 1066-7, 1082, 10,492, cp. B.57,113,480. On *Dur*, value, cp. 3331. And see *Aś, Dara, Dur, In-Duru*, Lord Dur or Thor.

Ak.—*Adar*, god Adar. *Ea*, god Ea. *Marduk*, god Marduk. *Adāśu=? Iddiśu*, shining. 24.

Eg.—*Anher*, "a human Sun-god, the local god of Thinis (Abydos) in Upper Egypt and Sabonnytos in the Delta." PRE.58 and cp. BGE.I. 172.

Sk.—*Indra*, king of the gods, with human traits.

Goth. & Anc. Br.—*Andvari* or *Eindride*, a title of King Thor the Asa, or Dur in the Eddas.

E.—*Andvari* or *Eindride*, a title of King Thor, the first king of the Goths in the Edda epics, and the source of the name and in great part of the legend of St Andrew: see WPOB. 246, 259 f., 315 f., 321 f.

ANU

Su.—**ANU**, Ear of Corn. 440-1. B.13.

Ak.—*Śubultu*, ear of corn. 1003.

Eg.—*Anh, Ankk*, corn, grain, wheat. 126a.

Sk.—*Anna*, bread, corn.

Goth. & Anc. Br.—*Ögn*, chaff, husk. EI. *Ahana*, chaff. U.

Nor.—*Avne*, chaff. DN.

Co. & Celt.—*Arne*, beard of corn. S. *Eorna*, barley. GI.

O.E.—*Awn*, beard of corn.

E.—Awn, beard of corn or grass, husk : Awn-ed, Awn-less, Awn-y.

AR, ĀR, ARA

Su.—**AR, ĀR, ARA**, Plough, encase, bond, shackle, uplift. Pictured by a Plough, essentially identical with the Egyptian hieroglyph of *Ar*, a plough, see pl. I. 5775-6, 5783. B.261. And see *Har* plough, and *Ub, Up*, plough or the "Uplifter."

Ak.—*Iluru*, encase, bond, shackle. 49. *Na'adu*, uplift. 627.

Eg.—*Ar*, a plough. This phonetic value for the plough hieroglyph has not previously been recognized; but it is seen in *Ar-par* or granary or "storehouse of plough (-produce)." 130a, *Ar-it*, 130b, *Ar-n*, 130b, *Hab-ar*, 441a, and many other words. Pictured by a plough essentially the same as in Sumerian, pl. I. *Ari-seka*, to plough. 66b. N.B.—The ordinary Egyptian word for plough, *Hab*, is seen to be from the Sumerian synonym *Ub*, the plough as "the *Up*-lifter." See *Ub, Up*, up.

Sk.—*Ara*, a probe. (*Hal*, a plough, from Sumerian, *Ar*, with *l* for *r*).

Gr.—*Aroō*, I plough, or plough up. *Harstron*, a plough.

Lat.—*Aro*, I plough.

Goth. & Anc. Br.—*Ar*. *Al*, a small plough. I.

Ard, Arth, a plough. EI. *Eria*, to plough. EI. *Arjan*, to plough. U. *Arin*. L.

Co. & Celt.—*Ar*, plough. GI. *Arat*, a plough. Co. *Aru, Aras*, to plough. Co.Cy. *Ar, Arati*, ploughed land. Cy.

A-S.—*Erian*, to plough.

O.E.—*Eren*, to plough.

E.—Ear, to plough or "ear the ground" (cp., Deut. 30, 4, Isaiah, 30, 24, etc.) and see WPOB.345, 361. Arable, plough-able, or fit for ploughing and tillage. Harrow, see *Har*.

AR, ARA, ARALI

Su.—**AR, ARA, ARALI**, Arable land, a region, territory. Pictured by the Plough sign. 5781-2, 5788. B.261. And see *Har*, to dig, and *Arata*, earth.

Ak.—*Karmu*, arable land. 437. *Kibratu*, region, territory.

Eg.—*Har*, a field. PV.327. *Ari(t)*, land, estate. 72a.

Sk.—*Irā*, the earth. *Hār*, arable land. IP.

Gr.—*Era*, the earth. '*Aroura*, a field.

Lat.—*Arva*, ploughed fields, regions. *Are*, unit of land measure. F.

Goth. & Anc. Br.—*Aurr*, loam, soil, mud, wet clay. EI. *Arbi*, heritage. U. *Arbja*, heir. U.

Co. & Celt.—*Ār, Har*, land, ploughed land. Co. *Ar*, do. Cy. *Era, Erw*, a field. Co. *Aor*, earth mould. Co. *Uir*, earth mould. GI.

A-S.—*Ear*, earth mould. *Ar*, an estate, wealth, money, property.

O.E.—*Er, Ear*, a spike or head of corn.

E.—Arable land. Are, the unit of the French land-measure. Area? a large space. Earth, see *Arata*, Earth. Heritable?, real property in land, etc., as opposed to moveable property: Heir, Heri-tage, Heri-tor, a land-holder in a Scottish parish. Urry, a dark clay near a bed of coal.

AR, ARA

Su.—**AR, ARA**, Exalted, lofty, high, glorious. Pictured by the Plough sign with the idea of "uplift." 5775-6, 5779, 5783, M.4101, B.261.

Ak.—*Na'adu*, be exalted, lofty, high, glorious. 627. *Tēlu*, lofty, sublime. 1161.

Eg.—*Ara*, up, be high. 7a. *Aār, Ār*, ascend, go up. 29a, 129a. *Ar*, ascent, stairs. 129a. *Hari*, sky, heaven (?·air). 498b. *Har*, a mountain, lofty. 422a.

Sk.—*Arya*, exalted, noble. *Āruh*, ascend. *Ir*, raise, elevate. *Aur*, more. IP.

Gr.—*Airō*, exalt, lift up, raise. *Oros*, mountain. *Orthos*, erect, upright. *Aēr*, air, the atmosphere.

Lat.—*Or-ire*, to rise, arise. *Oriens*, the rising sun. *Ārea*, a *high* lying open space.

Goth. & Anc. Br.—*Hār*, high, tall. EI.

Co. & Celt.—*Ero*, a ridge. Co. *Ard*, high. GI.

A-S.—*Ir*, *Aar*, glory, honour.
O.E.—*Orient*, eastern, of sunrise.
E.—*Ar-*, "high, exalted," prefix in names of hills, mountains or high sites, e.g., Ar-den in York and Warwick, the Ar-dennes, forest hills in France, Arra Mountains in Ireland, *Aran*, peak on Snowdon range, etc., *Aran*, holy isles of Galway. *Arran*, mountainous isle of the Clyde. Ar-arat in Asia Minor. And see *Arata*, high land. Area, an open space, originally meaning a "high" lying open space. Orient, the rising sun, the east: Or-iental, Or-ientalise, Or-ientalism, Or-ientalist, Or-ientate, Or-ientation. Orology, relating to mountains: Oro-graphy, Oro-logist, Oro-meter. Air ?, the atmosphere and sky: "The Lift" title of Air.

AR, ARA, HARA, HARRI

Su.—**AR, ARA, HARA, HARRI**, Aryan, Aryans. "The Lofty, exalted, famous (ones)." Pictured by the Plough sign (*Ar, Ara*). 5784, 5794, B.261. They are also called "The host of the Hara nation" (5915 and cp. on *Ha*, value, 8206). Later the Amorites, Hittites and Mitani, or Early Medes call themselves and are called Harri or "The Warriors." See on this title WPOB. and WISD. references in last para.
Ak.—*Arha*, lead, conduct. P(BP.15). *Tanattu*, loftiness, majesty, glory, fame. 1179. *Hara*=*Kiššat niši*, the host of the *Hara* nation. Br.5915.
Eg.—*Hari, Heri*, a chief, chiefs, governors 494a. *Harit*, a chieftains, mistress, goddess. *Ari*, one who goes up. 129a. *Arit*, mankind. 67a. *Harita*, a man, men. 495b. *Ari*, friend, companion. 69b.
Sk.—*Arya*, the exalted, or noble, master, lord. *Arya*, an Aryan, one of the "exalted" ruling race. *Arya-man*, a companion (Aryan). *Airya*, racial title used by Darius on his tomb.
Gr.—*Areiōn*, better, stronger, braver, usually derived from *Ares*, war, but probably cognate with *Airō*, exalt. *Ar-istos*, best. *Herōs*, a hero, a freeman. '*Arios* or *Harios* a title of Medes and Persians. *Aeria* or *Heriē*, a Greek name for Egypt (Æschyl. *Supp.*), also for Crete (Pliny).
Goth. & Anc. Br.—*Harri*, lord or king. EI. *Hera* a title of King Thor of the Holy Grail in the Eddas, see *Dur*. *Her*, famous or noble man. I. *Har-sir*, a chief, a lord. EI. *Earl, Jarl*, a hero, warrior. EI.
Nor.—*Herre*, lord, master, gentleman. DNS.
Ger.—*Herr*, lord, master, gentleman.
Co. & Celt.—*Arhu*, command. Co. *Aire*, chief. GI.
A-S.—*Hearra*, lord, master. (*Eorl*, a chief, leader, hero, man of rank or valour).

O.E.—*Erl*, a lord. (*Erl*, a chief, a man of rank or valour).
E.—Aryan, as a racial ruling title (see WPOB.5, 132, 257 f., 345 f.). Aristo-cracy, a government of the "best or strongest" men, the nobility, from the Greek: Aristo-crat, Aristo-cratic. Earl ? a nobleman of high rank—formerly a "title of a hero"—see *Ur*, a hero. *Ara, Aryan*, names of old lands of the Aryans: Ariana, Eran, Iran, names of Medo-Persia, Aryavarta, n. of India, 'Aeria or *Heriē*, name for Egypt and for Crete. *Harios*, an old n. for the Medians. *Her*, a title of King Thor of the Early Goths (or Sumerians), whom I show in my new literal translation of the Gothic Edda epics is the remote historical source of King Arthur or Ar-Thur or *Her-Thor* or "Arthur." The Sumerian legend of him and his Holy Grail and his contests with the Serpent-cult matriarch, transplanted by the Amorites and Phœnicians to Ancient Britain is disclosed to be the source of the Arthurian Legend in Britain with its various memorials and King Arthur's seats, Great Orme's Head, etc. See *Dur* and WPOB.191-195. f.

AR

Su.—**AR**, Arid ground, desert. 5781. P.38, B.261. And see *Ar* Ruin.
Ak.—*Karmu*, ruined land. 437.
Eg.—*Harr, Khar*, waste ground, desert. 532b. *Ar*, pebble, mountain, rock. 129b.
Sk.—*Āranya*, desert.
Lat.—*Āreo*, be dry. *Arēna*, sand, a sandy place. *Aridus*, dry. *Arido*, dry, arid. I.
E.—Arid, dry, parched: Arid-ity, Arid-ness. Arenaceous, sandy.

AR, ARA

Su.—**AR, ARA**, Harry, ravish, ruin—War. Pictured by the Plough sign, with the idea of "ploughed up" in destruction. 5781, P.36, B.261. And see *Ari*, Enemy, *Haru*, *Uru*, Lion and *Urur*, War.
Ak.—*Arn*, to shriek out. P.(BP.15). *Karmu*, a ruined land, a ruin heap. 437.
Eg.—*Ar*, capture, strangle. 7a. *Ar*, be oppressed. 69b. *Ar-ti*, be hurt. 69a. *Ar-ut*, to rob. 72a. *Har*, oppress, be hard. 442a. *Hurā*, robber, n. of a devil (as an enemy). 473a. *Ari*, a fiend, devil. 72a. *Ar*, a lion (as enemy). 129a. (*Uras*, serpent, as enemy. See *Ari*).
Sk.—*Ar*, to injure. *Ar-ma*, ruins. *Ari*, hostile. *Arar, Arus*, wounded. *Har*, ravish. *Hara*, ravisher, destroyer, a n. of Shiva, as a demon. *Hary*, demon of disease. *Arya-man*, the Devil. *Ahriman*, the Devil in Pers. *Hari*, *Hary*, a lion. *Uraq*, a serpent. See *Ari*.

Gr.—*Ara*, ruin. *Arēs*, war, slaughter. *Aireō*, seize, grasp, kill.
Lat.—*Ira*, ire, anger, wrath. *Guerre*, war. F. (*Ursa*, a bear as enemy ?).
Goth. & Anc. Br.—*Herja*, to harry, ravish, lay waste, despoil. EI. *Herjan*, ravisher, a title of Wodan in the Eddas. *Æra*, run furious, wild, run mad. EI. *Arr, Oer*, a scar. EI. *Aras*, assault. I. *Jara*, war, fight, battle. EI. *Jörmun*, Wodan, as a devil. E.
Nor.—*Herge*, to ravage. DN. *Art*, a scar. DN.
Ger.—*Heeren*, ravage. *Aar*, an eagle.
Co. & Celt.—*Ár, Aor, Hár*, slaughter, murder. Co. *Aer*, war. Cy. *Ár*, war, battle. GI. *Ear*, scar. G. *Aer*, a snake. Co.
A-S.—*Hergian*, to lay waste. *Hearm*, harm. *Uuerre, Wyrre*, war. *Irming*, a devil.
O.E.—*Herien, Harwen*, to harry. *Werre*, war.
E.—Harry, to plunder, ravage, lay waste: Harri-er, one who harries, a hunting, harrying hawks, a hunting-dog, Harry-ing, Harrow-ing, "The Harrowing of Hell." Harass, to torment, annoy: Har-assed, Har-assedly, Harasser, Har-assing, Har-assingly, Har-assment. Harm, injury, also moral wrong: Harm-ful, Harm-fully, Harm-fulness, Harm-less, Harm-lessly, Harm-lessness, and see *Erim*, Harm. Harpy, a mythic harrowing monstrous woman. War, hostility, a contest between states by force of arms: War-cry, War-fare, War-like, War-office, War-paint, War-path, War-rior, War-ship, War-tax, War-wearied, War-worn, War-whoop, War-wolf. Holy war, and see *Urur*, War. *Ahriman*, the Devil of the Zoroastrian Fire worshippers. Old *Harry*, n. for the Devil, and see *Ari*, Enemy.

AR

Su.—**AR**, Shine, light, brilliance, burn. Pictured by an Eye plus the sign for shine. It also means "Burn" through its synonym *Lakh*, to burn, shine. 9424-5, B.408.
Ak.—*Namāru*, shine, light, bright. 684. *Samū*, burn through synonym *Lakh*, burn. 5319, M.5805.
Eg.—*Ari*, light, fiery oven. 130b. *Ar(t)*, fire, flame. 130a. *Har*, furnace. 499b. *Ar*, eye. 68a, G.12. Pictured by an Eye as in the Sumerian sign, see pl. II. under *As-aru*. *Ar-tua* or "One-eyed," a title of the Sun.
Sk.—*Aro*, shine. *Arci*, ray, flame, shine. *Ara-ni*, wood-fire drill. *Aru, Aruna*, the Sun.
Gr.—*Argos*, shining, bright.
Lat.—*Uro*, glow, burn. *Ard-ere*, to burn, glow. LI. *Aurora*, the dawn (the shining) the goddess of the dawn.
Goth. & Anc. Br.—*Arinn*, fire-hearth. EI.
Nor.—*Arinn*, fire-hearth. DN.
O.E.—*Aurora*, the dawn, the goddess of the dawn.
E.—Aurora, the shining Dawn: Auro-ral, Auro-ra Borealis. Ardent, burning, fiery: Ard-ently, Ard-ency, Ard-our, Ard-ent spirits. Argus, quick eyed, quick sighted: Ar-gus-eyed, Ar-gus pheasant. Arson, felonious burning, incendiarism.

ARA

Su.—**ARA**, Copper, bronze. 8584, P.37. And see *Aiar*, Silver and *Urudu*, Bronze.
Ak.—*Erū*, copper, bronze. 94.
Eg.—*Har*, copper facings. 493a.
Sk.—*Ara*, brass. *Arū*, ruddy, tawny yellow.
Lat.—*Aes-Aeris*, copper. (*Aurum*), gold. *Airain*, brass. F.
Goth. & Anc. Br.—*Eir, Eyri*, bronze, ore, bronze or brass rings as money. EI. *Aurar*, ingots as money. EI.
Ger.—*Erz*, brass.
Co. & Celt.—(*Ouer*, gold. Co.).
A-S.—*Ár*, brass. *Or*, ore.
O.E.—*Āre*, bronze. *Ore*, ore.
E.—Ore, a metalliferous mineral. Its name, says Skeat, "seems to be merely another form of *Ár*, brass."

ARA

Su.—**ARA**, Hurry, go, go swiftly, rove, bring flow. Pictured by a Foot or by a Leg. 4858, 4870-2, B.207. And see *Er, Eri*, and *Ir*, to hurry.
Ak.—*Arh*, to convey. P(BP.15). *Alāku*, go, go swiftly, rove, cause to go, roam, flow. 45f. *Alaktu*, a route or course. *Abāla*, bring, take away. 7.
Eg.—*Ari*, to go, to visit. 65a. *Ar*, river (or "hurrier"), the Nile. 69a. *Aur, Iar*, river. 35b, 142b. *Arāa*, the Nile. 69a, as "The Hurrying Water."
Sk.—*Ara*, going, swift, speed. *Arane*, hurry, haste. *Ar-vant*, a horse as the "swift goer."
Gr.—*Ar-gos*, swift. *Erinyes*, or "The runner," one of the Furies. (*Archē*, a beginning).
Lat.—*Ire*, to go. *Err-are*, to wander.
Goth. & Anc. Br.—*Arr, Eyrandi*, an errand, a messenger. *Örr*, swift. EI. *Airus*, a messenger. U. *Aur*, n. of a stream in E. *Ar-*, a river in compounds in EI.
Nor.—*Hurr*, hurry. S. *Ærende*, errand. DNS.
Co. & Celt.—*Ire*, progress. GI.
A-S.—*Ærende*, errand.
O.E.—*Hori, Hory*, hurry. *Arende, Erande*, errand.
E.—Hurry, to hasten on, to urge on: Hurr-ied, Hurr-iedly, Hurr-iedness, Hurry-ingly, Hurry-skurry. Argo, or "the swift," the vessel in which Jason and his heroes sailed in the quest of the Golden Fleece: Argo-naut, Argo-nautical, Argo-sy. Arrant, thorough-going, downright, notorious: Arr-antly. Err,

to wander, to go astray: Err-able, Err-atic, Err-atical, Err-atically, Err-atum, Err-oneous, Err-or. Errand, a message, a commission to go. Errant, roving, wandering: Err-antly, Err-antry, Knight-err-ant. Urge, to press on, to cause to go, to drive, to incite: Ur-gency, Ur-gent, Ur-gently. *Ar* or " the Hurrier," in river-names, e.g., Arre in Cornwall, Aray in Argyle, Are and Aire in York, Ayr in Cardigan and Ayr, Arro in Warwick, Arrow in Sligo and Hereford, Arw in Monmouth, Arun in Sussex, Yare, Yarrow, Ware, etc. *Ar*, the Nile, *Aar* in Switzerland, Ara and Ohre in Germany, Arve in France, Era and Arno in Italy, Arva in Spain, Araxes at Mt. Ararat. And see, *Ir*, to flow, to hurry, *E*, *Eku* and *Eśa*, stream names.

ARA, ADA, ADU

Su.—ARA, ADA, ADU, Time, course, event— Era, also "Times" in multiplication. Written by the sign of Water + a Foot. 11,493, 10,472, P.19, LSG.123.

Ak.—*Ark*, a long time. P(BP.15). *Adî, Adŭ, Enu*, time, a course, event. 16, 67.

Eg.—*Ar(t)*, time, year, season (cp. the signs in) 100a.

Sk.—*Ahar*, a day, day by day, daily. *Varsha*, a year. *Yātu*, time, from Sumer synonym *Adu*, time.

Gr.—*Ŏra*, a year, season, an hour. *Aion*, an age, eternity, from Akkad *Enu*. (*Arche*, beginning of time).

Lat.—*Hora*, time, time of year, season, time of day, an hour. *Annus*, a year, from Akkad *Enu*. *Ætus*, time, an age, from Sumer *Adu*. *Æternus*, eternal, from Sumer *Adu*, time, course. *Jour*, a day. F.

Goth. & Anc. Br.—*Ar*, a year. EI. *Ar*, early. EI. *Jer*, a year. U. *Air*, early. U.

Nor.—*Ar, Aur*, a year. DN.

Ger.—*Jahr*, a year. *Eher*, early.

Co. & Celt.—*Awr*, an hour. Cy. *Er, Our, Ur*, an hour. Co. *Uair*, an hour. Gl. *Aor*, an age. I. *Arvis*, early. Co.

A-S.—*Gear*, a year. *Gearre*, yore. *Aar, Ær*, soon or early.

O.E. *Aera*, an era. *Yer*, a year. *Yore*, yore. *Erly*, early.

E.—Era, a series of years reckoned from a particular date, or that point or period itself: Christian era, Gothic era, Phœnician era, Roman era, Sumerian era. Early; in the beginning of time, in the beginning of the day or year, in the near future: Ear-liness, Ear-ly Britons, Ear-ly English. Ere, earlier than. Hour, a definite space of time: Hour-glass, Hour-hand, Hour-ly, Hour-plate, Horo-graphy, Horo-logue, Horo-logist, Horo-scope, Horo-scopist, Horo-scopy. Journal, a daily record or diary: Jour-nalise, Jour-nalism, Jour-nalist. Journey, a day's travel, a tour: Jour-neyman, Jour-ney-proud. Year, a period of time: Year-book, Year-ling, Year-long, Year-ly, Leap-year. Yore, in olden time. Æon, Eon, a long period of time, an age, eternity, from the Akkad *Enu*, time: Æonian. Annual, yearly, from the Akkad *Enu*, Time: Annu-ally, Annu-ity, Annu-itant, deferred Annu-ity. Day, time of light from sunrise to sunset, from the Sumerian *Ada*, Time ?: Day-book, Day-break, Day-dream, Day-fly, Day-labour, Day-labourer, Day-light, Day-long, Dai-ly, Day-scholar, Day-school, Day-star, Day-time, Day-work, Dooms-day, Dooms-daybook. ? Dawn, to become day, and see *Udu*, Day, Dawn. Et-ernal ? everlasting time, from the Sumerian *Adu*, a course, time. Archæ, a beginning, ancient, prefix in words from the Greek: Archæ-ology, etc.

ARATA, ARATTA

Su.—ARATA, ARATTA, Earth, land, massive, heavy, high, hard. Pictured by land, or Mountain + High. 9049, 9051-2, P.39. And cp. B.389 and *Ar*, Earth, *Arata-gar*, and see *Gi, Ki, Kur*, Land, earth.

Ak.—*Aras*, land. P(BP.15). *Kabtu*, heavy, high, massive, hard. 370. *Etu*, be high.

Eg.—*Arit*, land. 72a. *Arat*, stairs, ladder, ascent. 130a. *Har*, hard. 442a.

Sk.—*Ira*, earth. *Ūrdhva*, high. *Arādhas*, hard. *Adri*, stone, rock, mountain.

Gr.—*Era*, earth. *Ardēn*, lifted up. *Orthos*, erect, upright.

Lat.—*Arduus*, high, steep. *Arête*, a sharp, high ridge. F. *Arduo*, steep, difficult. I.

Goth. & Anc. Br.—*Iŏrth, Jŏrth*, earth. EI. *Airtha*, earth. U. *Hard, Herda*, hard. EI. *Hardus*, hard. U.

Nor.—*Jord*, earth. DNS. *Haard, Hărd*, hard. DNS.

Ger.—*Erde*, earth.

Co. & Celt.—*Oor, Oar*, the earth. Co. *Herda*, headland. Co. *Ard*, high, lofty. Gl. *Aradh*, a ladder. Gl. *Airtain*, a pebble. I. *Hard*, hard. Co.

A-S.—*Eorthe*, earth, mould. *Heard*, hard.

O.E.—*Erthe*, earth, mould. *Hard*, hard.

E.—Earth, soil, dry land: Earth-born, Earth-en, Earth-enware, Earth-full, Earth-hunger, Earth-iness, Earth-ly, Earth-nut, Earth-quake, Earth-ward, Earth-work, Earth-worm, Earth-y. Arduous, hard, difficult to perform, from the sense of the word as "high, steep": Ard-uously, Ard-uousness. Arête, a high sharp ridge. *Ard*-" high," prefix in place-names of high sites. Arad, the famous Phœnician seaport with extant colossal buildings in Phœnicia. Ard-el-Burājineh on the flanks of Lebanon, near the Phœnician seaport of Beirut. Ardagh, Ardglass, Ardfert, etc., etc., in Ireland, Ard-chattan, Ard-lui, Ardrishaig, Ardlamont, etc., in Scotland, Ard-udwy, etc. in Wales. Ortho-"upright, erect," prefix in words derived from the Greek: Ortho-dox, Ortho-doxness, Ortho-doxy, Ortho-epy, Ortho-grapher, Ortho-graphic Ortho-graphy, Ortho-pedist.

ARATA-GAR, ERETI

Su.—ARATA-GAR, ERETI, The Earth of the Four Quarters (*Gar*) or The World or Region. It is used with the addition of "King" as the title for universal dominion or empire. 5782, 5800, 6643 and cp. HOB. 134; MD.368 f. And see *Gar*, four, and WPOB.241-3 and *Arata*, Earth.
Ak.—*Kibrat-arba*, the four quarters of the world. 386 f.
Eg.—*Aratta, Aritta*, belonging to the earth. 71*b*. *Ariuta*, denizens of the earth. 71*b*. *Aat*, direction. 28*a*.
Goth. & Anc. Br.—*Jörth, Iörd*, the earth, the world. EI.
Nor.—*Jord*, the earth. DN.
Ger.—*Erde*, the earth.
Co. & Celt.—*Aird, Ard*, quarter of the earth, direction, cardinal points. GI. *Airt*, quarters of the earth, direction (Scot). *Harz*, a limit or boundary. Co.
A-S.—*Eorthe*, the earth.
O.E.—*Erthe*, the earth.
E.—Earth (The), of the four quarters, as the World. Airt, direction or quarter (Scot.)

ARAZU

Su.—ARAZU, Prayer, supplication — Urge. 11,548, P.39.
Ak.—*Teslitu*, prayer, supplication. PSL.39.
Eg.—*Arq*, swear on oath. 131*a*.
Sk.—*Arih*, prayer, petition, supplication. *Arzi*, prayer, petition. IP.
Gr.—*Eirq-ein*, constrain. *Ergō*, therefore—in agreement or appeal.
Lat.—*Urg-ere*, to urge, drive. *Or-are*, pray. *Oraison*, prayer, orison, speech. F.
Goth. & Anc. Br.—*Örva*, exhort. EI.
Nor.—*Örva*, exhort.
Co. & Celt.—*Ars, Arsa*, saying, asseveration on oath. Co. ? *Airc*, distress. GI.
E.—Urge, to pray earnestly, entreat, drive: Urg-ency, Urgent, Urg-ently. Argue, to discuss, appeal, try to press: Arg-uable, Arg-uer, Arg-umentable, Arg-umental, Arg-umentation, Arg-umentative, Arg-umentum ad hominem. *Ergo*, therefore, in appeal or argument. Orison, a prayer: Oracle seems cognate here.

ARI

Su. ARI, Enemy, foe—Harass. 11,447-8. P.39. And see *Ar, Ara*, Harry and *Erim*, Enemy, foe.
Ak.—*Āru, Ābu*, enemy, foe. 4, 91. (*Eru*, poison. 94). (*Arū*, lion. 91).
Eg.—*Ari*, hostile, fiend. 72*a*. *Hura*, robber, n. of devil. 473*a*. *Ār*, lion (? as enemy). 129*a*. *Ar-hes*, lion-god. 73,*a*. *Aār(t)*, Uræus serpent. 29*a*. *Art*, a serpent fiend. 73*b*. *Arārti*, serpent goddess. 72*a*, 130*a*.
Sk.—*Ari*, hostile, enemy. *Araru*, a demon. *Harita*, enemy or child-stealing goddess or demon.
Gr.—'*Ara*, goddess of revenge. *Arē, Arēs*, god of war and destruction. (*Ursa* ? a bear, as enemy).
Lat.—*Ira*, ire, anger. *Harasser*, to vex, disquiet. Old F.
Goth. & Anc. Br.—*Arr*, evil. EI. *Ær*, furious, mad. EI. *Jara*, war, battle. EI. *Orm*, the great serpent or worm as the devil. EI.
Co. & Celt.—*Aer*, a snake. Co. *Arth*, a bear ? as enemy. Co.
O.E.—*Harras, Harrasse*, harass.
E.—Harass, to torment, plague, vex, see *Ar, Ara*, Harry, ravish. War, see *Ar, Ara*, Harry, ravish. Old Harry, see *Ar, Ara*, Harry. Uræus, Serpent, Lion and Bear, as enemy, see *Ar, Ara*, to harry and *Er, Eri*, to seize.

ARI

Su.—ARI, Eagle, as "The Soarer." 11,448, and see *Ar*, Lift up, ascend, and *Akh*, Eagle as "Bird of the Winds."
Ak.—*Aru, Erū*, eagle. 91, 94.
Eg.—*Haru*, or "soarer," a title of the Horus Sun-hawk. G.20.
Sk.—(*Garura* or *Garuda*, n. for eagle).
Gr.—'*Ierax*, a falcon, a hawk. *Ornis*, a bird in general.
Lat.—*Ornis*, a bird in general.
Goth. & Anc. Br.—*Ari, Orn*, eagle. EI. *Ara*, eagle. U.
Nor.—*Örn*, eagle. DNS.
Ger.—*Aar*, eagle.
Co. & Celt.—*Er*, eagle. Co. *Eryr*, eagle. Cy. *Ever*, eagle. Br. *Aro*, eagle. I. *Earn*, eagle. Sc.
A-S.—*Earn*, eagle.
O.E.—*Erne*, eagle.
E.—Earn, Erne, a name for the Eagle, and see *Akh*, eagle. *Ornis*, the Greek term for a bird in general appears to be derived from the Gothic *Örn* for the king of birds: Ornith-ology, Orn-ith-ological, Orn-ith-ologist.

ARI

Su.—ARI, Amorite, Akkad—Aryan. M.5328, B.316. And see *Ar, Ara*, Aryan.

SUMER-ARYAN DICTIONARY AŚ—AŚ

Ak.—*Ammurū*, Amorite. 61. *Akkadū*, Akkad. 33.
Eg.—*Hari, Heri*, chiefs, governors. 484a.
Sk., Gr., Lat., Goth. & Anc. Br., Nor., Ger., Co. & Celt.—For equivalents in these languages see *Ar, Ara, Hara, Harri*.
E.—Aryan, as a title of Amorites and Akkads.

AŚ

Su.—**AŚ**, One, as the "Ace." Written by a short stroke, rod or bar or as in modern Aryan numerals for One. 17, 18, 6549, 10,070, 13,474, B.1 and 439. Also written in early lapidary script in Mesopotamia, Ancient Britain, etc. as a circular depression or "cup," or as a semi-circle. See for representations, etc. WPOB.240 f. And see *Ana*, One and *Iś*, a bar of wood.
Ak.—*Akkd, Ahd*, one. P(IP.135). *Êdu*, one. 28. *Ishtĕn*, one, single, alone. 24.
Eg.—*A, Ua (Wā)*, one. 105a, G.37. Pictured by a short bar or rod. *Asa*, a mace or baton. 83a. *As*, a beam. 79b. *Aza*, a chip or splinter of wood. 14b.
Sk.—*Eka*, one, from the Phœnician *Akhd* ?. *Isha*, a pole. *Aksha*, an axle.
Gr.—*Eis*, one. *Axōn*, axle.
Lat.—*As*, an unit. *Assula*, a splinter. *Axis*, axle-tree, axis. *Acus*, a needle. *Asso*, the ace in cards and dice. I. *Ais*, a plank. F. *Asse*, a plank, axis. I. *Asta*, a pole. I.
Goth. & Anc. Br.—*Ass*, the ace at dice. I. *Ass*, a pole, main rafter. EI. *Asto*, a twig. U. (*Ekkia*, a widow or "the alone." EIU).
Nor.—*Ass*, a pole, main rafter. DN.
Ger.—*Aas*, ace. *Achse*, axle.
Co. & Celt.—*Ag*, a nick or notch. Cy. *Eag*, ditto. G. *Aydn*, one. Co. *Asser*, a beam. I. *Asen, Aisean*, a rib. Co.GI.
A-S.—*Aex*, axis. *Eax*, axle.
O.E.—*As*, an ace.
E.—Ace, One at dice or cards. Axis, the axle or pin, real or imaginary, on which a body revolves : Ax-ial, Ax-ile, Ax-ially, Axis of the earth, equator, eye, etc. Axle, the pin or rod in the nave of a wheel : Axle-tree. *Aydn*, Cornish for "One," from the late Phœnician, *Ahd*, One.

AŚ

Su.—**AŚ**, Unity, alone, complete, perfect. Written by the same stroke as foregoing. 16, B.1.
Ak.—*Gitmālu*, perfect, complete.
Eg.—*Asa*, full, fill full, satisfied. 83a. *As*, conjunction "As," to wit [i.e., one with]. 79b.
Sk.—*Aś*, pervade.
Gr.—*Eis*, one.
Lat.—*As*, an unit.
Goth. & Anc. Br.—*Aimo*, eternity. U.
Co. & Celt.—*Uz, Huis, Hyies*, an age. Co.
O.E.—*As*, conjunction. *As*.
E.—? As, the conjunction and adverb, meaning "just so," i.e., "One with." *As*, Roman unit of weight and money.

AŚ, AŚŚA

Su.—**AŚ, AŚŚA**, Lord as God, heaven, star. Pictured by a Star, 419,425, B.13. And see for representations, etc. WPOB.240 f. WISD. 36 f., and *Ana*, God as "the One" and *Asaru*, Osiris.
Ak.—*Ilu*, god. *Belu*, lord. *Kakkebu*, star. *Samū*, heaven.
Eg.—*Aśar*, Osiris, Father-god. 83a. *Asther*, a star. 10a.
Sk.—*Iś, Iśa*, lord, supreme spirit, title of god. *Asura*, a god as the supreme spirit, a title of Indra.
Gr.—*Astēr*, a star.
Lat.—*Astrum*, a star.
Goth. & Anc. Br.—*Ass, Āsa*, God, gods as the deified hero Thor and his relatives. EI. *Anse*, ditto, in later Gothic.
Co. & Celt.—*Usgar*, holy, sacred. G.
E.—*Asa* as "Lord-god," a title of the deified Gothic King Thor in the Eddas. Aster, a star, and star-like rayed flower of that name : Ast-ral, Ast-ral body, Ast-ral spirits, Ast-erism, Ast-eroid, Ast-eroidal, Astr-olabe, Astr-olatry, Ast-rology, Ast-rologer, Ast-ronomy, Ast-ronomer, Ast-erisk, a star used in printing. China-ast-er.

AŚ, AŚ-AŚ

Su.—**AŚ, AŚ-AŚ**, Lady, as wife of the Father-god, and Lady of Heaven. Pictured by the Star sign. 45, 419, 426, M.351, B.13. And see *Azu Sib* and *Bartu* (*Aś-*), Lady of Heaven as Britannia.
Ak.—*As*, Isis. P(BP.14). *Beltu*, wife of Bel, the Lord. 170. *Antu*, lady. 73. *Iśtārītu*, Ishtar—goddess. 125.
Eg.—*As(t)*, Isis, wife of Osiris. 9a, 81a. *Āst(t)*, Isis, queen of Heaven and Earth. BG.22,207. *Has*, a n. of mother-goddess. BGE.1433. *Ashtar(t)*, Ishtar, the mother goddess of Syrio-Phœnicians. 136b.
Sk.—*Iśvarī*, n. of the mother-goddess. *Aśi* of Ur (*Urv-aśi*), w. of the first king of the Aryans, Purū of the Sun (*Purū-ravas*).
Gr.—*Isis*, w. of Osiris. *Astarte*, mother-goddess of late Phœnicians.
Lat.—*Astraea*, goddess of justice who left the earth in the Iron Age and became the star Virgo.
Goth. & Anc. Br.—*Āsynia* a title of *Āsa* Thor's wife. E. *Āsynjar*, the female Āsas. E.
E.—Isis, the mother-goddess of the Egyptians

and wife of Osiris; as Āsimia, wife of King Thor the Goth, and latterly deified as Astarte and Ashtoreth or Diana. See (Aś) *Bartu* or "Lady of Heaven" as Britannia with representation in WPOB. 9, 55 f.

AŚ

Su.—**AŚ**, Lord, as human king or master. 12, 428, 439. B.1 and 13.
Ak.—*Aś*, a lord, a citizen. P(BP.16). *Amelu*, man. *Belu*, lord or master. *Śarru*, king.
Eg.—*Ansu*, king. 63b.
Sk.—*Īsa*, lord, master, king.
Gr.—*Anax*, king.
Goth. & Anc. Br.—*Āsa*, *Anse*, lord, title of King Thor and his royal Goths in the Eddas.
Nor.—*Anse*, a judge, of high standing, stately, notable. DN.
E.—*Asa* or *Anse*, title of "lord," "lady," for the royal Goths in the court of King Thor in the Eddas; and see WISD.36 f.

AŚ

Su.—**AŚ**, Wish, desire, prayer, curse or spell. 6745-47.
Ak.—*Haśāhu*, wish, desire, prayer. *Arratu*, a curse.
Eg.—*As*(*t*).
Sk.—*Āśa*, *Esh*, *Āsis*, *Ish*, *Iccha*, wish, desire, request. *Wa*(*n*)*ksh*, wish. *Aśas*, bless. *Aesha*, wish. Z.
Gr.—*Aisa*, fatal decree, curse of Fate or of a god. *Asē*, loathing. *Asai*, to hurt.
Goth. & Anc. Br.—*Æskia*, *Ösk*, wish. EI. *Ask*, ask. EI. *Oski*, the wishing god, a n. of Wodan. EI. *Æsa*, terror. I.
Nor.—*Æsk*, ask. DN. *Æska*, ask. S. *Önska*, wish. S.
Co. & Celt.—*Asig*, ask. GI. *Achain*, prayer. GI. *Ais*, wisdom. GI. *Azrek*, sorrow. Co.
A-S.—*Wysc*, *Wusc*, wish. *Ascian*, *Æsce*, ask.
O.E.—*Wisch*, *Wissh*, wish. *Ask*, *Asch*, ask.
E.—Wish, to desire, to have a desire, to long for: Wish-er, Wish-ful, Wish-fully, Wish-fulness, Wish-ing-bone, Wish-ing-cup, Well-wisher. Ask, to pray, request, question.

AŚ

Su.—**AŚ**, Six, sixth. 12,197 f. B.435, 534.
Ak.—*Śaś*, *Śeś*, six. P(SB.183). *Śiśśu*, six. 1125.
Eg.—*Sys*, *Sas*, six, sixth. 643b.
Sk.—*Shash*, six. *Sash*, *Che*, six. IP.
Gr.—*Ex*, six, from Sumer.
Lat.—*Sex*, six, from Phœnician or Akkad.
Goth. & Anc. Br.—*Sex*, six. EI. *Saihs*, six. U.
Nor.—*Sex*, six. DNS. *Szeszi*, six. L.
Ger.—*Sechs*, six.
Co. & Celt.—*Sē*, *Sēa*, six. GI. *Chwech*, six. Cy. *Chouech*, six. Br.
A-S.—*Syx*, *Siex*, six.

O.E.—*Sixe*, six.
E.—Six, the number five and one, from the late Phœnician *Śeś* or *Śaś*, the sibilized Sumerian, *Aś*, Six: Six-fold, Six-footer, Six-pence, Six-shooter, Six-th or Sis-tine, Six-thly, Sixteen, Six-teenth, Six-ty, Six-tieth.

ASARU, ASARI

Su.—**ASARU, ASARI** (As-), Lord or God, *Asaru* as "The Eye of the Throne"—a title of the supreme god. Pictured by an Eye within the sign for Throne and is identical with the Egyptian hieroglyph for Osiris, see plate II. It first appears in the inscription of the Phœnician King Uruash, c. 3100 B.C., see WISD.30 f., 918 f., M.557, P.40, B.44.
Ak.—*Il Iśhuru*, the god Ishuru. *Haru*, inspect. 333 and Br.5974. *Aśur* or *Ausar*, god of the Assyrians, cp. CEA.170.
Eg.—*Asar*, *Asir*, god Osiris, 83a, with hiero. as in Sumer, see pl. II.
Sk.—*Aśira*, the Sun. *Asura*, God, as the supreme spirit, a title of Indra. *Iśwara*, lord, a title of God as the supreme being.
Gr.—*Osiris* or *Poly-ophtalmos* or "The Long Eye" (Over-seer). Cp. BED.83a. This is the Greek spelling and etymology for the n. of the Egyptian god *Asar* or *Asir*.
Lat.—*Osiris*, the Father-god of Egyptians. *Assar*, n. of god among Etruscans. Suet, Aug. 97.
Goth. & Anc. Br.—*Āsa-Ottar*, a title of King Thor the *Asa* or lord.
E.—Osiris, the solar Father-god of the Egyptians is disclosed to be the supreme solar god of the Early Sumerians. He had human traits of a traditional solar king, and died a violent death and was posthumously deified; and we shall find that he is identical with King Thor, the *Asa* of the Gothic Eddas. See *Dur*.

AŚŚA

Su.—**AŚŚA**, Horse. Pictured by the Head and neck of a Horse. See for representations and reading WPOB.257-8, WISD.31, etc. 4981, 4984-6, B.211. The sign read in Br. as *Ansu* is written in Assyrian cuneiform by the compound sign of *As* (high, lofty, 419) and *śa* (a foot, 4866), defining the horse as "The high-footed or high-legged." This is confirmed as regards the first syllable by the Neo-Babylonian which writes the sign as *Iś* (wood 5698) and *śa* (foot) or "the wooden or solid footed"—the latter being the title also adopted by scientific modern zoologists for the Horse Family.
Ak.—*Sisū*, a horse. 773.
Eg.—*Sas*, a horse. 618b, 695b, etc. (from the Akkad *Sisū*).
Sk.—*Āśu*, *Aśwa*, *Aśva*, a horse.

SUMER-ARYAN DICTIONARY

Gr.—*Ikkos*, a horse in old Greek, later *Hippos*.
Lat.—*Equus*, a horse. *Eōus*, one of the horses of the Sun in Ovid.
Goth. & Anc. Br.—*Ess*, a horse, a steed. EI. *Hest*, *Hross*, horse. I. *Aihva*, horse. U. "*Aesv*" legends with Horse on Ancient Briton coins. WPOB.284-5, 413.
Nor.—*Hest*, horse. DN. *Hast*, horse. S.
Co. & Celt.—*Each*, *Ech*, a horse. I. *Asen*, an ass. Co. *Asyn*, *Azen*, ass. Cy. GI.
A-S.—*Henges*, *Hors*, a horse. *Assa*, ass.
O.E.—*Hors*, a horse. *Asse*, an ass.
E.—Horse, the well-known quadruped. This form of the name is presumably derived from the Sumerian *Assa*—a form which runs through most of the other Aryan languages—by aspirating the word and intruding an *r* cockneywise: Horse-back, Horse-box, Horse-boy, Horse-breaker, Horse-car, Horse-cloth, Horse-dealer, Horse-doctor, Horse-flesh, Horse-guards, Horse-hair, Horse-leech, Horse-litter, Horse-man, Horse-manship, Horse-marine, Horse-power, Horse-race, Horse-racing, Horse-ring, Horse-shoe, Horse-whip, Horse-woman, Hors-y, and as name for plants and trees: Horse-chestnut, Horse-radish, Horse-tail, Horse-thistle, Horse-tongue, Horse-vetch. Ass the parent of the early wild horse—the horse being also called by the Sumerians "The mountain Ass." *Æsv*, *Asvp*, *Eciv*, *Eisw*, legends with figures of the Sun-Horse on the Pre-Roman coins of the Ancient Briton kings. See for representations and descriptions WPOB.284 f., 413.

AŚTE, ASTI

Su.—*AŚTE, ASTI* (*Iś*-), seat (wooden), a rest. 47, 61-2. P.43. Pict. by throne as in Egy. hiero. See under *Asaru*, pl. II.
Ak.—*Kuśśu*, a seat, a throne. *Nāru*, a rest.
Eg.—*Ast*, a seat, a throne. 79*b*. *Aasb*, a seat. 25*b*, with hiero. as in Sumer.
Sk.—*Āsa*, a seat. *Āśi*, rest. *Aste*, easy. IP. *Kūrsī*, a seat. IP. From Akkad, *Kuśśu*.
Gr.—*'Astu*, a dwelling-place. *Igō*, sit, settle down. *Aesa*, sleep. *Khuśi*, pleasant, easy. IP. From Akkad, *Khuśśu*.
Lat.—*Sedes*, a seat. *Aise*, ease. F. *Agio*, ease. I.
Goth. & Anc. Br.—*Æja*, rest. EI. *Sæti*, a seat. EI. *Azets*, easy. U.
Nor.—*Sæde*, a seat. DN. *Sāte*, a seat. S.
Ger.—*Sitz*, a seat.
Co. & Celt.—*Aise*, *Aizia*, easy, easier. Co. *Usa*, ease. I. *Suidha*, seat. GI.
A-S.—*Set*, *Sett*, a seat.
O.E.—*Eisa*, easy. *Sete*, a seat.
E.—Ease, rest from work, disturbance or pain: Ease-ful, Ease-ment, Eas-ily, Eas-iness, Eas-y, Easy-chair, Easy-going, Dis-ease. Seat, that on which one sits: Sed-an-chair, Sit, Sett-le, sett-lement, Sett-ler. Cushion, from the Akkad, *Kuśśu*, a seat, a throne. *Cooshy*, easy, pleasant in Anglo-Indian: Cooshy-job, a sinecure.

ATTI

Su.—*ATTI*, dialectic for Khatti, Hatti, or Hittite, q.v. C.p. 11,816.
E.—"*Att*," legend on the coins of the Pre-Roman *Catti* or "Hittite" kings of Ancient Britain, see WPOB.6 f., 203.

AUM

Su.—*AUM*, Mystic title of the solar Father-god as Lord of the Waters, a variant of *Aa* or *Ai* and *Ia* (or *Jah*). 11,686, 3896, 11,690.
Ak.—*Ea*, god of the waters. *Abu*, father.
Eg.—*Am*, *Ym*, n. of Horus, the Sun-god. 49*a*.
Sk.—*Aum*, *Om*, mystic title of the supreme god and trinity.
Gr.—*Omega*, title of God in the Apocalypse.
Goth. & Anc. Br.—*Om*, title of Wodan in Eddas.
E.—Omega, mystic title of God in the Apocalypse. *Aum* or *Om*, mystic title of God or the supreme spirit amongst Hindus and Northern Buddhists, derived from the Sumerian, cp. WBT.139, 143, 148, 160, 165.

AZAG

Su.—*AZAG*, Bright Metal, silver, tin, bronze, money. Literally "The Shining bright (metal)." Tin and bronze is also read by Sayce and others. *Azaggi*=Gold in the shining cane (coloured metal), cp. 9898, and *Aujase* in "The Shining" is also a name for gold in Sanskrit. 9887, 9891, 9908, B.428. And see *Aiar*, silver and *Bar* or *Far*, Iron.
Ak.—*Kaspu*, silver, money in the form of rings (*Kaspa Unqa* or silver finger-rings) or stamped ingots. 417 f. *Ellu*, bright, shining. 40.
Eg.—*Has-man*, bronze. 512*a*.
Sk.—*Ayas*, bronze. MKI.131. *Ka(n)sa* or nasalized *Kasa*, "white copper (bronze)" bell-metal, brass, presumably derived from Akkad, *Kaspu*. *Ojas*, lustre, shining.
Gr.—*Kassi-teros*, tin? from Akkad, *Kaspu*. *Kassi-terides*, Phoenician tin islands off or near Cornwall. *Aiglē*, shining bright or metals.
Lat.—*Aes*, bronze, copper. *As*, copper coin.
Goth. & Anc. Br.—*Aiz*, brass or copper. U.
Co. & Celt.—*Azroue*, a token (? coin). Co.
E.—*As*, copper unit coin of the Romans. Cassi-terides or "Catti-terides," tin islands of the Phoenicians off or near Cornwall and usually identified with Cornwall itself, possibly derived their former name from the Akkad name for Tin *Kaspu*. See WPOB.160, 201-2, 209, 415 f.

AZAG

Su.—AZAG (*Aś-tu*), Lord Azag, the Incanter or Enchanter; also called "Lord *Azag* of the Plants" and *Bakuś* or *Būśu* of the Jar of Plenty (*Gar-Būśu* 9890), a title of the son of King *Dar* or *Andara*, afterwards deified as Bacchus. 9887-88, 9890, 9906. On *tu*=incanter or enchanter cp. 781 and on "plant." 9906. And see his titles *Ag, Aka, Bakuś, Bazuzu, Buz* and *Gan* (Gany-mede) and *Khunu*.

Ak.—*Il Ellu*, the shining god. 40.

Eg.—*Akhkhu*, god of vegetation. 9a. And see *Besa*, god of corn. 223a under Sumerian *Buz, Buzu,* Bacchus. *Hakau*, god of incantations, spells and magic. 515a. And see *Aka*, augury.

Sk.—*Āyus*, son and successor of first Aryan king of first dynasty, see *Bur*, king. *Āyavasa*, conquering solar king in Vedas. (1, 122, 15).

Gr.—*Iakchos*, n. of Bacchus.

Lat.—*Iacchus*, n. of Bacchus.

Goth. & Anc. Br.—*Ægi, Ægis*, the lord of Ale in the Eddas.

E.—Iacchus, a name for Bacchus from the Sumerian *Azag* and see *Bakuś*, Bacchus. "Jack" of the Bean-stalk of the nursery tale appears to be the Sumerian prince *Azag*, afterwards deified as Iacchus or Bacchus.

AZU, AZA, UZU

Su.—AZU, AZA, UZU, Wise man seer, priest, physician, conjurer, augur. Literally, "One who has deep knowledge," *Zu.* 3868, 4663 f., 11,378, P.46,366, B.188. And see *Aka*, Augury.

Ak.—*Asū*, physician, wizard. 74. *Aśśapu*, a diviner, soothsayer, conjurer. 117.

Eg.—*Hakai*, physician, enchanter, sorcerer. 514. *Aq*, a priest who reads service. 138b. *Aakhu*, mystical words, protective spells. 22b. *Hak*, spells, magic. 515a. *Has*, spell against evil spirits. 509a.

Sk.—*Ajnya*, a physician, augur. *Ojas, Ausadh*, medicine. *Oja*, medicine-man, sorcerer. IP. *Hāgim*, a doctor. IP. and Arabic.

Gr.—'*Agios, Hagios*, devoted to the gods.

Lat.—*Augur*, an augur. ? *Uis-ere*, go to see.

Goth. & Anc. Br.—*Vis*, wise. EI. *Weis*, wise. U. *Vitki*, wizard. EI. *Haga*, to arrange. EI. *Hagr*, skilful. EI.

Nor.—*Vis*, wise. DNS.

Ger.—*Weiss*, wise. *Weissager*, a soothsayer. *Hexe*, a witch.

Co. & Celt.—*Ais*, wisdom. GI. *Aswonas*, know. Co.

A-S.—*Wīsa, Wicca. Wīs*, a sage, wise man. *Wīsdōm*, wisdom.

O.E.—*Wise*, wise.

E.—Wise, having knowledge, discretion, learned : Wis-dom, Wise-ly, Wise man, Wise woman. Wizard, one who practises magic, a magician : Wiz-ardly, Wiz-ardry. Witch, a woman regarded as having magical power : Witchcraft, Witch-ery, Witch's-broom, Witch-ing, Witch-ridden, Witch-wife, Be-witch ; and see *Buz*, Witch. Augur, see *Aka*, Augury. Hag, an old witch : Hag-gard, Hag-iarchy, see *Aka*, Augury. *Hākim* or "Hakeem" a physician, also a judge in Hindustani.

AZU, ṢIB

Su.—AZU, ṢIB (*Aś Aśzu-*), "The Lady *Aśzu* the enchantress, *Sib* (or Fate)," also called "The Lady Sib of the Father," i.e., Dar or Andara. She is disclosed as *Asi* the enchantress, *Sif* wife of King Thor or Dorr, the first king of the Goths in the Eddas, and the historical source of Isis. 68, 10,386. And see *Adueni* (Athena), *As*, Lady, *As*, *Bur* and *Dur*, Magic Bowl, *Edin, Nana*, the lady diviner of the Bowl, and *Sib*, Sibyl.

Ak.—*As*, Isis in late P(BP.16). *Ilat Zarpānitu*, The great Lady of Seed and Springtide (New Year, cp. 812 f.). The lofty offspring of Heaven and Earth, Lady of *Edin*, Queen of the Great Temple, Lady of Wisdom (*gaśmu — mudū*). Br.2224, 2659. Wife of Bēl, the Lord. 894-5.

Eg.—*Uaz-it*, Lady of life and green crops, a title of Isis. BGE.2, 213 f. *Sept*, lady of Heaven and opener of the New Year, a title of Isis. BGE.2, 213. *Isis* or *Sept*, as "The Great Enchantress" and "Lady of Words of Power." BGE.2, 207.

Sk.—*Aśi*, of Ur (*Urvaśi*), wife of the first Aryan king, *Puru* of the Sun (-cult)—*Purū-ravas* and an enchantress.

Gr.—*Asia*, w. of Pro-Metheus. *Aīsa*, goddess of Fate.

Lat.—*Asia*, w. of Prometheus the Titan.

Goth. & Anc. Br.—*Āsynia* or *Sif*, priestess of *Urd* or *Ur*, and wife of Bur-Mioth or Thor. E. See *Bur*, Lord *Bur* or *Puru*.

E.—Asia, wife of Prometheus, the titanic benefactor of man and possessor of the sacred Fire and the Higher Civilization as the Gothic *Āsynia* or *Sif*, the Sybil of the Well of Urd and wife of Thor. *Bur* or *Sig*, first traditional king of the Goths and identical with the first Sumerian king *Zagg* on the votive stone-bowl war-trophy record of his great-grandson *Udug*, Sumerian priest-king of Kish, c. 3300 B.C. See *An-Dara, Bur, Dar, In-Dara, Mid, Puru, Sakh, Udug* and *Zagg* or *Zagaga*.

B

BA, BI

Su.—BA, BI, Bisect, divide, cut off, apportion, half. Pictured by a mass bi-sected. 102 f., P.47, B.5. See *Bar*, cut, *Bi*, divide and *Bid*, *Bita*, both.
Ak.—*Naśaru*, cut off, tear, etc. 741. *Sapaxu*, break in pieces. 777. *Qāśu*, portion out. 934. *Zāzu*, half, divide. 276.
Eg.—*Bai(t)*, a cutting. 201a. *Pa(t)*, two halves, four quarters. 229a. *Pah*, to rend. 243b. *Pah*, to split, divide. 245b.
Sk.—*Bis*, *Bid*, to cleave, divide, split. *Vi-*, prefix of division. *Bhaga*, a bit, a portion.
Lat.—*Bi-*, prefix, divide in two ways. *Bi*, twice, *Bi-nus*, twofold. *Baia*, inlet of the sea. *Pars*, a part.
Goth. & Anc. Br.—*Bita*, divide. EI. *Bit*, a bite, a bit. EI. *Bai*, *Bādi*, both. EIU. *Beit*, bite. U.
Nor.—*Bit*, *Bide*, a bit, a bite. DN. *Bita*, bite. S. *Bugt*, a bay. DS.
Ger.—*Biss*, *Bissen*, bite, bit.
Co. & Celt.—*Barri*, divide. Co. *Ba*, twice. I.
A-S.—*Ba*, both, *Bit*, *Bite*, a bite.
O.E.—*Bite*, a bite. *Bit*, a bit.
E.—Bay or Bight, an inlet, a recess. Bite, to cleave with the teeth: Bit-er, Bit-ing, Bitt-en. Bit, a piece: Pitt-ance, Petty. *Bis*, twice, from sense of divide. *Bi-*, prefix in words: Bi-carbonate, Bi-centenary, Bi-ceps, Bi-concave, etc. Bi-cycle, Bi-fid, Bi-ennial, Bi-fold, Bi-furcate, Bi-gamy, Bi-lingual, Bi-metallic, Bi-metalism, Bi-monthly, Bi-nary, Bi-ped, Bi-sect, Bi-valve, Bi-weekly, etc. Bias, partisanship. Piece, a portion. Bate, to lessen or cut. A-bate.

BA, BI

Su.—BA, BI, conjunction And. Cp. LSG.170.
Ak.—*Ba*, conj., " and " in P(BP.18).
Sk.—*Vā*, conj. and, or, as.
Lat.—*Vel*, or.
Goth. & Anc. Br.—*Bai*, *Badi*, both. EIU.
A-S.—*Ba*, both.
E.—Both, in sense of a division into two parts, and see under *Bid*, *Bita*, " both."

BA, BE, BI

Su.—BA, BE, BI, passive prefix or suffix Be, Been. On *Ba* as passive prefix. LSG.134. See *Bē*, to be.
Ak.—*Ba* = " be " in P(BP.18). *Baśū*, be, exist. 197.
Eg.—*Pa*, to be. 230b.
Sk.—*Bhu*, to be.
Gr.—(*Phuō*, to make grow, beget).
Lat.—*Fui*, I have been.
Goth. & Anc. Br.—*Ver*, *Vas*, was. EI.
Nor.—*Blive*, to be. DN.
Ger.—*Bin*, am.
Co. & Celt.—*Be*, been. Co. *Byw*, be, exist. Cy. *Bi*, be, exist. G. *Bu*, was. I.
A-S.—*Beon*, been.
O.E.—*Bean*, been.
E.—Be, Be-ing, Been, Be-come and see *Bē*, to be.

BAD, BAT

Su.—BAD, BAT, a Stave, a wooden tool, sceptre, a bat. Pictured by a club or spear. 1508-9, 1526, B.70.
Ak.—*Hattu*, stave, sceptre.
Eg.—*Baāit*, a club, cudgel. 202a. *Bat*, a branch, a palm branch. 202a, 208a. *Pat*, staff, sceptre. 233.
Sk.—*Vadha*, Indra's bolt.
Lat.—*Baton*, cudgel. F.
Goth. & Anc. Br.—*Badm*, a beam. EI. *Vid*, wood. EI.
Co. & Celt.—*Batt*, stave. Co. *Bat*, a stave. GI. *Fiodh*, timber. I.
O.E.—*Batton*, cudgel.
E.—Bat, a cudgel: Brick-bat, Bat-on. Batt-en, wooden rod or scantling. Beet-le, a mallet. Batt-ledore.

BAD, BAT

Su.—BAD, BAT, Strike, strike down, destroy, kill. 1499 f:, 4390-91, B.70, 171, Pictured by Club, and see *Hat*, *Hit*, to strike.
Ak.—*Gamāru*, destroy, etc.
Eg.—*Patha*, *Pitha*, smite. 233. *Fat*, to cut or hack at. 263a. *Bata*, a god of War. 208a. *Bateu*, enemy. 208b.
Sk.—*Bādh*, strike. *Pith*, to strike, smite. *Bid*, to cleave. *But*, to kill. *Vadh*, slay, kill.
Lat.—*Bāt-ere*, beat. *Battre*, beat. F. *Buter*, to strike. F.
Goth. & Anc. Br.—*Bauta*, to beat. EI.
Ger.—*Fehde*, hatred.
Co. & Celt.—*Budh*, conquest. Co. *Baeddu*, beat. Cy. *Buaidh*, victory. GI. *Fuat*, enmity. I.
A-S.—*Beat*, beat. *Beada*, battle, war, slaughter.
O.E.—*Bate*, beat. *Butt-en*, to strike. *Bataile*, battle.
E.—Bat, Beat, to strike, Batt-er, Beat-er, Beat-ing: Batter, Batt-ery, Batt-ering, etc., Batt-le, Batt-le-ment. Com-bat, Com-bat-ant Batt-alion, Batt-ue. But, Butt, to strike. Bout, attack. Feud, hostility, revenge. Pat, Patt-er, to strike. Pet-ard, a war-engine.

BAD, BAT, BATU

Su.—**BAD, BAT, BATU**, Death, Fate, bad or wicked, rave, howl. 1491-3, 1510, 1517, 1527, 1536-37, 4389, B.70 and 171. On *Batu* and the three Fates in Sumerian, see WPOB.243 f.
Ak.—*Astu*, bad, wicked. *Matu*, *Mūtu*, death. *Simūtu*, fate, lot, destiny. 1065. *Idimmu*, demon. 20.
Eg.—*Bata*, *Bataui*, evil, wickedness. 208a, 226a. *Bath*, evil destruction. 212a. *Pat*, the dead. 235b. *Bati*, horror. 208a. *Batiu*, devils. 208a. *Beden*, the enemy, evil spirit. 228a.
Sk.—*But*, to kill. *Vadh*, slay, kill. *Bad*, bad. IP. *Pat*, to fall down, to kneel. *Pāta*, n. of demon of ill-fortune, *Rāhu*. *Pāt-āla*, Hell or abode of *Pāta* (Ill-fate). *Bhūt*, *Baital*, devil in IP.
Gr.—*Pathos*, suffering.
Lat.—*Fatum*, fate, *Pedus*, bad. *Fata*, a goddess of Fate. *Fata morgana*. I. *Fatal*, fatal. F. *Bête*, brute-beast. F.
Goth. & Anc. Br.—*Bauta*, slay. I. *Ŏd(r)* or *Ŏth(r)*, evil mind. EI. *Ŏd(r)* or *Oth(r)*, mad, frantic. EI. *Wods*, mad. U. *Wodan*, as the Fury opposed to Thor in E.
Ger.—*Wuth*, madness.
Co. & Celt.—*Badoes*, mad. Co. *Beud*, hurt, mischief. G. *Baodh*, giddy, foolish. G. *Wud*, mad. S. *Buathad*, mad. G. *Badb*, a demon. I.
A-S.—*Wite*, evil, affliction, torment, plague. *Wod*, mad.
O.E.—*Badde*, bad. *Wood*, mad.
E.—Bad, evil, wicked: Bad-ly, Bad-ness. Both-er, trouble, Both-ersome. Pathos, suffering: Path-etic, Path-ology, Path-ologist, Path-ogenic, Path-ognomonic. Pat-ient, bear suffering: Pat-ience, Im-pat-ience. Fate, Fatal (denoting the deadliness of Fate): Fatality, Fat-alism, Fat-ed, Ill-fated. Fat-uous, in-fat-uated, etc. The Three Fates. (*B* interchanging with labials F, P).

BAD, BAT

Su.—**BAD, BAT**, Open, open a way, be far away, removed, escaped, departed. Pictured by the "Spear (*Bad*) or Way-opener." 1525, 1529, etc., B.70.
Ak.—*Pitū*, open. 849. *Nisū*, far removed, departed, etc. 698.
Eg.—*Path*, to open. 254b. *Baa*, a path. 202a. *Pat*, *Paut*, remote ages. 230b. *Pat*, creator, father-god "Ptah." 253b.
Sk.—*Bhid*, *Pat*, to open. *Patha*, a path. *Pāta*, width, expanse. *Bādh*, to remove. *Pitri*, father, fore-father. *Pitā*, father. P.
Gr.—*Patos*, a trodden path or way.
Lat.—*Pat-ere*, to lie open. *Puteus*, a pit. *Viduus*, void. *Void*, empty. F.
Goth. & Anc. Br.—*Braut*, a path or road. EI. *Vid*, wide. EI. *Vidd*, width. EI. (*Fœdr*, father, as Opener of the Way?).
Nor.—*Vid*, wide. DNS.
Ger.—*Weit*, wide.
Co. & Celt.—*Byth*, *Vyth*, nothing, void. Co. *Vidhe*, distance. G. *Wyth*, a wide field. Co.
A-S.—*Peath*, a path. *Pyt*, *Pytt*, pit. *Wid*, wide.
O.E.—*Path*, a path. *Pit*, *Put*, a pit. *Wid*, wide.
E.—Path, Path-way, Path-less. Pat-ent, lying open, public, patently: Pat-ent, official document conferring rights for invention, etc. Pit, opening in the earth: Pit-man, Pit-fall, Cock-pit, etc. Wide, far extended: Wide-en, Wide-ly, Wide-awake, Wide-spread, Wide-ness, Width. Void, empty, destitute, evacuated, Void-ance, A-void, Una-void-able. Widow (bereft), Wid-ower, Wid-ow-hood, etc. ? Father, as "the opener of the way"—a supposed meaning of that name: Father-hood, Father-ly, Pater-nal, Patri-arch, Patro-nym, Patr-iot, Patr-iotism, Patr-on, etc.

BAD, BAT

Su.—**BAD, BAT**, a Vessel, enclosure of Pot, etc., a Vat or Pot. Pictured by the sign "Open" and "Open within" an "Enclosure." 1526, 1540, 4385, M.869, 872, 876, B.70 and 171.
Ak.—*Asāru*, a vessel. 23. *Nuta-bur*, a vessel, a bowl, cistern. On *Bur*, bowl, see 186 f.
Eg.—*Bātha*, pot or vessel. 213b.
Sk.—*Avat*, a pot. *Bahat*, a vat.
Gr.—*Butis*, a flask.
Lat.—(*Pot-are*, to drink). *Poterie*, pottery. F. *Butila*, a kind of vessel.
Goth. & Anc. Br.—*Pott(r)*, pot. NI. *Bothn*, vessel for mead. EI. *Pudas*, pot. L. *Fat*, vat. EI. *Bytha*, a pail, a tub. EI.
Nor.—*Potte*, pot. DN. *Fad*, vat. DN. *Fat*, vat. S.
Co. & Celt.—*Pot*, a pot. Cy. *Poit*, pot. G. *Pota Potadh*, pot, a vessel. I. *Pat*, pot. S. *Buidael*, bottle, cask. G.
A-S.—*Faet*, a vessel, a cask.
O.E.—*Pot*, pot. *Botel*, bottle. *Fat*, a vat.
E.—Pot, Pot-age, Pot-able, Pott-er, Pott-ery, Pot-sherd, Pot-ash, Pott-le, a little pot, Bott-le, But-ler, etc. Vat, Wine-vat. Butt, a tub, a barrel.

BAD, BAT

Su.—**BAD, BAT**, Deep, dark, strike down, the end. 1499, 1520, M.857, 860, 2909, B.70 (44).
Ak.—*Nagbu*, deep. *Gamaru*, end. 222.
Eg.—*Paht*, the end of anything. 244a. *Pahuit*, fundament, *podex*. 244a.
Sk.—*Budhna*, bottom, deep. *Ahi Budhnya*, or

serpent of the Bottom, the Devil. *Bād*, to bathe, to dive.
Gr.—*Bathus*, deep. *Puthmēn*, bottom. (? *Pous, Podos*, a foot).
Lat.—*Fundus*, bottom. *Pat-ere*, to be open, extended. *Podex*, fundament.
Goth. & Anc. Br.—*Botn*, bottom. EI. *Angr Bodo*, "Angry Bodo," a title of Wodan in E.
Nor.—*Fod*, bottom. DN. *Boten*, bottom. S.
Ger.—*Boden*, bottom.
Co. & Celt.—*Bodo, Bodun*, the deep. Co. *Bedh*, a grave. Co. *Weath*, below. Co.
A-S.—*Botm*, bottom.
O.E.—*Botym, Bothem*, bottom.
E.—Bott-om, Bott-om-less, Bott-om-less pit. Butt, an end, or Bottom-end, Butt-ock, diminutive of Butt. Butt-ress, a base support. Funda-ment, Funda-mental, Foundation. Fathom, as measure. Pathos, deep feeling. ? Bath, as the deep. ? Ped, foot from end or foundation, Ped-al, Ped-estrian, etc.

BAD, PAD

Su.—**BAD, PAD**, Food, meal, etc. Bread. Pictured by a cake or loaf. 9925, 9929-30, B.429(4-5).
Ak.—*Kurmatu*, food, meal, etc. 438.
Eg.—*Bast*, a cake or loaf. 209a. *Pāt*, food, loaf, bread. 234a. *Paut*, food, bread. 230b. *Bat*, grains. 226b. *Bāht*, abundant food. 213b. *Fat*, a cake, a loaf. 259b. *Past*, a loaf, a cake (? pastry). 233b.
Sk.—*Pitu*, food. *Bhāt*, cooked rice. IP.
Gr.—*Biotos*, subsistence, means of life.
Lat.—*Pāte*, cake, pastry. F. *Pāture*, pasture. F.
Goth. & Anc. Br.—*Faeda, Faedi*, food. EI.
Nor.—*Fōde*, food. DN.
Ger.—*Futter*, food.
Co. & Celt.—*Būyd*, food. Co. *Bwyd*, food Cy. *Biadh*, food. Gl.
A-S.—*Fōda*, food. *Bat*, bait.
O.E.—*Fode*, food.
E.—Food (F for BP.), Food-stuff, Feed, Feed-ing, etc. Fodd-er. Bait, food set as lure. Patti-cake. Bread. ? Past-ry. Past-ure, Past-ure-land.

BADUR, BA-DUR

Su.—**BADUR, BA-DUR**, Water. 128, 11,319.
Ak.—*Mū*, water. 503.
Eg.—*Bāir*, water, a mass of water. 213a (Where the *i* is omitted in transliterating the signs).
Sk.—*Va, Vār*, water, ocean. *Udan*, water, river. *Udān*, ocean.
Gr.—*Udōr*, water.
Lat.—*Ūdus*, wet, moist. *Unda*, flowing water, a wave.
Goth. & Anc. Br.—*Vatn*, water. EI. *Voda, Wandu*, water. L.
Nor.—*Vand*, water. DN.
Ger.—*Wasser*, water.
A-S.—*Wæter*, water.
O.E.—*Water*, water.
E.—Water (W. for B. and *d* for *t*): Water-y, Water-ish, Water-closet, Water-course, Water-cress, -fall, -fowl, -logged, -man, -mark, -mill, -pipe, -pot, -power, -proof, -shed, -spout, -tight, -wheel, -work, etc.

BAES

Su.—**BAES**, a Vessel, a vase. P.48 and cp. Br.5892.
Ak.—*Kub-dugga*, a vassal, written with sign of *Dug*, a Jug or pot, q.v.
Eg.—*Bas*, a vase or bottle. 222b. *Baza*, a kind of pot, a vessel. 208b. *Pag, Peg*, a bowl or vessel. 253a.
Sk.—*Vāsana*, a water-jar.
Lat.—*Vas, Vasum*, a vase or vessel.
Nor.—*Vas*, a vase. DN.
Ger.—*Vase*, a vase.
O.E.—*Vase*, a vase.
E.—Vase, Vess-el, Vas-cular, Vas-culum, etc.

BAK, BAG, PAG

Su.—**BAK, BAG, PAG**, A bird, Bird of the Winds (*Hawk*). Identical with *Akh*, q.v. Also defined as "Caged bird," i.e., Hunting falcon. And as sacred Sun-Hawk is defined as The Great *Uku* Lord (*Uku-zu-umun*) and Lord of the Land, the Judge of the *Uku* (Achaian), people; and same name and sign in Egyptian. See pl. II. 2047, 2051-53, B.83 and cp. 346, and see *Akh* and *Ukh*.
Ak.—*Issur Šāri*, wind-bird. 1106.
Eg.—*Bak*, hawk. 206a and G.20. *Bāk*, Hawk-god. 210b, 211b. Sun-hawk of Horus. *Baak*, hawk. 210b. *Aākh*. Hawk of Setting Sun. 29b. Hieroglyph is essentially the same as in Sumerian, see plate II.*
Sk.—*Pāji-ka*, falcon. *Pdksha*, the Sun as "The Winged." *Vajja*, the winged thunder-bolt of Indra. *Bāj, Bāz, Basha*, sparrow-hawk IP. Cp. Blanford's *Birds of India*, III, 402 f.
Lat.—*Busis*, Low Latin for *Buteo* or sparrow-hawk used by Pliny.
Goth. & Anc. Br.—*Hauk*, hawk. EI.
Nor.—*Hōg, Hōk*, hawk. DN.
Ger.—*Habicht*, hawk.
Co. & Celt.—*Barges*, a kite. *Faucun*, a falcon. Co.
A-S.—*Heafoc*, hawk.
O.E.—*Hauk*, hawk. (*Faucon*, a falcon).
E.—Hawk (and see *Akh*, "Hawk,") a rapacious bird allied to the falcon; Hawk-ing, Hawk-bell, Hawk-eyed, -nosed, Hawk-moth, Hawk-weed, etc. Buzz-ard, an allied bird to hawk and falcon.

BAKUŚ, BA-KUŚ

Su.—BAKUŚ, BA-KUŚ, Wine-lord of Sumerians, now disclosed as historical original of Bacchus, and identical with King *Bazuzu*, son of *Zagga* of the Udug Bowl, from Kish, c. 3400 B.C. : and see WPOB.348 f. 122, 6018, re Kuś. And see *Ag, Aka, Azag, Bazuzu, Buzur, Dias* and *Maga*.
Ak.—*Bau* (Confused by later Assyrians with *Bau*, a title of the Mother-goddess).
Eg.—*Bag*, god of the Date-palm. 224a. i.e., of the "Toddy-palm," yielding fermented wine. *Basa* or *Besa*, Corn-god. 223a. *Basa, Besa*, the lion- (or feline-) headed and dancing god with harp. 205b. *Bakhis*, a bull-god. 601a.
Sk.—*Bhaga*, "The dispenser," God of welfare, good fortune and prosperity. *Basu* or *Vasu*, Lord of Wealth. *Bagha*, god of destiny. Z.
Gr.—*Bakchos*, god of wine and fruits and animals, in lion-drawn car. *Bagaios, Zeus*, a god of plenty.
Lat.—*Bacchus*, wine-god of wine and revels.
Goth. & Anc. Br.—*Bauge* or *Bōgvi*, giant of agriculture and mead in E. *Bogu*, god in L.
O.E.—*Bacchus*, god of wine.
E.—Bacchus, god of wine and revels: Bacch-ic, Bacch-anal. Booze or Bouse, deep wine-drinking: Bous-er, Bous-y, Bous-ing.

BAL, BUL, PUL

Su.—BAL, BUL, PUL, Spindle, baton—Pole. Pictured by a sign which appears to a knob-headed spindle or shaft. 262, 275, 278, M.162, B.9.
Ak.—*Palū*, a baton, a royal insignium. *Pilaqqu*, a spindle, an axe. *Balu*, a spear. 159.
Sk.—*Vala-ka*, a pole, a beam. *Palā-la*, a stalk.
Gr.—*Belos*, a dart. *Ball-nos*, a bolt-pin.
Lat.—*Palus*, a pale or stake. *Baleno*, lightning bolt. I.
Goth. & Anc. Br.—*Bol, Bul*, stem of a tree. EI. *Voll*, a staff. EI.
Nor.—*Bul*, a log, stem, stump. DN. *Pil*, a bolt. DN. *Bāl*, stump. S.
Ger.—*Bolzea*, a bolt.
Co. & Celt.—*Bul*, an axe. Co. *Falh*, bill-hook. Co. *Paal*, a spade. Co.
A-S.—*Bolt*, a bolt, an arrow.
O.E.—*Bolt*, a shaft or arrow.
E.—Bole, the stem of a tree. Bolt, a bar or shaft or arrow: Bolt-hard, Bolt-sprit, Bolt-upright, Thunder-bolt, Bludgeon. Pale, a stake, pail-ing, a fence of pales, Beyond the Pale. Pole, a long piece of wood: Pole-axe, from the Akkad, *Pilaqqu*, Plank. Pole, an axis on which anything turns: North Pole, South Pole, Polar, Pole Star, May-pole. Bails, sticks for wickets. Baluster, a rail of a stair-case: Bal-ustrade. Block, a log: Block-ade, Block-house, Block-head, Block-tin.

BAL

Su.—BAL, Turn, turn around, return, cross over—Ball. Pictured by the preceding knob-headed spindle. 262, 266, B.9.
Ak.—*Taru*, turn around. 1185. *Eberu*, cross over, yonder, beyond. 9.
Eg.—*Bal-bal(t)*, any rounded thing, a berry, etc. 204a.
Sk.—*Val*, to turn, move or roll.
Gr.—*Ball-igo*, I dance.
Lat.—*Volu-ere*, to roll. *Boule*, a ball, a globe. F. *Bal*, a dance. F. *Ballet*, a little dance. F. *Pallone*, a balloon. I. *Balls*, a dance. *Ballade*, a ballad. F.
Goth. & Anc. Br.—*Böll*, a ball, globe. EI. *Vŏlo-spā*, or *Vŏlu-spā*, the speech of the Balladist, the chief song in the Eddas. E.
Nor.—*Bal*, a ball. DN. *Ballade*, ballad.
Ger.—*Bal*, ball. *Ballade*, ballad.
Co. & Celt.—*Bail*, a berry (=round). Co.
O.E.—*Balle*, a ball. *Ballade*, a ballad.
E.—Ball, a spherical body: Ball-cartridge, Ball-proof, Ball and socket, Billiard-ball, Cricket-ball, Eve-ball, Foot-ball, Golf-balls, Snow-ball. Ball, a dance: Ball-room, Ball-et. Ballad, a spirited narrative poem, being originally a song sung to the rhythmic movements of a dancing chorus: Ball-adist. Bowl, a wooden ball for rolling: Bowler, Bowl-ing, Bowl-ing-green. Voluble, rolling forth. *Vŏluspa* or "The Speech of the Balladist," the chief song in the Gothic Edda epics. Volve, to turn over: E-vol-ve, E-vol-ution, E-vol-utioning, E-vol-utionist, E-vol-ution theory.

BAL, BUL, PUL

Su.—BAL, BUL, PUL, Pull, draw, outgoing, pour out, cross over, a measure of time, Fly. Same sign of Bow and Arrow with the idea of pull, draw of the bow, and issue or out-going of the arrow. 262-3, 265, 268, 271, 275. B.9.
Ak.—*Elēqu*, pull, draw, pass away. *Dabū*, draw. *Naqu*, pour out. *Eběru*, cross over, *Palū*, a year of reign. 802.
Sk.—*Palāy*, to flee, fly. *Pala*, a measure of time.
Gr.—*Ballō*, to throw. *Pallain*, hurl a missile. ? *Palaios*, old (in sense of flown time).
Lat.—*Vell-ere*, to pull. *Pell-ere*, to drive or propel. *Fluo*, flow. *Flu-men*, a river (or the flower). *Volée*, a flight. F.
Goth. & Anc. Br.—*Bola*, push. I.
Co. & Celt.—*Buille*, a blow. I. *Buail*, strike. I. *Bel*, long, far off. Co. *Bulah*, a passage. Co.
O.E.—*Pulle*, pull.
E.—Pull, Pull-ing, Pull-ey, Pull, as a drink. Pelt, Pro-pel, Pro-pell-er, etc. Blow, Volley, a flight. Fling, Flung, Fly, Flee, Flow, Fluid,

Flown. Palæ-o-logy, or study of bygone times, Palæ-ologist, Palæ-ography, Ply, to bend, bow.

BAL, BUL, PUL

Su.—BAL, BUL, PUL, Valour, strength, strong, bold. Same sign of Bow and Arrow with the idea of strength and valour in pulling and marksmanship. 262. B.9. And see *Al*, strong.
Ak.—*Abāru* be strong. 9.
Eg.—*Pal(t)*, *Par(t)*, strength, vigour. 240*b*. *Pali, Pari*, bold warrior, fighting man. 240*b*. (*l* and *r*, interchangeable in Egyptian).
Sk.—*Bala*, strength, might.
Gr.—*Palā*, wrestling.
Lat.—*Valor*, strength. *Violentia*, violent. *Baldo*, bold. I.
Goth. & Anc. Br.—*Ball(r)*, bold, daring. EI. *Valor*, might. EI. *Balthic*, boldness. U.
Nor.—*Wala*, strength. L.
A-S.—*Beald, Bald*, bold. *Baldor*, the bold.
O.E.—*Bald*, bold. *Valoure*, valour.
E.—Bold, daring, Bold-ly, Bold-ness. Val-iant: Val-our, Val-orous, Valor-ously. Viol-ence, Viol-ent, Viol-ently. Bully.

BAL, BUL, PUL

Su.—BAL, BUL, PUL, Hostile, evil, ruin, dig up, destroy. Same sign of Bow and Arrow with the idea of enemy and battle and destruction. 262, 269-70, 272-4 and B.9.
Ak.—*Bal*, negation in Phœnician. (BP.20). *Bakāru*, hostile. *Vagaru*, break, destroy. *Hiru*, dig up. *Nabal Katu*, rebellion. *Napālu*, destroy.
Sk.—*Bhal*, to hurt. *Balā*, troops of war, an army. *Bala*, a demon conquered by Indra.
Gr.—*Bal, Ballō*, to fall, to tumble.
Lat.—*Bellum*, war. ? *Fallere*, to deceive. *Falsus*, deceive. *Fello*, traitor. Low L.
Goth. & Anc. Br.—*Balli, Böll*, evil, deadly, fatal, misfortune. EI. *Val(r)*, the slain, slaughter. *Val-höll* or *Hall*, of the slain, abode of Wodan. *Balwjan*, plague, torment. U.
Ger.—*Balo*, destruction. HG.
Co. & Celt.—*Bal, Val*, plague and a place dug up. Co. *Balas*, to dig. Co. *Balin* grinding mill. Co. *Feull*, treachery. I.
A-S.—*Balo, Balu, Balewe*, wicked, hateful. *Fel* fierce. *Wael*, slaughter, the slain. *Balewa*, the hateful wicked one: Satan. *Wal*, slaughter. *Wal-crigge*, goddess of War.
O.E.—*Bale*, evil. *Fel*, fierce, cruel.
E.—Bale, evil, Bale-ful, Belial, ? Bally, curseword. Belli-cose, Belli-gerent. E-vil, The E-vil one. Fall, Fall-en, Fall out, etc., and see *Bul*, throw down. False, False-ly, Falsehood, etc. Fell, fierce, cruel, Fel-on, etc. Vile, wicked, base, Vil-ify, Vill-ain, Vill-ainous, etc.

Val-halla, Wodan's Hall of the Slain. Valkyries, Wodan's harpies of War, see *Firig*.

BAL, BUL, PUL, BALAG

Su.—BAL, BUL, PUL, BALAG, Bawl, bellow, roar, swear, interpret, and see *Balag*, cry of Woe. P.51. Same sign of Bow and Arrow with the idea of hostile battle-cry and roaring and interpreter between the two sides. 262, 271, 283-4, 702*b*. B.9.
Ak.—*Tamū*, talk, speak, swear, conjure, incantation, etc. 1166. *Naqu*, to howl. 719.
Eg.—*Bal-aka*, bless. 204*a* (through idea of incantation as with *Aś*, "curse" also= "bless).
Sk.—*Boli*, speech. IP.
Lat.—*Baul-ere*, to bark like a dog. *Dia-bolos* The Devil as The Slanderer. *Palavra*, a word, parole.
Goth. & Anc. Br.—*Bölva*, to curse, swear. EI. *Bala*, Boar. EI. *Vāla, Vola*, wail. *Balvjan*, to curse. U. *Belia, Belja*, to bellow. I.
Nor.—*Ballra*, make loud noise. N.
Ger.—*Poltern*, clamour.
Co. & Celt.—*Bolder*, thundery. Co. *Ballart*, clamour. Gl. *Flyte*, to scold. S.
A-S.—*Bell*, roar. *Bellan*, to bellow, make a loud noise. *Belle*, a bell.
O.E.—*Belor*, bellow. *Balle*, a bell. *Balder*, to use coarse language in prov. E.
E.—Bawl, to shout; Bawl-er, etc., Bla-tant. Bal-derdash, jumbled, empty or coarse talk. Bell, the loud sounding. Bell, Bellow, to roar like a bull. Blare, roar of trumpets. Bull, probably cognate with Bellow. Palaver, a parley.

BAN

Su.—BAN, Son, daughter, young, small, of man and animals, weak, also "The Child-creating goddess"—Venus. Pictured by a pair of breasts as in Egypt., pl. II. 4075 f., M.2729, B.161. And see *Bir*, Birth.
Ak.—*Ban*, son. P(BP.20). *Binu, Māru*, son. *Mārtu*, daughter. *Il Ban-Māri*, Ishtar. 175.
Eg.—*Bann*, to be begotten, to beget. 217*a*. *Ban(t)*, pair of breasts. 203*a*, 217*a*, with hieroglyph essentially identical with the Sumerian. See pl. II. *Ban-en*, deity of generation. *Fan, Fent*, weak, helpless, faint. 260*b*, 261*a*. *Bennu-Asar*, n. of Venus as "The Star of the Ship." BGE.303.
Sk.—*Vansa*, son, offspring. *Bansa*, descent, family, lineage. IP. *Bhānu*, a wife. *Banh*, to grow, increase.
Gr.—? *Pan-dora*, a form of Venus (usually translated "Every-gift").
Lat.—*Puine*, the younger. F.
Goth. & Anc. Br.—*Barn*, child. EIU. *Venia* or *Venja*, to wean. I.

Nor.—*Barn*, child. DNS.
Co. & Celt.—*Bodn*, a teat. Co. *Bennen-Bennen*, a woman. Co. *Benyw*, woman. Cy. *Ban, Bean*, woman, wife. Gl. *Bainne*, milk. I. *Wan*, weak. Co. *Bairn*, child. S. *Wain, Wean*, child. S.
A-S.—*Bearn*, a child.
O.E.—*Barn*, a child.
E.—Wain, Wean, a child (Scot.). Bairn, child and see *Bar*, bear, and *Bir*, breed, brood. Puny, small, inferior in size and strength. ? Faint, weak, through the Egyptian. Venus, the goddess of Love (Ven-ery). ? Wean, to give up suckling a child (*re* the breasts of pictograph): Wean-ed, Wean-ing. Wench, young girl.

BAN, PAN

Su.—BAN, PAN, a Bow. 9097, 9100 f., B.394 (2-4)
Ak.—*Qaštu*, a bow. 936.
Eg.—*Fan*, bow-legged, bandy-legged. 260*b*. *Ban*(t), *Ben*(t), a harp. 203*b*, 216*b* (the Bow was the primitive harp as shown by Mr. H. Balfour, Oxford). *Ban*, to [? cause to] flee, go on. 216*b*.
Sk.—*Ban*, a part of an arrow, an arrow.
Gr.—*Bainō*, to make to go. P.
Lat.—*Pando*, bow, bend, curve. *Bandé*, bent, of a bow. F.
Goth. & Anc. Br.—*Benda*, stretch, strain. El. *Beygia*, to make bend. El. *Bogi*, a bow. El. *Bugan*, to bend. U.
Nor.—*Bānda*, stretch. S. *Bōie*, to bend. DN. *Bue*, a bow. DN. *Bage*, a bow. S.
Co. & Celt.—*Ben*, bent. Co.
A-S.—*Bugan, Bend*, bend.
O.E.—*Bowen*, to bend. *Bende*, bend, bow.
E.—Bandy, bowed or bent. Bandy-legged, bow-legged. Bandy-ball (Hockey), played with a bowed or bent stick. Bend, to bow or curve, Bend-ing, Un-bend-ing, Bent, Un-bent, etc. Bow, Bow-man, to Bow, Bow-ed, Bow-ing. Banjo, a stringed (bow-like) instrument.

BANA, BAN-DA, BAN-DISH, BĀNNA

Su.—BANA, BAN-DA, BAN-DISH, BĀNNA, A kind of vessel with a handle (*Da*), a measure of capacity (10 *sila* or about 15 pints)—a ? Pan. 907, 1725 in which latter the *Da* also reads *A*(6542), 1826, 5893, B.77, 264 and cp. PSL.52. In 907 the word reads *Ba-an-na*.
Ak.—*Bandū*, vessel. 179. *Paššura*, a "bowl." 846.
Eg.—*Bān*, a pot with a handle i.e., a pan]. 212*b*. *Banu*, a vessel, a bowl. 218*a*. *Ban*, a wooden box. 203*b*. ? *Pans*, to cook, to roast. 237*a*.
Sk.—*Vana*, a vessel for Soma juice. *Bhanda*, a utensil.
Lat.—*Panna*, a pan. (Low L.).
Goth. & Anc. Br.—*Panna*, a basin or pot. El. *Fen*, a fen, a morass.
Nor.—*Panna*, a pan. S.
Ger.—*Benne*, a kind of basket.
Co. & Celt.—*Pan*, pan. Cy. *Panna*, pan.
A-S.—*Panne*, pan. *Fenn*, a fen.
O.E.—*Panne*, pan. *Fen*, a fen.
E.—Pan, Pan-try, Pan-cake, Fry-pan, Ash-pan, Brain-pan, etc. ? Puncheon, a cask. ? Fen, a morass.

BANA, BAN-DA

Su.—BANA, BAN-DA, Adversary, hostile, injure, ruin, kill—Bane. 1725, 1776, etc., B.77.
Ak.—*Zairu*, adversary. *Ahū*, hostile. *Balu*, ruin. *Nasāqu*, injure. *Parāra*, kill.
Eg.—*Ban*, enemy. 203*a*. *Bann, Benn*, the Evil eye, witchcraft. 217*a*. *Bana*, evil, wretchedness and wickedness. 216*a*. *Behen*, baleful, deadly. 221*a*. *Pan*, to overthrow. 236*a*. *Ban, Ben*, a "god" of Evil. 216*b*. *Fennu*, the great Worm or Serpent of Evil. 260*b*.
Sk.—*Bāna*, a demon, enemy of Vishnu, the Sun-god.
Gr.—*Phonos*, murder.
Lat.—*Venenum*, poison. *Ven-ari*, to hunt.
Goth. & Anc. Br.—*Bani*, a bane, Death. El. *Fiendi*, a foe, enemy, hater. I. *Banja*, a wound. U.
Nor.—*Bane*, death. DNS. *Fiende*, enemy. DNS.
Ger.—*Feind*, enemy, foe, fiend.
Co. & Celt.—*Bana*, murderer. I.
A-S.—*Bana*, a murderer. *Feond*, hater, enemy. *Winnan*, to fight, to labour.
O.E.—*Bane*, destruction. *Fend*, an enemy, foe, hater. *Wan, Won*, gain by contest or labour.
E.—Bane, harm, destruction, death: Bane-ful, Bane-fully, Dog-bane, Hen-bane, Wolf-bane, Witch-bane, etc. Cp. *Fi* a viper. Fiend, an enemy, Fiend-ish, etc. Venery, hunting: Veni-son, Ven-om, poison: Ven-omous. Win, to gain by contest or labour: Win-ner, Winn-ing, Win-some.

BANA, BAN-DA

Su.—BANA, BAN-DA, Exorcise, remove, overthrow, separate. 1725, 1786, 1779, 1844, 1848, M.1006, 1083, B.77.
Ak.—*Āšipu*, exorcise. *Nisū*, remove. 697. *Parāšu*, separate.
Eg.—*Bannhu*, to turn away. 217*a*. *Band*, to bind with spells. 219*a*. *Pana*, to overthrow. 236*a*.
Sk.—*Bhan*, to call, to proclaim.

SUMER-ARYAN DICTIONARY

Lat.—*Bannir,* to proclaim. F. *Banditto,* proclaim. I. *Bando,* a ban. I. (*Pun-ire,* to punish, chastise).
Goth. & Anc. Br.—*Bann,* to ban. EI. *Banna,* to forbid. EI. *Bannan,* a curse. EI. (for exorcism). *Bandva,* to ban. U. *Bandja,* a prisoner. U.
Nor.—*Bann,* to ban. DNS.
Ger.—*Bann,* to ban.
Co. & Celt.—*Beneas,* banned. Co. *Wyn, Benegys,* blessed. Co.
A-S.—*Bannen,* to prohibit, to curse. *Ben,* a deprecation.
O.E.—*Feuden,* to ward off.
E.—Ban, to banish, proscribe, excommunicate. Ban-ish, to exile, expel, Ban-ish-ment. Ban-dit, Ban-ditti. Banns, proclamation of marriage, to forbid the banns. Fence, a guard, protection, ward off. Fend, toward off: Fend-er, De-fender. ? Pun-ish.

BAR, BĀR, PAR, BA

Su.—BAR, BĀR, PAR, BA, A sprout of wood, a reed or cane, a mace or sceptre=a Bar. And see *Bar.* Pictured by a staff. Firesceptre. 1722, 1723, 1813, M.982-4, 1019, 1067, B.77.
Ak.—*Isu,* wood. *Uššubu,* sprout. *Parussu,* a staff. 838.
Eg.—*Par, Parr,* a sprout, a plant. 242b. *Pa(t),* a sceptre, a staff. 253b.
Sk.—*Pala,* a stalk (*l* for *r*).
Lat.—*Veru,* a spit. *Verber,* a cudgel. *Fer-ula,* a rod or cane. ? *Baro,* blockhead.
Goth. & Anc. Br.—*Bar, Bar(elli),* a rod, a club. EI. *Bord,* a plank.
Ger.—*Bord,* beam. OG.
Co. & Celt.—*Baar,* a bar, a bolt. Co. *Ber,* a spit. Co. *Pren,* a stick, a divining rod of Druids. Co. *Bar,* bar, nail. Cy. *Bar,* branch of tree. Br. *Barra, Bior,* a bar, spike. GI.
O.E.—*Barre,* a bar.
E.—Bar, a rod of wood. Board, a plank, a table, see *Bar,* to bear. *Fer-ule,* a rod or cane. ? Branch. ? Bough from *Ba.* ? Forest, a wood.

BAR

Su.—BAR, Barrier, fence, a bridge, side, enclosure, boundary. Pictured by a cross. 1755, 1760, M.992, 102, B.77.
Ak.—*Itiātu,* side, enclosure. *Kamātu,* enclosure, ring, wall. 399. *Ballurtu,* a fence.
Eg.—? *Bra,* a basket (plaited). 219a.
Sk.—*Vara,* enclosing, environing, circum-fer-ence. *Varana,* a rampart, a bridge. *Vrita,* a fence.
Gr.—*Peri,* around. *Para,* by the side of, beside. *Or-os, Ouron,* a boundary.
Lat.—*Paries,* a wall. *Borne,* a boundary. F. *Barrière,* a barrier. F. *Para-petto,* a rampart, breast high. I. ? *Bara,* a bier, a litter. I.
Goth. & Anc. Br.—*Biorr,* a wall, a screen. I. *Bordi,* border. EI. *Bord,* side of a ship. I. *Byrge,* fence. *Bera,* a shield. EI. *Brū, Bryggia,* bridge. EI. *Barm,* brim or border. EI. *Võr,* a fenced place, weir.
Co. & Celt.—*Bart,* a side. Co. *Bers,* defence, Armoric. *Bord,* a border. *Brē,* a hill. Co. *Brae,* a hill. S.
A-S.—*Bord,* a border, a shield, a hedge.
O.E.—*Barrere,* barrier. *Bourn,* boundary. *Bordure,* border.
E.—Bar of a door, Barr-ed, Barr-ing, Bar-maid, Toll-bar, Sand-bar, De-bar. Barr-ier, a boundary, side. Barri-cade, Barri-caded. Barrage. Para-pet. Border, edge or boundary. Bourn, a boundary. Bor-der, Bor-dering. Brae, a hill (Co. and S.). Brim, border or edge: Brim-ful, Brim-ming. Period, time of a circuit or round. *Peri-* "around," prefix of word: Peri-phery, peri-patetic, Peri-phrase, Peri-anth, Peri-carp, Peri-cardium, Peri-helion, Peri-meter, Peri-plus circumnavigation, Peri-osteum, Peri-tonitis, Peri-scope, etc. *Park,* enclosed ground. ? Bridge. ? Barr-el, cask of bars. Ward, a guard, a means of guarding, a guardian: Ward-en, Ward-er, Ward-robe. Ste-ward, Ste-wardship. Weir, a fence or dam.

BAR, BARA

Su.—BAR, BARA, House, palace, chapel. Pictured by crossed bars of wood and by a stockaded or buttressed building essentially similar to the Egyptian sign. See pl. II. 1809, 6872, 6881, B.77 and 301.
Ak.—*Subtu, Tiltu,* dwellings. *Parakku,* a sanctuary.
Eg.—*Par,* a house, a palace. 237b. Hieroglyph of palace is essentially similar to the Sumerian pictograph. See plate II.*
Sk.—*Vara,* a room. *Bāri,* a house (Bengali).
Lat.—*Baraque,* a barrack. F. *Baracca,* a tent. I.
Goth. & Anc. Br.—*Būr,* a house, a chamber. EI. *Bær, Byr,* house. EI. *Vera,* a dwelling. EI.
Nor.—*Bur,* house chamber, a cage. DNS.
Co. & Celt.—*Barth,* house (Devonsh). *Byre,* a cow-house. S. *Baircinn,* side timbers of a house. G.
A-S.—*Bur,* cottage, chamber, bower.
O.E.—*Fort,* a hold. *Boure,* bower, lady's chamber.
E.—Fort, Fort-ress, forti-fy, and see *Bar,* strong. Bower, lady's chamber. Barrack, from Akkad. Byre, a cow-house. ? Barn, a granary. Ward, a room.

BAR

Su.—BAR, City, large city, metropolis=Borough or Burg. 1767, B.77.

Ak.—*Marāzu*, city, metropolis. 521.
Eg.—*Bak*, a city. 206b.
Sk.—*Pura*, city.
Goth. & Anc. Br.—*Bœr*, a town, a village. *Borg*, fort, castle. I. *Baurg*, a town. U. ? *Fern*, a region, district. U.
Nor.—*Borg*, fort. DNS.
Ger.—*Bürg*, city.
Co. & Celt.—*Ber-ges*, a citizen. Co.
A-S.—*Burh*, *Burg*, a town.
O.E.—*Buric*, *Borwe*, *Borewe*, a town.
E.—*Boro*, Borough and Burgh, suffixes of the City and town names, most of which are pronounced "Boro": Edin-boro' or Edin-burgh, Peter-boro, Scarborough, Marl-borough, Jed-burgh, Rox-burgh, etc. Burg-ess, Burgh-er, citizen. *Bury*, suffix in city names, Canter-bury, Glaston-bury, Salis-bury, Shrews-bury, Bans-bury, etc. Broch or Brogh, "Pictish" castle-towers in Scotland.

BAR

Su.—**BAR**, Strong, lead, captive, grace—Brave. 1759, M.975-7, 1034, 1066, B.77.
Ak.—*Ezzu*, strong. *Kamū*, lead captive. 392. *Naplusu*, grace. 708. *Biru*, hero. CT.18, 7.
Eg.—*Parā*, strength, bravery, hero. 241a. *Parā*, mighty man, hero. 241a.
Sk.—*Bīra*, brave. *Va*, strong, powerful.
Lat.—*Fors*, strong, brave. *Brav*, brave, gay, fine. F. *Bravo*, brave, valiant. I.
Goth. & Anc. Br.—*Barr*, strong, vigorous. EI. *Bragi*, heroes. I.
Nor.—*Brav*, brave, goodly DN. *Bra*, good. S.
Co. & Celt.—*Breo*, *Brav*, fine. Br. *Breagh*, fine. G. *Braw*, fine, good-looking. S.
O.E.—*Brave*, valiant, brave, fine. *Fors*, Force, strength, power.
E.—Brave, valiant, fine: Brav-ery, Brav-ado. Bravo! well done. Force, Force-ful, Force-fully, Forc-ible, Forc-ibly, Force-ibleness, Forcing, Force-less, Force-pump, etc. Fort-ress, Fort-itude, Fort-ify, etc., see *Bar*, "House." Pr-owess, bravery, valour. Braw, Scottish for fairly dressed, showy, handsome, pretty. ? Brawny, muscular. Fair, captivating, pleasing, beautiful, from the "grace" and "captivating" meaning of Sumerian word: Fair-ness, Fair-ly. Vir-ile, vir-ility, and see *Ur*, hero.

BAR

Su.—**BAR**, Great, large, wide, burly. 1800. B.77.
Ak.—*Sadādu*, large, etc.
Eg.—*Ur*, great, great size, greatness, very. 170b.
Sk.—*Brihart*, great, large, vast, wide. *Bara*, great, large, very. IP.
Gr.—(*Hy-per*, in sense of excess).
Lat.—*Probus*, excellent, fine.
Goth. & Anc. Br.—*A-far*, *A-var*, very much, much. EI. *A-br*, great. U. *Forr*, haughty. I.
Co. & Celt.—*Brās*, great, gross. Co. *Berri*, fatness. *Borr*, great. GI.
O.E.—*Burli*, *Burlie*, burly, large.
E.—Burly, large, huge. Very, as intensive, greatly, in great degree: Very good, Very bad, Very fine, Very coarse, Very wet, Very cold, Very hot, Very warm, Very much, Very true, Very false, etc., Veri-est.

BAR, PAR, BARA

Su.—**BAR, PAR, BARA**, Far away, across, over, the future, past, eternity—all from the idea of "open" (*Ba*). "The far-off Land," *Bar* or *Par*, as the Sumerian title for "The West" and for "The land of the *Maru*, *Maruta*, *Martu* or "Amorites." 1732-7, 1793, 5528, 5530-4, B.77, 244.
Ak.—*Pitū*, open. 79. *Ahrū*, the future. 30. *Rīgātu*, distance. *Sātu*, remote past, eternity. 899. *Arkātu*, behind, after. *Suparuru*, spread out. *Aḫharū*, west, western, behind (i.e., behind worshipper at sunrise), land of the *Muru* or *Amurri* (Amorites). 30.
Eg.—*Bar*, outside. 219b. *Barg*, to open. 219b. *Par*, go forth, beyond. 240a. m *Bahā*, before, of old time. 205a.
Sk.—*Para*, far, future. *Par*, cross over. *Pra*, before, forth, away. *Var*, to overspread *Purva*, *Purana*, ancient. *Apar*, *Varum*, West, Western. *Aparāntya*, the Western division of the world, in which the Indian Emperor Asoka (3rd cent. B.C.) placed the *Yavans* or Ionians (I.A.1893, 173). (*Paśca* "West," literally "behind," i.e., behind the Sun-worshipper at sunrise) is strictly analogous to the Sumerian title for "the West.") *Bahar*, outside. IP.
Gr.—*Para*, beyond, beside. *Pro*, in front of. *Poros*, a way through. *Hyper*, over, across, beyond. *Bara-thron*, the abyss, the lower world.
Lat.—*Præ*, before, in front of. *Su-per*, above, over, beyond. *Bar-Bar*, foreign. *Bara-thrum*, the abyss.
Goth. & Anc. Br.—*Fiara*, far. EI. *Far*, *Fara*, to fare forth, voyage by ship. EI. *Yfir*, over, above, beyond. EI. *Fyrir*, before. EI. *Fairra*, far off. U. *Faura*, far, before. U. *Ufar*, over, above, beyond. U.
Nor.—*Fjern*, far. DN. *Öfver*, over. S. *For*, before. DN. *For*, before. DNS.
Ger.—*Fern*, far. *Vor*, before. *Uber*, over.
Co. & Celt.—*Per-ag*, before. Co. *Per-grin*, a foreigner. Co. *Pres*, *Prez*, *Prys*, time. Co.
A-S.—*Feor*, *Feorr*, *Fior*, far. *Fore*, before. *Ofer*, over. *Fær*, *Faru*, a journey.
O.E.—*Fer*, *Feor*, far. *Fore*, before, in front.

E.—Far, Far-ther, Far-thest, A-far. Fare, travel, voyage, Far-ing, Sea-faring, Ferry, Ferry-boat, Ferry-man. First, foremost. Fore, in front, fore-most or First, be-fore and their compounds. For-mer, For-ward, Fore-arm, fore-bears, fore-fathers, Fore-bode, Fore-cast, Fore-castle, Fore-close, Fore-date, Fore-father, Fore-finger, Fore-foot, Fore-front, Fore-ground, Fore-land, Fore-head, Fore-judge, Fore-know, Fore-knowledge, Fore-lock, Fore-man, Fore-woman, Fore-noon, Fore-ordain, Fore-part, Fore-runner, Fore-see, Fore-sight, Fore-shorten, Fore-stall, Fore-taste, Fore-tell, Fore-thought, Fore-word, pre-face, etc. Forth, go Forth. Foreign, distant, Foreigner. Over, above, across and its compounds : Over-arch, Over-awe, Over-balance, Over-bear, Over-board, Over-burden, Over-cast, Over-charge, Over-cloud, Over-coat, Over-come, Over-do, Over-dose, Over-draw, Over-dress, Over-drive, Over-flow, Over-grow, Over-hang, Over-haul, Over-head, Over-hear, Over-joyed, Over-lade, Over-land, Over-lap, Over-lay, Over-leap, Over-lie, Over-laid, Over-look, Over-match, Over-pass, Over-pay, Over-plus Over-power, Over-rate, Over-reach, Over-ride, Over-rule, Over-run, Over-see, Over-set, Over-shadow, Over-shoot, Over-sight, Over-spread, Over-step, Over-stock, Over-strain, Over-take, Over-task, Over-throw, Over-top, Over-turn, Over-value, Over-weening, Over-weigh, Over-whelm, Over-wise, Over-work, Over-wraught, etc. *Pre-*, before, beforehand and its compounds : Pre-amble, pre-bend, Pre-caution, Pre-cede, Pre-centors, Pre-cept, Pre-cession, Pre-cinct, Pre-cipice, Pre-cise, Pre-clude, Pre-conceive, Pre-cursor, Pre-decessor, Pre-destine, Pre-determine, Pre-dicate, Pre-dict, Pre-dilector, Pre-dispose, Pre-dominate, Pre-eminence, Pre-empture, Pre-engage, Pre-exist, Pre-face, Pre-fect, Pre-fer, Pre-fix, Pre-gnant, Pre-hensile, Pre-historic, Pre-judge, Pre-judice, Pre-late, Pre-liminary, Pre-lude, Pre-mature, Pre-meditate, Pre-mise, Pre-monish, Pre-occupy, Pre-ordain, Pre-pare, Pre-pay, Pre-ponderate, Pre-position, Pre-possess, Pre-posterous, Pre-rogative, Pre-sage, Pre-science, Pre-scribe, Pre-sentiment, Pre-side, Pre-sident, Pre-suppose, Pre-text, Pre-vail, Pre-varicate, Pre-vent, Pre-vious, Pre-warm, etc. *Pro-*, before, forward, in front, and its compounds : Pro-bation, Pro-ceed, Pro-claim, Pro-clivity, Pro-crastinate, Pro-create, Pro-cure, Pro-duce, Pro-ffer, Pro-ficient, Pro-file, Pro-found, Pro-genitor, Pro-geny, Pro-gnostic, Pro-gramme, Pro-gress, Pro-hibit, Pro-ject, Pro-jectile, Pro-lix, Pro-logue, Pro-long, Pro-menade, Pro-minent, Pro-miscuous, Pro-mise, Pro-montory, Pro-mote, Pro-noun, Pro-nounce, Pro-pagate, Pro-pel, Pro-pensity, Pro-portion, Pro-pose, Pro-position, Pro-pound, Pro-rogue, Pro-scribs, Pro-sect, Pro-secute, Pro-spect, Pro-sper, Pro-stitute, Pro-strate, Pro-tect, Pro-tract, Pro-trude, Pro-tuberance, Pro-vide, Pro-vidence, Pro-vost, etc. Prow, forepart of ship, the bow. *Pariah*, outcaste. " The Far-off Land in the West," the Sumerian title for " The Land of the *Maru, Maruta* or Amorites."

BAR, BA, BURU

Su.—BAR, BA, BURU, High Heaven (*Imin*)—Heaven, " The dwelling of the Lord (*Ŝer*)," presumably from the idea of *Bar*, " over," above. 1722-3, 1751, 8748, 8767-8, B.77, 365. And see *Aŝ-Bartu*, Lady of Heaven and *Imin* (Gothic *Himin*), Heaven and *Uru-u-wa-nu*, the God of Gods or Lord of Lords. Br.40 and WPOB.243, 251 ; WISD.94, 97.

Ak.—*Elātum*, the zenith. *Elati*, the firmament, the upper world. *Elim, Imin*, high heaven. Cp. 47, 51 and Br. 1751. *Samū*, heaven.

Eg.—*Baa*, Heaven, the sky. 210b. *Ba-qt*, Land of Heaven and the Sky. 224a. *Par-ur*, Heaven or Sky. 238b.

Sk.—*Ba*, the enveloping sky. *Varuna*, the all-enveloping sky. *Ambara*, the sky.

Gr.—*Ouranos*, Heaven, the fault of Heaven and the sky. *Ourios*, a title of Zeus.

Lat.—*Urania*, the heavenly. *Ver-tex*, the summit, the head, the pole of the heavens, the zenith.

Goth. & Anc. Br.—*Ofar* above, high up. EI.

Co. & Celt.—*Bar*, the top, the summit. Co. *Barr*, top. Cy. *Wartha*, on high. Co. *Worthyans*, glory. Co. *Bārr*, the top. GI.

E.—*Ouranos*, Heaven or the sky, and its deity. Urano-graphy, descriptive astronomy. Urano-metry, measurement of the heavens and constellations. Uranus, a primary planet. Ver-tical, the pole of the sky, the zenith : Ver-tically or perpendicular. And see *Bar*, over.

BAR

Su.—BAR (*Iti*), First month of the Agricultural New Year—Ver-nal or Spring. It is called " The establisher or leader of the Months," and began at the Vernal or Spring equinox, about March 21st, i.e., the date of the New Year in Britain until 1752 A.D. 6871, 6876-7, 6903, B.301. And see *Bar*, to open.

Ak.—*Nisanna*. (*Arath*, Month of *Nisan*, 1st month of the year (c. 21st March to 20th April).

Eg.—*Par(t)*, the Vegetative season of the Ancient Egyptian year. 242b. *Par(t)*, a sprout, a plant. 242b. *Par*, to rise (of the Sun). 242a. *Pirūit*, season of Vegetables. MDC.207. *Hapar, Khapar*, the Spring equinox (21st March). 525a.

Gr.—'*Ear*, the Spring, Spring-tide.
Lat.—*Ver*, the Spring. (*Aprilis*, April usually derived from *Aperire*, to open). *Avril*, April. F.
Goth. & Anc. Br.—*Vār*, *Vor*, the Spring tide.
Nor.—*Vaar*, the Spring. DN. *Var*, the Spring. S.
Co. & Celt.—*Errach*, the Spring. I.
O.E.—*Vernall*, Vernal. *Aueril*, *Aprille*, April.
E.—April, the opening month of Spring. Vernal, belonging to Spring, which bebins at the Vernal equinox; about 21st March, which was the Sumerian New Year *as it also was in Britain* down till 1752 A.D. when it was changed by Act of Parliament to the 1st of January.

BAR, BA

Su.—BAR, BA, Cut, break, tear, open, divide—Break. From *Ba*, to cut, break. 1786, 1814, 1849, B.77.
Ak.—*Barā*, to cut. P(BP.23). *Uṣṣuru*, cut, cut in two. *Parāsu*, separate. *Parāru*, break, break in two.
Eg.—*Bahan*, to cut in pieces. 220b. *Baha*, *Beha*, break, tear in pieces. 220b. *Fakhkh*, to break. 261b. *Parkh*, to divide, separate. 243b. *Berg*, to force (or break), open a door. 219b. *Perasht*, destruction, ruin, perish. 243b. *Perza*, to split, divide, separate. 243b.
Sk.—*Vrasc*, to cut off, or down, or asunder. *Vrikna*, broken, cleft ro torn.
Lat.—*Pars*, a part, a portion. *Fragor*, a crack. *Frang-ere*, to break. *Brevis*, short. *Bref*, short. F.
Goth. & Anc. Br.—*Par*, a paring, a scrap. I. *Braca*, break. EI. *Brot*, a fragment. EI. *Brik*, break. U.
Nor.—*Brākke*, break. DN. *Brag*, crack. DN. *Brud*, a breach or rupture. DN.
Ger.—*Brechen*, to break.
Co. & Celt.—*Barri*, to divide. Co. *Byr*, cut short, brief. Co. *Ber*, short. Co. *Parad*, a separation. Co. *Bragh*, a burst. GI.
A-S.—*Brece*, break.
O.E.—*Breke*, break. *Parcel*, a portion.
E.—Pare, to cut off. Break, to fracture, Breach, Break-er, Break off, Break-water, Break-fast. Brief, Brief-ly, Brief-ness. Par-cel, a little part: Parcel-out, parcel-office, parcel-post. Part, a portion: A-part, Part-ial, Part-icle, Part-ing, Part-isan, Part-ition, Part-ly, Part-ner, Part-ake, Part-y. Portion, Portion-ed, Pro-portion, Ap-portion. Fract-ure. ? Perish, to be destroyed, to be ruined, decayed, Perish-able.

BAR, BIR, BAR-GAIL AŚ-BAR

Su.—BAR, BIR, BAR-GAL, AŚ-BAR, Iron, as "The Bar of kings or of Protection," "The heavenly or lordly Bar." *Aś-bar*. From *Bar* to cut. 1789, 1924, 7787, B.77. The spelling may be *Bir* in 1789.
Ak.—*Br-zl*, *Bar-zal* (or *Bir-zal*). P(BP.23). *Par-ṣillu*, iron. 828. On *ṣillu*, "protect." 875.
Eg.—*Par-ihar*, iron (weapons). 232a. [As "protecting Bar"—on *thar*=protect, see 851a]. *Ban-pi*, iron [as "The banisher," see *Ban* above]. 203b. *Baa-an-pat* or Iron of the sky (meteoric iron). 210a.
Sk.—*Ayas*, iron, from the Sumerian synonym, "*Aś-bar*."?
Lat.—*Ferr-um*, iron. *Fer*, iron. F.
Goth. & Anc. Br.—*Iārn*, *Jārn*, Iron. EI. *Fōra*, armour. I. *Eis-arn*, iron. U. (from *As*-bar synonym).
Nor.—*Jern*, iron. DNS.
Ger.—*Eisen*, iron. (From *As*-bar synonym).
Co. & Celt.—*Baar*, a bolt. Co. *Haiarn*, iron. Cy. *Iarann*, iron. G.
A-S.—*Iren*, *Isen*, *Iassern*, iron.
O.E.—*Iren*, iron. *Isen*, *Yzen*, iron.
E.—Ir-on, the now common and most useful metal as "The Lordly Bar," and "The protective Bar" of the Sumerians and Ancient Egyptians: Iron-age, Iron, for golfing, Iron-bound, Iron-cased, Iron-clad, Iron-er, Iron-founder, Iron-foundry, Iron-gray, Iron-handed, Iron-hearted, Iron-heater, Iron-ing, Iron-master, Iron-monger, Iron-side, Iron-smith, Iron-stone, Iron-ware, Iron-work, Iron-crown, Cast-iron, Pig-iron, etc. Ferr-ic, Ferr-eous, Ferr-uginous, Ferro-type. Uranium, a metal resembling iron.

BAR

Su.—BAR, Savage, hostile, devastating, wild beast—Bear, Barbarous. From idea of *Bar*, "side," as beside, opposed, hostile and *Ba Bar*, cut and tear. 1729, M.1005-6. See *Firig*, fierce and *Ur*, *Paru*, leopard.
Ak.—*Akhū*, hostile, stranger, evil, enemy, also jackal, leopard. 28. *Barbar*, leopard. Br. 11,276.
Eg.—*Parā*, war. 214a. *Pari*, battle. 240b. *Pari*, warriors, soldiers. 243b, 340b. *Ba*, a leopard. 200b.
Sk.—*Vair(n)*, war, war-fare. *Vyāghra*, a tiger. *Bagar*, a leopard. IP.
Lat.—*Fur-ere*, to rage. *Fera*, wild beast. *Ferr-us*, wild. *Fer-ox*, fierce. *Bar-barē*, *Guerre*, war. F. *Pardu*, leopard.
Goth. & Anc. Br.—*Bar*, *Bar-āttu*, war. EI. *Berja*, to beat. EI. *Ber*, *Bera*, a bear. EI.
Co. & Celt.—*Braw*, fear. Cy. *Bresel*, war (Armoric).
A-S.—*Wyrre*, *Uuerre*, war. *Fierd*, *Fyrd*, an army. *Bera*, a bear.
O.E.—*Werre*, war. *Bera*, a bear.
E.—Barbarous. War, Warr-ing, War-fare, Warr-

ior, War-like. Ferocity, Feroc-ious. Fierce, Fierce-ly, Fierce-ness. Fury, Fur-ious, Fur-iously, Fr-antic, Fray, Af-fray. ? Fear, Fearful. Bear, an animal, Bear-ish. Pard, a leopard.

BAR, BARA

Su.—BAR, BARA, Privative, prohibitive, negative prefix and preposition, meaning, Not, to be, away from, without, extinguished, from the idea of *Ra*, divide, *Bar*, side, outside, and cut off. 123, 1742, M.1014, B.5 and 77.
Ak.—*La*, negative. *Balū*, without, not to be, etc. 159.
Eg.—*Baa*, negative. 209a. *Bu*, negative, not. 213b.
Sk.—*Vi-*, prefix of opposition, away from, without, opposition, etc.
Goth. & Anc. Br.—*Vid*, *Vith*, against.
E.—Bar, prohibit. *For-*, appears to be used as a negative prefix, in sense " away from," in such words as, For-bid, For-get, Fore-go, For-sake, For-swear (swear falsely). Bare, void.

BAR

Su.—BAR, Brother, a peer, pair or twin, companion, kin. From idea of *Bar*, side and parity in " cut in two " (*Ba*). 118, 1763, 1774, 1806-7, 1851-3, B.77. On " brother " as title of a priest, see *Bar*, Priest.
Ak.—*Akhu*, *Axu*, brother, friend, companion. 27. *Tappu*, companion, twin. *Kimtu*, kindred.
Eg.—*Ari*, companion, friend. 69b f.
Sk.—*Bhrātra*, brother, friend, companion. *Prati*, likeness.
Gr.—*Phrātēr*, brother.
Lat.—*Frāter*, brother. *Frère*, brother. F. *Par*, alike, equal. *Pair*, equal, like. F. *Pare*, alike. I. *Pari*, a pear. I.
Goth. & Anc. Br.—*Brōthir*, *Brōdir*, brother. EI. *Bar-mi*, a brother. EI. *Friā*, a friend. EI. *Brothar*, brother. U. *Par*, a pair.
Nor.—*Broder*. DN.S.
Ger.—*Bruder*.
Co. & Celt.—*Beur*, brother. Co. *Brathair*. G.
A-S.—*Brothor*, brother. *Fera*, *Gefera*, a companion.
O.E.—Brother. *Peire*, a pair. *Pere*, a peer.
E.—Brother, Brother-ly, Brother-liness, Brother-like, Brother-hood. Friar, Friary. Friend, companion: Friend-ly, Friendli-ness, Friend-ship. Par, equal, equal value. Pair, Par-ity, Paramour, Non-pareil. Peer, Peer-less, Peerage, Peer-ess. Par-allel, side by side, Par-allelism, Par-allelogram. ? Fellow, as companion (*l* for *r*).

BAR

Su.—BAR, Bear, Carry, Carry off, remove, transport. 1779, B.77.

Ak.—*Nisū*, carry off, remove. 697.
Eg.—*Fa, Fai*, bear, carry, lift up. 258a. *Fi*, bear, carry, bring. 260a.
Sk.—*Bhara*, bearing, carrying, bringing. *Vah*, to bear, carry, transport, convey, bring.
Gr.—*Pherō*, to bear. *Baros*, a burden.
Lat.—*Fero*, to bear, carry. *Porto*, bear, carry.
Goth. & Anc. Br.—*Bera*, *Færa*, to bear, carry. EI. *Bairan*, to carry. U. *Briggan*, to bring or fetch. U.
Nor.—*Bœra*, to carry. DN.
Ger.—*Ge-bären*, to bear.
Co. & Celt.—*Beir*, bear. I. *Far*, freight.
A-S.—*Beoran*, *Beran*, to bear, bring or fetch. *Bringan*, *Brengan*, to fetch.
O.E.—*Bere*, to carry. *Bring*, bring.
E.—Bear, to carry. Bear-er, Bear-ing, Bear-able. Bear-ing-rein, Bear-dom, Bear-out, Bear up, Bear with, Bear in mind, Bring to bear, One's bearings, For-bear. Borne, Up-born. Bring, to fetch, Brought. Ferry: Ferry-boat, Ferry-man. Por-ter, carrier, Por-terage. Fer-tile, bearing produce, Fer-tility, Fer-tilize, Fer-tilizer.

BAR, BIR, PIR, GARZA or MAŚ

Su.—BAR, BIR, PIR, GARZA or MAŚ, Mace, wood-sceptre, the shining wood in hand. " The sceptre of the king and of the Sun-God," the Fire-Cross emblem of the Sun. Pictured by the crossed twin fire-producing sticks, identical with Egyptian hieroglyph, and see WPOB.289 f., 334 f., WISD.83, 128, 136. 1724, 1745, 1750, 1802, 5644, 5647, M.984, 989, B.77 (27-28). And see *Garza*, Cross-sceptre.
Ak.—*Isa*, wood. *Ita-bruru*, shining in hand. 194. Cp. *Ita*, 127. *Ellu*, shining bright. 40. *Samsu*, the sun.
Eg.—*Par-ami*, fire-stick, that supplied the Sun-god Rā with Fire. 238a. Its *ami* (or " inset ") hieroglyph is identical with the Sumerian, cp. with GH. 37. Nos. 78, 169.
Gr.—*Phry-ktos*, a fire-brand, fire-signal of enemy's approach.
Co. & Celt.—*Ber*, a spit. Co. Fiery-Cross of Scottish clans in warfare.
E.—The Bar mace, as emblem of the Sun. The Fire-Cross, " The Fiery - Cross," and Red Cross of St. George. See WPOB.262 f., 278 f., 289 f.; WISD.83, 138 f. On "Cross," see *Garza*.

BAR, BIR, PIR

Su.—BAR, BIR, PIR, Fire, burn, bright, shine, the Fire-god, *Bil* or *Gi-Bil*. Pictured by Fire-cross. 1724, 1744-5, 1756, 1810, 1845, M.998, 1028, B.77. And see, *Bir*, Bright, *Bil*, *Pil*, Glaze and *Fir*, *Pir*, Fire.

Ak.—*Titaltu*, fire, flame. *Kabābu*, burning fire. *Nūru*, fire, light. *Gibil*, fire-god. 209.
Eg.—*Pā'h*, Fire, flame. 234a. *Bar*, shine, sunrise. 242. *Bar-ga*, give light. 204b.
Sk.—*Barhis*, fire, light. *Bhraj*, bright, parch. *Prā-kaś*, shine, illumine, irradiate.
Gr.—*Pyr, Pur*, fire. *Phyrgō*, to roast, to fry.
Lat.—*Fer-uare*, to be hot, to glow. *Fer-vor*, heat, raging heat. *For-nax*, a furnace, oven. *Frive*, fry. F. *Brio*, fire. I. *Brace*, burning cinders. I.
Goth. & Anc. Br.—*Fyri, Fūrr*, fire. EI. *Bri-mi*, Fire. EI. *Biarmi*, beaming. I. *Biart*, bright. EI. *Brenna*, burn. EI. *Varm*, warm. EI. *Varda*, a beacon. I. *Baer*, hearth. I. *Friō*, fry. EI. *Brinnan*, burn. U. *Bairhts* bright clear. U.
Nor.—*Fyr*, fire. DNS. *Brāende*, burn. DN. *Varm*, warm. Fro, fry. DNS.
Ger.—*Feuer*, fire. *Brennen*, burn. *Warm*, warm.
Co. & Celt.—*Par-et*, baked. Co. *Fria, Frya*, fry. Co. *Frio*, fry. Cy. *Forn*, an oven, a furnace. Co. *Brwd*, warm. Cy.
A-S.—*Fyre, Fir, Fyryne*, a fire. *Bærn, Byrn*, burn. *Wearm*, warm.
O.E.—*Fyr*, fire. *Bern, Bren*, burn. *Warm*, Warm. *Frie*, fry.
E.—Burn, to consume or injure by fire : Burn-er, Burn-ing, Burn-ing-glass, Burn-ing-kiln, Burnt-offering, Burnt sienna, Burn-ing bush, Burn-ing question, Burn out, Burn-up. Brand, a piece of wood burning a mark burned into anything, a trade-mark : Brand-ed, Brand-er, Brand-ing, Brand-ing iron, Brand-y, ardent spirit, Brand-new, Best Brand. Bright, shining, full of light : Bright-en, Bright-ly, Bright-ness, Bright-some. Fire- in words and compounds, and see *Fir*, Fire.

BAR, BARU

Su.—**BAR, BARU**, Priest (of Fire-cult), seer, conjurer, exorcist, lord, elder brother. Pictured by Fire-Cross sign. 1752, 1758, 1844, 1852-3, M.994, 998, 1083-4, B.77. And see *Bar-ama*, Brahman and for *Baru*, WISD.31.
Ak.—*Barū*, seer, priest. *Ásipu*, exorcist, conjurer. *Enitiu*, lordship. *Uri-gallu*, elder brother. 92. *Piristu*, divine decision, oracle, man of the mysteries. 835.
Eg.—(*Par-ā-a*, Pharaoh, and later a title of his chief officials as well. 238a).
Sk.—*Brahman*, priest and priestly caste (and see Barama). *Puro-hita*, domestic priest. *Bharu*, lord, master. *Vartikka*, a conjurer, a physician.
Gr.—? *Presbys*, elder. *Presbeis*, elders, chiefs, princes.
Lat.—? *Presbyter*, elder. *Færie*, enchantment. OF.
Goth. & Anc. Br.—*Bragi*, the best of bards. E. *Frey(r)*, a lord. *Frauja*, lord, master, king. U. *Forn*, sacrifice, religious offering.
Co. & Celt.—*Bronter, Braonter, Prounder*, a priest. Co. *Fairo-me*, prophecy. I. ? *Prim, Priom*, chief, principal (derived apparently from "prime"). I. *War-lock*, a wizard. S.
A-S.—*Freā*, a lord. *Brego*, chief. *From*, a physician (Northumb.). *Preōst*, priest. ? *Frod* wise, prudent. *Bryta*, an author.
O.E.—*Preest, preost*, priest. *Færie, Fairye*, enchantment.
E.—Priest. This word has been supposed to be derived from the ecclesiastic Latin *Presbyter*, "an elder," through the Greek. But "elder brother," is a meaning of the Sumerian *Bar*, "priest." The latter name "Priest." would now appear to be derived from the Akkad synonym of *Piristu* or "Man of the mysteries—the divine decision or oracle." Priest-craft, Priest-hood, Priest-ly, Priest-ridden. And see *Bar*, to pray. Brahman, Indo-Aryan priest, see *Barama*. Fairy, properly "the enchanter." Warlock, a wizard (Scot.) (Friar, see *Bar*, Brother). ? Bar-on, the bearer of the *Bar* or sceptre of the lord ?

BAR

Su.—**BAR**, See, look, inspect, i.e., Peer, pry. Pictured by Priest and Fire-Cross sign and thus probably relating to vision of seers, which is in keeping with its modern usage. M.1001, 1030, 6998, B.77.
Ak.—*Natalu*, see, look, look up, inspect. 667.
Eg.—*Par*, sight, vision. 243a. *Bar*, eye. 219b.
Sk.—*Vipra*, a seer, inspired. *Pra-kēś*, become visible, make visible.
Lat.—*Pār-co*, appear, become, visible.
Co. & Celt.—*Faire*, see, watch. I.
O.E.—*Pere*, peep, pry, also appear. *Prian*, to pry. *Pore*, to pore over.
E.—Peer, to peep : Peer-ing, Peering into the dark. Pry, to inspect closely, especially into things closed, Pry into the future, Paul Pry. Pore, to look steadily at, Pore over books. Appear, Appear-ance and Appar-ition, seems related to the same root.

BAR

Su.—**BAR**, Pray, beseech, supplicate, speak. M.1039. B.77.
Ak.—*Barak*, bless. P.(RP.381). *Suppū*, pray, beseech, supplicate, prayer. 774 f.
Eg.—*Par, Paru*, speech, words. 240b. *Baroka*, to bless. *Barth*, a covenant. 204b.
Sk.—*Barh*, to speak. *Pra-bhi*, to pray to deity and man. *Prac*, to ask. *Pra-cit*, to make known. *Prā-kaśa*, to proclaim. *Pra-syva*, to preach.
Gr.—*Phaō*, to speak, to say especially of gods and oracles.

Lat.—*For*, to speak, to say especially of gods and oracles. *Prex*, prayer. *Verbum*, a word, a spoken word. *Par-ler*, speech, talk. F. *Prière*, prayer. F.

Goth. & Anc. Br.—*Prata*, to prate. I. *Brag(r)*, poetry. EI. *Bragi*, the muse of poetry. EI. *Ord*, *Orth* (*Vord*), a word, report, message. EI. *Waurd*, word. U.

Nor.—*Prat*, talk. DNS. *Ord*, a word. DNS.

Ger.—*Wort*, a word.

Co. & Celt.—*Pro-gath*, a speech, oration. Co. *Barf*, a bard, a poet. Co. *Bar-dd*, a bard. Cy. *Bar-za*, a bard. Br. *Bard*, a poet. GI.

A-S.—*Word*, word.

O.E.—*Preie*, *Preye*, pray. *Parley*, talk, speech, speak. *Preise*, praise. *Verbatim*, spoken. *Word*, word.

E.—Pray, to entreat, ask earnestly: Pray-er, Pray-er book, Pray-erful, Pray-erless, Pray-er rug, Pray-ing, Pray-er flag, Pray-ing machine, Prayer-mill, Pray-er wheel. Par-ley, conference, talk with enemy (in Sumerian sense of praying, beseeching). Par-ole, Par-lance, Par-liament with its Speaker, Par-lous. Pra-te, loquacious, idle talk, Pra-ter, Pra-ting, Pra-ttle, Pra-ttler, Pra-ttle-box. Preach, to pronounce in public on religious matters: Preach-er, Preach-ing, Preach-y, Preach-down. Ver-bal, spoken as opposed to written. Verb-ally, Verb-atim, Verb-ose. Word, an oral utterance, message, promise: Word-bound, Word-ed, Word-ing, Word-iness, Word-y, The Word, Pass-word. Bard, a poet, Bard-ic. Brag, Braggart. Brogue, peculiar pronunciation or dialect.

BAR

Su.—**BAR**, Council seat of wisdom, decision, decree. Pictured by Fire-Cross sign or *Bar*. 1752, 1788, M.1051, 1065, B.77.

Ak.—*Mérišu*, decision, wisdom. 593. *Purussū*, decision, decree. 834. *Tišmittu*, *Tašrmtu*, decision, wisdom, prudence. 1200.

Eg.—*Par-ebu*, judgment hall of Osiris. 238a. *Par-matu*, house of Speech, council chamber. 238a. *Par-maza*, registry, chancery. 238b.

Sk.—*Pari-kshak*, a judge. *Pāri-cchid*, to decide, discriminate, judge. *Pra-kkrip*, to decree.

Lat.—*Forma*, government, constitution. *Forma*, to form, order, regulate. *For-um*, place of legislative and political and commercial business. *For-ensis*, relating to the Forum as seat of Justice, legal. *Verus*, true.

Goth. & Anc. Br.—*For-seti*, an umpire. EI. *Frōd*, *Frædi*, knowledge, learning. EI. *Frodi*, wise, prudent, learned, a title of scholars. I. *Froth*, wise. U. *Var*, heed, caution, warn. I. *Vārar*, pledge, covenant, treaty, truce. EI. *Wars*, heed, caution. U.

Nor.—*Var*, caution, heed. DNS.

Ger.—? *Wahr*, true, veritable.

Co. & Celt.—*Bres*, judgment. Co. *Bar-ner*, a judge. Co. *Barn*, judgment. G. *Pour*, dominion. Co. *Peruez*, learned, an expert. Armorica. *Fur*, wise. Co.

A-S.—*Wær*, *Waere*, a covenant, an agreement, a pledge, a fine, cautious.

O.E.—*Verytie*, truth. *War*, wary. *Barner*, a judge.

E.—Bar, in regard to Courts of Justice, would appear to have referred originally to the Court itself or its *bar* or mace of authority, rather than the wooden railing or bar dividing the judge's seat from the prisoner, see Bar, a barrier. Bar of Justice, Barr-ister, a pleader at the bar. Board, as a committee may possibly be related to this *bar*. For-ensic, legal, For-ensic medicine, medical, jurisprudence. Forum. Form, order, regularity, established practice, system of government. Form-al, Form-ally, Form-ality, Form-ulate, Good form, Bad form. Prud-ence, direction sagacity: Prud-ent, Im-prud-ent. Ver-ity, truth, Ver-itable, Ver-ify, Ver-ifiable, Verification. ? Ware, Wary, cautious, War-ily, War-iness, A-ware, Be-ware. ? Warn, Warning.

BAR-AMA

Su.—**BAR-AMA**, "Brahman," priest. This is a fuller form of *Bar*, *Baru*, priest, which is found on the Sumerian seals from the Indus Valley. See WISD.35 f., 40 f.

BARDI, BARTI, BARDU

Su.—**BARDI, BARTI, BARDU**, Historical Sumerian king of Mesopotamia at Adab. 3250 B.C., founder of *Barat*, clan of Aryans. BB. 201, 266, with inscribed statue of king. On *di*, *ti* and *du* elements, see Br.9518, 9577.

Ak.—*Parat* and *Prydi*, a Barat or Brit-on in Phœnician. WPOB.53.

Sk.—*B'arata*, *Brihad* or *Brihat*, famous Aryan king and fire-worshipper, and founder of the *B'ārata*, clan of Indo-Aryans. WPOB.52 f.

Gr.—*Pretanoi*, Britons. *Pretanikai nēsoi*, British Isles. WPOB.54, 146. *Peirithsos*, Trojan hero.

Lat.—*Britannus*, a Briton. *Brito*, a Briton, a Breton. *Britannia*, *Britanniae*, Great Britain, British Isles.

Co. & Celt.—*Prydain*, *Prydein*, *Prydyn*, *Brytaen*, Britain. Cy. *Brutus*, 1st k. of Britons.

A-S.—*Bryten*, *Bryton*, *Breoton*, *Breoton*, *Breten*, *Broten*, *Brittan*, *Britten*, *Brytten*, Britain.

O.E.—*Brit-on*, *Brit-ish*, *Brit-ain*.

E.—*Barat* or *Brihat* or *Brit*, patronym of Aryan clan of Barats of the Phœnicians, Britons and Indo-Aryans: Brit-on, Brit-ain, Bret-on, Britt-any (Armorica). Great Brit-ain, Greater

Brit-ain, Brit-ish, Brit-isher, Brit-ish Isles. Brit-ish Fleet, Brit-ish Government, Brit-ish Parliament, Brit-ish trade. All Brit-ish. See details of name in WPOB.10, 52, 188 f. WISD.10, 53, 98, 107.

BARTU, BARTI(AŚ-)

Su.—BARTU, BARTI(AŚ-), Lady of Heaven, The Answering Lady (Oracle), tutelary goddess of Sumerians—Britannia. 9540. And see *Di*, Oracle-lady, Akkad, *Dai-anu*, Diana.
Ak.—*Barat.* U. *Bĕrouth*, later n. for Phœnician goddess of water. Eusebius, 1, 10, 14. *Gebartu* lady replier, answerer, cp. *Gabaru*, *Gabri*, 210. *Bel-tu*, Ish-tar, w. of Bel, 170 and WPOB.9 f.
Eg.—*Bārta*, "consort of Ba'al." 213a. *Bāirthy*, goddess of the Waters, mother of the Waters, supporter of the boat of the Sun-god and Lady Protector. BGE.2, 281, and see WPOB.59-60.
Sk.—*Bhāratī*, Vedic, goddess of rivers and prosperity. A fire-priestess who shows the light, food-bestower and protector of her votaries.
Gr.—*Parthenos*, title of Diana. *Brito-martis*, Phœnician sea-goddess. WPOB.63-64. *Ourania*, the heavenly one, muse of astronomy with crown of stars. See *Aś Bar* as *Aśtar* or Ishtar.
Lat.—*Britannia*, tutelary sea-goddess of Britain and the Britons. *Urania*, muse of astronomy.
E.—Britannia, tutelary sea-goddess of Phœnicians, Briton and Indo-Aryans. For details of her image and representations in Phœnician, Asia-Minor, Carthage, Gades, Egypt, etc., see WPOB.55 f.

BAT

Su.—BAT, Stave, a Bat, see *Bad*, *Bat*, a Stave.

BAT

Su.—BAT, Strike, strike down, battle, see *Bad*, *Bat*, strike, etc.

BAT, BATU

Su.—BAT, BATU, Fate, see *Bad*, Death, Fate.

BAZUZU

Su.—BAZUZU, historical form of the name of King Bakus' or "Bacchus," on the votive bowl of his grandson Udug. HDB. Nos. 108-109.

BE, BĒ, BI, BA

Su.—BE, BĒ, BI, BA, Be, become, exist, live. Pictured by an arrow-head. 1477, 1494-5, B.70 and see *Ba* to be and *Bil*, to be, to live. 163.
Ak.—*Baśū*, to be, exist, become. 197. *Balatu*, live, 163.
Eg.—*Pa*, to be, to exist. 230b.
Sk.—*Bhu*, to be. *Vas*, to dwell, to live.
Gr.—(*Phuō*, to make, grow, beget).
Lat.—*Fui*, I have been. *Vi-ta*, life. *Vi-vere*, to live.
Goth. & Anc. Br.—*Ver*, *Vas*, was. EI.
Nor.—*Bliv*, to be. DN.
Ger.—*Bin*, I am.
Co. & Celt.—*Be*, been. *Biu*, *Beu*, alive. Co. *Byw*, be, exist. Cy. *Bu*, was. I. *Beō*, *Biot*, living, life. I. *Bi*, exist. G.
A-S.—*Beo*, be. *Beon*, to be, become, exist. *Wæs*, was. *Wære*, wast.
O.E.—*Be*, be. *Been*, been. *Vytayelles*, *Vitailles*, meat and drink. *Vital*, vital.
E.—Be, to Be, exist, live: Be-en, Be-ing, Become. Bio-graph, living pictures, cinematograph. Bio-graphy, written account of a life, Bio-grapher, Bio-graphist. Bio-ology, science of life: Bio-logical. *Vic-tuals*, properly "Vi-ttles," nourishment for life, food. Victualler, Vi-and, see *Buz*, vegetable food. Vital, containing life, Vi-talise, Vi-talism, Vi-tality, Vi-tally, Vi-tals, Vi-tal functions, Vi-tal power, Vi-tal principle. Viv-id, lively, life-like, Viv-acious, Viv-idly, Viv-idness, Viv-ify, Vivi-parous, Vivi-sect. Vivi-section, Anti-vivi-section, Con-vivi-al, Re-vive, Survive. Was, from Akkad, *Baśū*, to be, Was-t. Were, from Gothic *Wer*.

BI, BA

Su.—BI, BA, Bisect, divide, half, portion, diminish. 103, 108, M.65, B.5, PSL.47-8. See *Ba*, divide and *Bar*, cut.
Ak.—*Naśāru*, *Zāzu*, etc., see *Ba*, bisect.
Eg.—*Bait*, a cutting. 201a.
Sk.—*Vi-*, division, asunder, as prefix. *Bid*, divide, cleave.
Lat.—*Bi-*, prefix for divide. *Bis*, twice.
Goth. & Anc. Br.—*Bita*, divide. EI.
Nor.—*Bid*, *Bide*, a bit. DN.
Ger.—*Biśo*, a bit.
Co. & Celt.—*Ba*, twice. I. *Wee*, small. S.
A-S.—*Ba*, both.
O.E.—*Bite*, a bit.
E.—Bit, a portion, Bite. Piece, a portion. Wee, small (Scottish): Wee-ny. *Bi-*, prefix of division, see *Ba*, divide.

BI, PI

Su.—BI, PI, Drink, pour out, libation, strong drink, wine, vessel or cup. Pictured by a drinking-jar with spout. 5119, 5126, M.3479, B.217.
Ak.—*Sikāru*, drink, wine. 1033. *Nazū*, pour out, libation. 717. *Kannu*, a vessel or can.
Eg.—*Ba-ba*, *Beb*, drink. 202a. *Pa(t)*, drink, liquor. 230b. *Paur*, new wine (beer). 231b.

SUMER-ARYAN DICTIONARY BI—BID

Sk.—*Pi, Pa,* drink. *Pi-na,* to drink. IP. *Piy-āla,* a cup. IP.
Gr.—*Phi-alē,* a bottle.
Lat.—*Bib-ere,* to drink. *Vi-num,* wine. *Boir,* drink. F. ? *Vin,* wine. F. *Bere,* to drink. I.
Goth. & Anc. Br.—*Bior, Bjor,* beer. EI. *Vin,* wine.
Nor.— *Vin,* wine. DNS.
Ger.—*Bier,* beer. *Wein,* wine.
A-S.—*Beor,* beer. *Wīn,* wine.
O.E.—*Bibb-en,* to tipple, imbibe. *Ber,* beer.
E.—Bib, to drink, to tipple, Bib-ber, Bib-ulous, Im-bibe. Bib, a drinking napkin. Beer, Beer-y, Bitter beer. Phial, a Vial, a little bottle. Pipe, a cask for wine or beer. Wine, Wine-bibber, Wine-bibb-ing, Wine-biscuit, Wine-cask, Wine-cellar, Wine-drinker, Wine-drinking, Wine-flask, Wine-merchant, Adam's wine.

BI, BE

Su.—BI, BE, to be, see *Be* to be.

BI, (BID)

Su.—BI, (BID), Bid, command, speak, say, proclaim, incant, swear. 5119, 5124, 5129, M.3841, B.217. And see *Di,* to speak.
Ak.—*Qibu,* command, order, speak. 904. *Qabū,* speak, say, announce. 903. *Tamū,* incant, swear, take an oath, cast a spell, bewitch. 1166.
Eg.—*Ba(t),* speak, cry. 209a. *Beg,* cry out ? Beg). 225b. *Path,* pray, ask. 254b.
Sk.—*Bid,* to speak harshly, to swear. *Vad,* speak, words. *Path,* to recite, invoke, to read. *Bāt,* speech. IP.
Gr.—*Paida-gogos,* a tutor.
Lat.—*Fatum,* an utterance. *Peda-gogus,* a teacher. *Dam-num,* harm and *Dam-nere,* to condemn (from Akkad *Tamū*). *Pedante,* a schoolmaster. I. *Baia,* joke, banter. I.
Goth. & Anc. Br.—*Bid-ia, Bith-ia, Beida,* to beseech, ask, beg or pray. EI. *Bida,* request, prayer. U. *Bidja, Biudan,* ask, beg, pray. U. *Geipa,* to talk nonsense. I. (From Akkad.)
Co. & Celt.—*Bis, Bys,* beseech. Co. *Pys,* to pray. Co.
A-S.—*Bydel,* to bid, to proclaim a beadle. *Bid,* to tell beads, pray. *Bad,* a pledge, a stake. *Fitt,* a song.
O.E.—*Bid,* to tell beads. *Bid-ding,* praying.
E.—Bid, command, propose, invite, proclaim, offer at a sale : Bid-der, Bid-ding, Bid-ding prayer. Bad-inage, jesting talk. Beadle, formerly " a crier of a court," now a petty officer of a church, college, parish, etc. Peda-gogue, a teacher, a pedant, Peda-gogy. Ped-ant, a schoolmaster, a vain displayer of learning : Ped-antic, Ped-antry. Quip, Gibe, Jibe, Gabble and Jabb-er (from Akkad, *Qibu, Qabū*). ? Dam-age, harm and Damn (from Akkad, *Tamū,* to swear, bewitch) : Dam-nable, Dam-nably, Dam-nation, Dam-natory, Dam-ned, Dam-ning, Con-demn, Con-dem-nation.

BID, BIT, BI

Su.—BID, BIT, BI, Abode, house, temple, a place or habitation in general. Pictures a building of (?) timber or bricks. 6235, 6238, 6545, B.281. On *Bi,* value, cp. 6235 and 6545. And see *Bar, Bara,* house.
Ak.—*Bat, Bit,* house or temple. P. *Bītu,* a house or temple, a place or habitation in general. 203. *Asurte,* a temple, a place of gathering. 121.
Eg.—*Bait,* a house. 202a. *Bat, Bet,* a house. 208a, 226a. *Baht,* a seat, throne. 221a. *Pait,* a house. 231b. *Ba,* abode. 202a.
Sk.—*Pad-am,* abode, a station, site, home. *Patt-an,* town, city. *Patam,* affix in place-names in India : Masuli-patam, Vizaga-patam, Nega-patam, Seringa-patam, Vizaga-patam. ? *Abad,* affix in city names, e.g., Allah-abad, Hyder-abad, Morada-bad.
Lat.—*Badia,* an abbey. I.
Goth. & Anc. Br.—*Bid,* abiding. *Bida, Bitha,* to bide, stay. EI. *Bygd,* abode, house. EI. *Vist,* abode. I. *Bū,* a house, to dwell. I. *Būth,* a booth, a shop. EI. *But-as,* home. L. *Byar-log,* town-law. I.
Nor.—*By,* town, city. DNS. *By-lov,* town law.
Ger.—*Bude,* a booth.
Col. & Celt.—*Bod, Bāk, Veth,* a house, a dwelling. Co. *Buth,* a cottage. Co. *Fod, Fed,* a place. Co.
A-S.—*Biddan, Abidan,* abide, stay, wait.
O.E.—*Abad, Abood,* a dwelling, staying.
E.—A-bode, a dwelling. A-bide, stay, remain, wait for : Abid-ing. Booth, a hut, Bothy, a cottage or hut for farm-servants. By-law or Bye-law : " Town "-law, supplementary regulations for towns. *By,* affix of " Abide, place or habitation "—the Sumerian *Bi*—in numerous place-names in England, especially associated with the Danes : Apple-by, Ash-by, Der-by, Grims-by, Kir-by, Malt-by. Orms-by, Rug-by, Sel-by, Sommers-by, Whit-by. In Lincolnshire alone are one hundred place-names ending in -by, see TW.

BID, BI-AD, BĀD

Su.—BID, BI-AD, BĀD, Evident, see, perceive, know, declare, consider or believe—Idea. Pictured by an Eye, as in the determinative hieroglyph of its Egyptian equivalent. 9258, 9267, 9273, 9283-4, M.6997, B.406. On *Bid* or *Biad,* cp. 9257 and 103. And see *Idi,* Idea, see and *Si* to see.
Ak.—*Amaru,* see behold, declare, consider. 59. *Ēnu,* eye. *Si,* see. *Idu,* know, perceive. 17.

Eg.—*Petr*, to see, look. 254a. Its hieroglyph determinative pictures an Eye as in Sumer sign, see *Asaru*, pl. II. *Petr-iu*, those who have sight, those who see. 254a. *Path* ("Ptah"), the creator, technician, master craftsman of the gods. 254b. *Bi*, wonder, wonderful. 213.

Sk.— *Vid*, to know, teach. *Veda*, knowledge. *Path*, to teach, recite. *Viśv-as*, faith. *Budh*, to perceive, observe, understand, know, think. *Buddha*, one who has achieved perfect knowledge of the Truth in ethics and religion.

Gr.—*Fidō*, old Greek for *Eidō*, to see, to know, to be skilled.

Lat.— *Vid-eo*, see, perceive, be thought, reflect, consider. *Fides*, faith. *Vue*, sight, survey, view. F.

Goth. & Anc. Br.— *Vita*, to see, know, understand. EI. *Vit*, wit, intelligence, sense, reason, understanding, opinion. EI. *Vitna*, to testify, to witness. EI. *Witan*, to see, observe, to know. U.

Nor.— *Vit*, *Vita*, wit, sense. DNS. *Vide*, know. DN. *Vidende*, knowing. DN. *Vidne*, witness. DN.

Ger.—*Wissen*, knowledge. *Witz*, wit.

Co. & Celt.—*Fidir*, know, consider. GI. *Faid*, a prophet. I.

A-S.—*Wittan*, to know, perceive, understand. *Wit*, understanding. *Wita*, a man of knowledge and understanding, a prophet, a witness. *Witenagemot*, supreme council of England in A-S. period.

O.E.—*Wit*, understanding, wise. *Wot*, *Woot*, know. *Feith*, *Feyth*, faith, belief.

E.—E-vid-ence, that which is visible or can be seen: E-vid-ent, E-vid-ential, E-vid-ently, Non-e-vid-ent. ? Fad, special "knowledge" or crotchet or craze. Faith, belief, Faith-ful, Faith-fulness, Faith-healing, Faith-less, and see Fid, faith. Fid-elity, faithfulness. Idea, see *Idi*, Eye, Idea. Pro-vide, fore-sight : Pro-vid-able, Pro-vid-ed, Pro-vid-ence, Pro-vid-ential, Pro-vid-ently, Pro-vid-er. *Veda* or "Knowledge," title of the Indo-Aryan hymns. View, a seeing, sight, opinion, belief : View-less, View-point, Re-view, Re-view-er, Re-view-ing. Vision, sight, see, etc., see *Igi*, synonym of *Bid*. Wit, understanding, knowledge, ingenious power of combining ideas with happy or ludicrous effect : Wit-icism, Wit-less, Witt-ing, Witt-y, Witt-ily, Witt-ingly, Un-witt-ingly. Wit-ness, evidence testimony. Wit-ness, evidence, testimony, Wit-nessing, etc. Wot, Weet, I know, he knows : To Wit, to say or cause to know. Buddha or "The-all-knower," title of the Indian sage, and teacher, Sākya : Buddh-ism, Buddh-ist, Buddh-istic. Non-Buddh-istic.

BIID, BIDA, BITA

Su.—BIID, BIDA, BITA, Both, and, or. 5153 and cp. *Ba*, *Bi*, divide, bisect.

Ak.— *U*, *U*, and, copula, or. 1.

Eg.—*Pat*, two halves (i.e., both). 229a.

Sk.—*Bha*, resemblance, likeness. *Vā*, either, or. *Bhī*, both, also. IP.

Gr.—(*Am-phō*), both).

Lat.—(*Aśv-bo*, both).

Goth. & Anc. Br.— *Badi*, *Badir*, *Bathu*, both (adj.-pron. dual). EI. *Bai*, *Bajoths*, both. U.

Nor.—*Baade*, both. DN. *Bācde*, both. S.

Ger.—*Beide*, both.

Co. & Celt.—*Baith*, both. S.

A-S.—*Ba*, both.

O.E.—*Bethe*, *Bathe*, both.

E.—Both, two together.

BIL, PIL, BI

Su.—BIL, PIL, BI, Blaze, flame, boil, burn, fire. Pictured by Fire-torch or Fire-brazier and by Friction of Fire-sticks. 4566, 4575. 4584, 4587-9 f., 4643, M.3081, 3085, 3100-1, B.185-6. See *Bar*, *Bir*, Fire, burn bright *Gi-Bil*, strong fire, *Izi* and *Pir*, Fire.

Ak.—*La'bu*, flame. 465. *Iśātu*, fire. *Irru*, firebrand or torch. *Napaxu*, blaze. 705. *Qualū*, burn. *Basālu*, boil. 201.

Eg.—*Pā*, flame, fire, spark. 234a.

Sk.—*Bahula*, fire.

Gr.—*Phle-gō*, to blaze up, kindle, to flame.

Lat.— *Fla-mma*, flame. *Feu*, fire. F.

Goth. & Anc. Br.—*Bāl*, a flame, a pyre. EI. *Bael*, to burn. EI. *Blys*, a torch. ? *Blid*, happy bliss. I. ? *Bleiths*, kind. U.

Nor.—*Blus*, a torch. DN.

Ger.—*Flamme*, flame, blaze.

Co. & Celt.—*Bale*, a beacon, faggot. S. *Bil*, good. I. *Bleeze*, blaze. S. *Lowe*, flame. S. (from Akkad).

A-S.—*Bael*, *Blaese*, blaze, flame. *Blæse*, torch. ? *Blids*, *Bliths*, Bliss.

O.E.—*Bele*, *Blase*, blaze, flame. ? *Blis*, Bliss, happiness.

E.—Blaze, a flame, to flame : Blaz-ing, Blaz-er, jacket of flaming colour. ? Bliss, happiness, from idea of cheerfulness of blazing fire. Bliss-ful, Bliss-fulness, Blithe, Blith-ely. Boil, Boil-er, Boil-ing, and see *Bul*, to blow. Flame, Flam-beau, a torch : Flam-ing, In-flame, In-flam-ed, In-flammation, In-flammatory. Flam-ingo, a bright red bird. Flare, Flash, see *Fil*, flame. Lowe, flame (Scot), from Akkad.

BIL

Su.—BIL, God of Fire and Light—Bil or Bel. Pictured as in foregoing signs. 4566, 4588, 4598, M.3120, B.185. See WPOB.2, 267 f., 318 f., WISD.78 f.

Ak.—*Bal* or *Bel*, Sun and Fire and Father-god of Phœnicians, see WPOB.2 f. *Urru, Ūru*, Light, day-light, day god. 92. *Kararū, Qararū*, fire, heat, god.
Eg.—*Bal, Baaul*, Bel,, Ba'al, 202a, 203b. *Bāl*, Syrian god of war. 213a.
Sk.—*Bali*, name of Indra. *Bahala* (or " Fire "), name of a Jina demigod.
Lat.—*Belus*, Fire-god.
Goth. & Anc. Br.—*Bil*, flashing light. EI. ? *Blot*, worship (pre-Christian), a sacrificial feast. EI. *Blot*, an idol. I.
Co. & Celt.—*Beal, Bel, Bil*, Fire. Co. *Bealtine*, Fires lighted to Belus. Co. *Bealltainn*, Bel's fire. G. *Bele*, a priest (? of Bel). Co. *Balerium*, (? land of Bel), an old name for Cornwall. WPOB.281. *Flaiteur, Flatur*, Heaven, sovereignty. I. ? *Flait*, a prince or chief. *Bel*, fire at fire-festival (summer solstice, or on May-day). GIS.
E.—Bel, fire at the old Fire-festival of *Bel-tane* in the British Isles, when bonfires are lit at the summer solstice or May-day : Bel-tane fires. See WPOB.2, 276 f., 318 f., WISD.78 f.

BIR, PIR

Su.—BIR, PIR, Bright, shine, pure, the Sun. 1724, 1744, 1802, 1854, 7764, B.77, 337, PSL.60. See *Bar*, Fire, bright and *Fir, Pir*, fire.
Ak.—*Utēbubu*, bright. *Berāru, Birratu, Namaru*, shine, be bright. 684.
Eg.—*Bar*, shine, sunrise. 242a.
Sk.—*Bhraj*, shine. *Barhi*, fire.
Goth. & Anc. Br.—*Biart*, bright. EI. *Bairhts*, bright. U.
A-S.—*Beorht*, bright.
O.E.—*Bright*, bright.
E.—Bright, shining, full of light : Bright-en, Bright-ly, Bright-ness, Bright-some. Brilliant, glittering, sparkling, Brill-iancy, Brilliance, Brill-iantness.

BIR

Su.—BIR, Break, tear, cut off. 8094-5, M.6063, B.342, PSL.60. See *Bar*, Cut, break.
Ak.—*Saratu*, tear, rend, cut. 1115. *Nakasu*, cut off, tear. 671.
Eg.—*Bar-bar*, to wreck. 219b. *Berg*, to force open. 219b.
Sk.—*Bhid*, break.
Lat.—*Frango*, break. ? *Brevis*, short. *Briser*, break. F.,
Goth. & Anc. Br.—*Braca*, break. EI. *Brik*, break. U.
Nor.—*Bråkke*, break. DN.
Ger.—*Brechen*, break.
Co. & Celt.—*Byr*, cut short. Co. *Bragh*, a burst. GI.

A-S.—*Brece*, break.
O.E.—*Breke*, break.
E.—Break, to fracture, and see *Bar*, cut, break.

BIR

Su.—BIR, Offspring, young, child, kid—Brood. Pictured by what is supposed to be a chicken being hatched from an egg. 2025, 2027, 2086, B.80, P.59. See *Bar*, to bear.
Ak.—*Biru*, young child, lamb. 187. *Lulu*, young offspring, a kid. 180.
Eg.—*Par(t), Per(t)*, progeny, descendants. 243a.
Sk.—*Bhar-na*, child.
Gr.—*'Arnos*, a lamb.
Goth. & Anc. Br.—*Bure*, son. *Barn*, a child. EI. *Burd, Burth*, birth. EI. *Baur*, son. U. *Brüten*, to brood. I. *Baur*, son, child. U.
Nor.—*Barn*, child. DN.
Ger.—*Brut*, brood. *Ge-burt*, birth. *Brüten*, to hatch.
Co. & Celt.—*Far*, grow, spring. I.
A-S.—*Brid*, the young of any bird, animal, a brood. *Beord*, birth. *Bredan*, to nourish or breed.
E.—Breed, Brood, Bred : Breed-er, Breed-ing. Bairn, child. ? Bird. Birth : Birth-day, Birth-mark, Birth-place, Birth-rate, Birthright. ? Brat, contemptuous name for a child : Brat-ling. And see *Bar*, to bear.

BU, PI, WI, FI

Su.—BU, PI, WI, FI, Serpent or Viper. 7501 f. B.325. See *Fi*, Viper and *Sir*, serpent.

BUGIN

Su.—BUGIN, Bag, receptacle for food and water, a pond or lake—a Bog. 10,289-91, M.7834, B.464.
Ak.—*Buginnu*, receptacle for food, and for water, ? a pond or lake. 147. *Sussulu*, a vessel, basket or jar. 774.
Eg.—*Ba*, a bag, sack. 209a. *Peg*, a vessel, bowl or measure. 253a. *Bak*, a frame. 206a. *Beka*, to bulge out, swell. 225a.
Lat.—*Bucca*, the inflated cheek cavity. *Poche*, a pouch, a bag. F. (? *Fossa*, a ditch). *Buca*, a hole. I.
Goth. & Anc. Br.—*Baggi*, a bag. EI. *Pok*, a bag. I. *Puggs*, a bag. U. *Bals*, wine-skin. U.
Ger.—*Poche*, a pustule.
Co. & Celt.—*Poca, Poc*, a bag. GI. *Bagack*, a bag. I. *Pucord*, a pustule. I. *Poke*, a bag. S.
A-S.—*Poc*, a pustule.
O.E.—*Bagge*, a bag. *Pock*, a pustule.
E.—Bag, a wallet, pouch or sack : Bagg-age, Bagg-y, Bag-man, Hand-bag and see *Bulug*, bulge. Bog, a march, swamp ; Bogg-y, Bog-moss, Bog-trotter. Box, a receptacle : Box-ing day. Pock, a pustule as in Small-pox,

Pock-ed, Pock-marked, Pock-pitted. Pock-et, a small pouch : Pock-et book, Pock-et money. Poke, a bag, a pig in a Poke. Pouch, a pocket.

BUL

Su.—BUL, Blow (of wind), etc., shake, tremble. 10,288, M.7828, 7831-2, B.463.
Ak.—*Śarbātu*, blow (of wind). *Radu*, thunderstorm. 954. *Nāśu*, shake, quake, tremble.
Sk.—*Va*, to blow. *Bal*, to whirl.
Gr.—*Pallō*, shake, quiver.
Lat.—*Flo*, blow of wind and mouth, etc. *Flatum*, blown.
Goth. & Anc. Br.—*Blāsa*, to blow, blast. EI.
Nor.—*Blase*, to blow, blast. S. *Flaga*, gust of wind. S.
Ger.—*Blähen*, to puff up. *Blasen*, to blow.
Co. & Celt.—*Blou*, blow. Co. *Blaw*, blow. S.
A-S.—*Blawan*, to puff or blow. *Blœst*, blast.
O.E.—*Blowen*, to puff or blow. *Blast*, blast. *Beli, Below*, a bellow.
E.—Blow, of air, breath or wind : Blow-er, Blow-n, Blow-pipe, Blow-y. Blast, a blowing or gust of wind, explosion of gunpowder, etc. : Blast-ed, Blast-furnace, Blast-ing. Bell-ows, an instrument for blowing. Blizz-ard, storm blast. Flatus, a puff of wind : Fla-tulence, Fla-tulency, Fla-tulent. In-fla-te, In-fla-ted. Flur-ry, sudden gust or blast, a fluttering : Flur-ried. Flute, a musical instrument for blowing : Flut-ist. Flutter, to vibrate : Flutt-ered, Flutt-ering.

BULUX

Su.—BULUX, Velocity, hasten, rush along. 79, B.2. See *Khal* or *Xal*, to run or gallop.
Ak.—*Hāśu*, hasten, rush along, hurry onward. 343.
Sk.—*Valg*, to gallop.
Lat.—*Velox*, swift.
Goth. & Anc. Br.—*Flag*, flight. EI.
Nor.—*Flugt*, flight. DN.
Ger.—*Flucht*, flight.
A-S.—*Flyge, Flyht*, flight.
O.E.—*Flight*, flight.
E.—Flight, Flight-y, Flight-iness (and see *Bal, Bul*, to fly). Veloc-ity, Veloc-ipede. Haste, Hasten (from Akkad).

BUR, BU

Su.—BUR, BU, Burn, glow. 7501-2, 7527, M.5536. See *Bar*, burn, for further details.
Ak.—*Napāhu*, burn, glow.
Eg.—*Burqa*, sparkle, shine. 215b.
Lat.—*Fer-uare*, to be hot, to glow.
Goth. & Anc. Br.—*Brenna*, burn. EI. *Brinnan*, to burn. U.
Nor.—*Brænde*, burn. DN. *Bränna*, burn. S.
Ger.—*Brennen*, burn.
A-S.—*Beornan, Byrnan, Barnan*, to burn.
O.E.—*Bern*, burn.
E.—Burn, to set on fire, be on fire : Burn-er, Burn-ing, Burn-t, etc.

BUR

Su.—BUR, Free, open, loose, unloose, salvation. 344, M.242, 244, 253, B.11.
Ak.—*Pitu*, open. *Paśaru*, unloose, set free, unloose of oaths and enchantment. *Tapśirtu*, salvation, redemption, delivery. 1182.
Sk.—*Pra*, forth, away.
Goth. & Anc. Br.—*Fri*, free. EI.
Nor.—*Fri*, free. DNS.
Ger.—*Frei*, free.
A-S.—*Freo*, free.
O.E.—*Fre*, free.
E.—Free, at liberty : Free-ly, Free-ness, Freedom, Free-hold, Free-holder, Free-man, Freemason, Free-thinker, Free-will.

BUR, BURU

Su.—BUR, BURU, Bore, open, cut through, dig a hole, burrow. Pictured by a Boring tool or drill and by circle or opening. 340, M.718, 8726-8, M.244, 248-9, B.11,365.
Ak.—*Pitu*, open. *Naqābu*, bore, pierce. *Palāśu, Palāxu*, bore, dig a hole. *Qarasu, Satata*, cut through, open.
Sk.—*Bāre*, an opening, aperture. *Prutrid*, to pierce. *Bar*, to cut. Z.
Gr.—*Phar*, in Phar-ygx, the gullet. Phar-agx, a ravine.
Lat.—*For-are*, bore. *Bur-in*, engraving tool. FI. *Percer*, to pierce. F. *Porciato*, pierced through. I. *Phar-ynx*, the gullet.
Goth. & Anc. Br.—*Bora*, to bore, pierce. EI. *Prike*, to prick, to stab. I. (*Byrgia*, to bury. I).
Nor.—*Bore*, bore. DN. *Borra*, bore. S. *Prick*, a prick. S.
Ger.—*Bohren*, to bore.
Co. & Celt.—*Bros*, a sting, a puncture. Co. *Brog*, a borer, an awl. GS. *Brod*, a goad. GI. *Prioca*, a sting. I.
A-S.—*Borian*, to bore.
O.E.—*Borien*, to bore. *Prike, Prikke*, a puncture.
E.—Bore, to perforate : Bor-er, Bor-ing, *Brog*, a borer, an awl. Bur-in, an engraver's tool. Burrow, to perforate : Burr-owing. Per-for-ate, to bore through : Per-for-able, Per-for-ator. Pierce, to make a hole, thrust through : Pierceable, Pierc-er, Pierc-ing. Prick, to puncture : Prick-er, Prick-ing, Prick-ly. Phar-ynx.

BUR, BURU, PU

Su.—BUR, BURU, PU, A Boring, hole, pit or well. Pictured by a well or pit or hole. 8632-3, 8664-5, 8685, 10,267, M.237, 7787. B.365, 460. And see *Bur*, Bore, and *Bur*, a Bowl.

Ak.—*Pitū, Patāru*, open. *Pithu*, a hole. *Būru*, a well or pit. *Hurru*, a hole, ravine. *Kannu*, a well or hole. 406.
Eg.—*Bar*, a well. 203*b*. *Barru(t)*, wells of water, pools. 202*a*.
Sk.—*Prahi*, a well. *Khani, Khāni*, a mine (from the Akkad).
Gr.—*Phrear*, a well. *Bothros*, a pit, a trench from Akkad. *Patāru*.
Lat.—*For-amen*, a hole. *Forame*, a hole. I. *Put-eus*, a pit, from Akkad, *pitū, pithu*.
Goth. & Anc. Br.—*Brunn*, a well, spring or burn. EI. *Byrda*, a large trough. I. *Brunna*, a well, spring. U.
Nor.—*Brönd*, a well.
Ger.—*Born, Brunnen*, well, spring.
A-S.—*Burna, Burne*, a stream, a fountain. *Pyt, Pytt*, a pit, from Akkad, *pitū*.
O.E.—*Bourn, Bourne*, a stream.
E.—Bore, a boring. Burn, a rivulet or brook as ? "The borer or burrower," and see *Bur*, water. Burr-ow, a hole in the ground, or along underneath a surface : Burr-owing. For-amen, a hole : For-aminated. Per-for-ation, a hole : A-per-ture. Prick, a puncture. Pit, a hole in the earth (from the Akkad synonym *Pitū, Pithu*) : Pit-coal, Pit-head, Pit-fall, Pit-man, Pit-ted, or marked with small pits. Pit-village. Bottomless Pit.

BUR, PUR

Su.—BUR, PUR, Flood water, river—the great river, *Bur-at* or Euphrates. Pictured by wavelet of Water. 8633, 8714, 11,318 11,331, 11,346, 11,444, B.521.
Ak.—*Mū*, water. *Butuqtu*, flood, eruption of water, inundation. 209. *Milū*, flood water, high tide. 544.
Eg.—*Bair*, mass of water. 213*a*. *Paur, Pair*, river, stream, The Nile, 231*b*. PV.145.
Sk.—*Bar-bura*, water. *Vari*, stream, river. *Var*, water, the ocean.
Goth. & Anc. Br.—*Ver*, the sea. EI. *Bāra*, a wave, a billow. I. *Brunn*, a stream. EI. *Fors*, a waterfall, brook, a stream. EI.
Co. & Celt.—*Bera*, to flow. Co. *Fairge*, the sea. I. (*Force*, waterfall. S.).
A-S.—*Wĕr*, the sea. *Brōc*, a rushing stream. *Force*, a waterfall. S.
O.E.—*Bore*, a tidal surge. *Brook*, a small stream of water.
E.—Bore, a tidal surge in a river (see *Ager*, Eagre). Brook, a streamlet : Brook-let. Burn, a rivulet or stream, and see above. Pour, to flow out. (This *Bur* or *Burat*, Sumerian river name may possibly be the source of such river-names as the Forth (Borderia of Ptolemy) : Bourne in Hants, Ware in Durham, Worse in Shrops., Barrow in Ireland (Bargou or Birgou of Ptolemy), etc.

BUR, BU, BURU

Su.—BUR, BU, BURU, Worm, a serpent. Figured as a borer, and as a serpent (the worm as a borer in the earth, and the serpent as living in holes, or ? a borer with its fangs). 334, 342, 7511, 7529, 8684, etc., B.11, 325. And see *Ara, Ari*, serpent.
Ak.—*Baśmu*, poisonous serpent. 202. *Arāku*, be long. *Nasahu*, bite. *Sarāpu*, burn. 1116. *Hurhumatu*, vermin living in holes. 337.
Eg.—*Fau*, a worm. 259*b*. *Fai*, a mythological serpent of Evil ("The Worm"). 259*b*.
Sk.—*Urag*, a serpent. *Bhujag*, a serpent.
Lat.—*Verm-is*, a worm. *Verme*, a worm. I.
Goth. & Anc. Br.—*Orm*, a worm, a serpent, the mythological serpent of evil. EI. *Waurm*, s serpent. U.
Nor.—*Orm*, worm. DNS.
Ger.—*Wurm*, worm.
A-S.—*Wyrm*, worm, snake, dragon.
O.E.—*Worm*, worm.
E.—Worm, the earth-worm, etc. : Worm-eaten, Worm-ed, Worm-holed, Worm-y, Earth-worm, Blind-worm, Glow-worm, Worm of a screw and distilling apparatus. To worm out. Vermicelli, wheat dough in worm-like rolls. Vermicular, relating to worms. Verm-in, obnoxious insects and small animals including snakes. *Orm*, "The great Worm," or Serpent of Evil in Gothic and Ancient Briton myth. Its name is preserved in several place-names associated with the Dragon and usually with serpent-like rock formations, e.g., Ormes-head, Orms-by, Orma-thwaite, Orms-kirk, Ormiston, Ormi-dale, Wurms-head in Wales, etc.

BUR, WUR

Su.—BUR, WUR, Ear, hearing, attention, intelligence, wisdom. Pictured by a hole and by a pair of ears. 7961, 7969, 8773, B.339, 365. On value, *Bur*, for, 7961, see 11,318.
Ak.—*Uznu*, an ear, hearing, attention, wisdom, understanding. 27. *Uznu, rapāstu*, intelligence. *Hasīsu*, wise, intelligent. 328.
Sk.—*Prajna*, wisdom, intelligence. *Wazn*, hear, hearing. IP. (from Akkad).
Gr.—*Ous*, ear, from Akkad. *Aiō*, hear.
Lat.—*Auris*, ear.
Goth. & Anc. Br.—*Aur, Eyra*, ear. EI. *Heyra*, hear. EI. *Ausa*, ear. U, from Akkad.
Nor.—*Öre*, ear. DN. *Ora*, ear. S.
Ger.—*Ohr*, ear.
A-S.—*Eāre*, ear. *Hyra*, hear.
O.E.—*Era*, ear. *Here, Huyre*, hear. *Her-sal*, rehearsal.
E.—Ear (from which the initial *B* of the Sumerian has dropped out), the organ of hearing, sense of hearing, attention : Ear-ache, Ear-drop, Ear-ed, Ear-less, Ear-lock, Ear-mark, Ear-

piercing, Ear-ring, Ear-shot, Ear-trumpet, Ear-wax, Ear-wig, Ear-witness. About one's ears, Lend an ear, Over head and ears, etc. Aur-icular, told in the ear, Aur-icle, ear lobe, Aur-ist, ear specialist. Hear, to perceive by the ear, Hear-er, Hear-ing, Hear-say, Hear-say evidence, Hear, Hear! Re-hear-sal. Hearken, Hark, Hark back, Aus-cultate, fr. Akkad.

BUR, BUR, PUR

Su.—BUR, BUR, PUR, A Stone Bowl, the Magic Wishing-Bowl of King Bur or Pur, priest-king, and of Lady Asza or Uzsa, "the decider of wishes" and "increaser of wisdom." 6971, 6973-5, 6979-80, 9519, 9527, B.306. And see *Epir* and *Kan*, a bowl or cup.

Ak.—*Abnu-būru* (or *pūru*), a stone bowl. 187 *Salātu*, libation. *Naptānu*, fear. *Azaru*, *Erēsu*, wish, desire. 27, 106. *Sutēsu*, pronounce an edict. 1135.

Eg.—*Bar-bas*, a pot or vessel. 204a.

Sk.—*Pura*, a receptacle. 635. *Bila*, a bowl. *Piyāla*, a drinking-cup. IP.

Gr.—? *Pialē*, a bottle, a vial.

Lat.—? *Boire*, to drink.

Goth. & Anc. Br.—*Hver*, magical, drinking stonebowl or cauldron of Sig or Thor in Eddas. *Byrd*, a trough. I. *Bolli*, a bowl. EI.

Co. & Celt.—*Bolla*, *Fiol*, a bowl, cup. Co. *Beol*, a trough. Co. *Bol*, a bowl. Cy. *Burie*, a milk or cream-jug. S.

A-S.—*Bolla*, a bowl.

O.E.—*Bolle*, a bowl.

E.—Bowl, a drinking vessel or cup (in which *l* for *r*): Flowing bowl, Magic bowl, Punchbowl, Devil's Punch-bowl, Witch's bowl or cauldron. Ewer, a water-jug, see *Ewir*, a vessel. ? Phial or Vial, a small bottle. Pour-*boire*, drink money.

BUR, BURU, PUR, PURU

Su.—BUR, BURU, PUR, PURU (*Aś*), Lord Bur or Pur or Puru, styled: The *Aś* Bur (or Puru), king, priest-king (*Iśakku*) of the Wishing Stone-Bowl, Lord Judge of the Land, the compassionate judge and counsellor. 6971, 6979-80, 8761, 9519, 9526, 9530-1. And see *Bur-ya*, *Dar*, *Dur*, *Induru*, *Mid* or *Mitra*, *Puru*, *Sig* and *Zakh*.

Ak.—*Maliku*, decider, king. 547. *Milku*, counsel, understanding. 548. *Dinu*, judgment. 259. *Iśakku*, priest-king. 114. *Silū satakalti*, decider of omen tablets. 1036.

Eg.—*Pa-Ra*, the flying Sun. 230a. *Par-ra*, the Sun Hawk. 239a. *Bar*, "Baal." 203b.

Sk.—*Purū-Ravas*, or "Puru of the Sun," husband of *Asi* of Ur (*Urv-asi*), founder of first Aryan dynasty in Lunar Epic King-lists. *Ikshvaku*, founder of first Aryan Solar dynasty in the Solar Epic King-lists.

Goth. & Anc. Br.—*Bur* or *Bor*, title of *Asa* Thor or *Öku* Thor or *Mioth*, husband of *Asyni* of Urd, 1st king of the Goths, in the Gothic Eddas, and capturer of the Magic Stone-Bowl.

E—Pro-metheus, husband of Asia, as first king of the Aryans and identical with *Bur-Mioth*, title of Thor the first king of the Goths and husband of Asyni in Gothic Eddas, and who is disclosed to be an historical Sumerian king, see *Azu Sib.* and *Mit*, *Mitra* and *Puru*.

BUR, BURU

Su.—BUR, BURU, Land, earth, a unit of land measure. 8689, 8663, B.365.

Ak.—*Erṣitu*, earth, land, a piece of land, a field. 104. *Bur*, a unit of land measure. 186.

Eg.—*Pehar* or *Pekhar*, ground, territory, land. 247a.

Sk.—*Bhū*, earth, land, a piece of land. *Prithvi*, the earth as "the broad one."

Lat.—? *Prae-dium*, an estate.

Goth. & Anc. Br.—*Bū*, land, estates. I.

E.—? Broad, wide. Pre-dial, consisting of landed estate.

BUR, BURU

Su.—BUR, BURU, Dig, cultivate, excavate. 8678-9, 8727-8, B.365. See *Bur*, to bore, burrow.

Ak.—*Harāru*, to dig, excavate. 341. *Habāru* or *Khabāru*, to dig. 331. *Habiri*, *Khabiri*, Hittite confederates allied to the Kassis. 302. Literally "The diggers"?

Eg.—? *Khabia*, the divine reepers of Osiris. 572a (from Akkad).

Sk.—*Vridh*, to cultivate. *Bhū-ru*, earth grower, a plant, a tree.

Goth. & Anc. Br.—*Bū*, tillage, cultivation. EI. *Byrgja*, to bury. I. *Hafr*, the diggers or cultivators and yeomanry of Thor in Eddas (confused with *Hafr*, a he-goat)—*Capra*.

Ger.—*Bau*, tillage, cultivation.

A-S.—*Byrgan*, to bury. *Gebur*, a tiller of the soil.

O.E.—*Beuir*, a cultivator. Burial, *Buryel*, a grave.

E.—Boor, a tiller of the ground, a cultivator, peasant: Boor-ish, Boor-ishly, Boor-ishness. Bury, to hide in the ground, Buri-al. Neighbour, originally designated an adjoining peasant or cultivator: Neigh-bour-hood, Neigh-bour-ing.

BURU

Su.—BURU, Fruit, Berry, fourfold, many fold. Pictured as a four-armed cross. 5905, B.266, PSL.65.

Ak.—*Inbu*, fruit, fruit of orchards (berry). 68.

Sk.—*Baer*, a wild berry. IP.

SUMER-ARYAN DICTIONARY

BUR-YA—BUZ

Lat.—*Fructus*, fruit. *Fruges*, corn.
Goth. & Anc. Br.—*Ber, Bär,* a berry. EI. *Fraiw,* seed. U.
Nor.—*Bär,* berry. DNS.
Ger.—*Beere,* berry.
A-S.—*Berige, Berga,* berry.
O.E.—*Berye,* berry. *Frut, Fruit,* fruit.
E.—Berry, a small round fruit. Fruit, produce of the earth, especially globular fruits: Fruit-age, Fruit-erer, Fruit-ful, Fruit-fully, Fruit-less, Fruit-lessly, Fruit-lessness, Fructify, Fruit-ion, Fruit-salad, Fru-menty.

BUR-YA, BUR-IA, BUR-INDURU

Su.—BUR-YA, BUR-IA, BUR-INDURU, Title of Bel or Iā (Jah) or Induru. 10,032, 10,038, B.434. And see *Bur,* Lord Bur and *Bur,* title of the deified *Thor* or *Dor* of the Goths and *Induru.*
Ak.—*Ia,* Father god of Waters. *Bēl,* the lord. 156.

BUZ, BŪZ

Su.—BUZ, BŪZ, Vegetation, produce, growth, increase, cut off, harvest— to Wax. 7503, 7531-4, 7518, 7531, 7542, M.5523, B.325. Pict. by same sign as in Egypt., pl. II.
Ak.—*Ebēru,* produce, fruit. *Pirhu,* a sprout, *Serū,* growth, vegetation, harvest. 1109. *Esipu,* harvest. *Ispu,* harvester 76. *Busū,* possession, property. 200. (*Buqlu,* vegetables. 182).
Eg.—*Bauk,* vegetables, grain. 210b. *Bākh,* abundant food supply, harvest. 213b. *Basha,* millet, crushed or ground flour or for beer. 223b. *Bes-en,* a kind of seed. 223b. *Uaz,* green things, vegetables. 150a. Pict. by same sign as in Sumer, pl. II. *Paz,* bread. 233a-b. (*Busa,* silver gifts. 215b). *Faa,* riches. 260a.
Sk.—*Bis,* to grow (literally to split. See *Bi*). *Vax,* make grow. *Bija, Vija,* see corn. *Bhoj,* food and drink. *Baksh* or *Bax,* eat or drink *Busa,* wealth and refuse corn. *Vasu,* plenty, abundance. *Bakshīsh,* gifts. IP.
Gr.—(F)*auxō, Auxō,* grow, increase, wax. *Foikos, Oikos,* goods.
Lat.—*Augeo,* grow, increase. *Vigeo,* flourish, thrive. *Vēgeo,* to quicken. *Victus,* food. *Uiuus,* living. *Uiu-ere,* to live (and cp. *Bi,* to exist, to live). *Pec-unia,* wealth.
Goth. & Anc. Br.—*Bug,* cultivation, stores. EI. *Bygg,* barley. EI. *Byggia,* harvest, money. I. *Auka,* to increase. EI. *Bugjan,* to buy in market. *Baug,* rings used as money. E. *Wahijan,* grow. U. *Aukan,* increase. U. *Faihu,* property. U.
Nor.—*Byg,* barley. DNS. *Öge,* increase. DN. *Öka,* increase. S.
Ger.—*Wachren,* grow. *Bau,* tillage.
Co. & Celt.—*Buz, Bes,* food. Co. *Bygg,* barley. S.

A-S.—*Weaxen,* grow or increase. *Ecan,* to increase. *Byegean,* buy. *Feoh,* cattle, property.
O.E.—*Woxen, Wexen, Waxen,* to grow, increase, wax. *Vegetives, Vegitals,* vegetables. *Eken,* to increase. *Buggen,* buy. *Fez,* property, payment.
E.—Veg-etation, growth, field produce. Vegetable, a plant for the table, a plant in general: Veg-etal, Veg-etarian, Veg-etarianism, Veg-etate, Veg-etative, Veg-etable kingdom, Veg-etable marrow, Veg-etable mould. Vict-ual, provision of food: Vict-ualled, Vict-ualler, Vict-ualling. Vig-our, vital strength, physical force: Vig-orous, Vig-orously, Vig-orousness. Wax, to grow, increase: Wax-en, Wax-ing. Aug-ment, increase: Aug-mentable, Aug-mentation. Bakhshish, Buck-sheesh, a present in the East. Bush, a clump of dense vegetation, a shrub with tufty branches: Bush-iness, Bush-man, Bush-ranger, Bushy, etc. Eke, to augment or increase: Ek-ing, Eke out. Fee, property, payment. Pec-uniary, re money, produce, or property.

BUZ, BŪZ

Su.—BUZ, BŪZ, Aboriginal Chaldean Earth and Vegetation Mother-goddess, Lady of the Earth —Witch. Figured as a serpent, see pl. II. as in Egypt. 7516, B.325, PSL.67.
Ak.—*Baau,* earth, Mother. P. *Bau,* Mother-goddess, Consort of La. 137. *Dam-kina,* or Lady of the Earth. Cp 253.
Eg.—*Waz*(t), *Uaz*(t), The Green goddess, goddess of the North, goddess mother of the Delta, Serpent goddess, with hiero. as in Sumer, pl. II. 150a-b, G.28. *Basi*(t), Serpent fire goddess. 222a.
Sk.—*Bīja,* primary cause, germ or seed of growth. *Vāeh,* mother-goddess of waters and sky, voice of the thunder. *Vijayā,* a name of Durga, the she-devil—mother-goddess of the Hindus.
Gr.—*Auxō,* goddess of growth and daughter of Zeus, called to witness in an Athenian citizen's oath.
Lat.—? *Pecc-are,* to sin. *Basso,* low, mean, base. I.
Goth. & Anc. Br.—*Veig,* or the witch, title of Gull, the aboriginal matriarch of the serpent-cult and arch-enemy of Thor in the E. *Vištor,* bewitched. I. *Puki,* wee devil. I. *Bangūs,* terrific. L.
Nor.—*Heks,* a witch. DNS.
Ger.—*Hexe,* a witch, a hag. *Spok,* a hobgoblin, a spectre.
Co. & Celt.—*Pisky,* a fairy. *Pestri-ores,* a witch. Co. *Buca,* a hobgoblin. Co. *Bwg, Pwca,* a hobgoblin. Cy. *Buitseach,* a witch. I. *Bocan,* a spectre. Gl. *Puca,* an elf. I.

A-S.—*Wicce*, a witch. *Hæg tesse*, a witch, a fury.
O.E.—*Pouke*, a goblin. *Wikked*, wicked.
E.—Witch, a woman supposed to have supernatural or magical power through compact with the Old Serpent or Devil: Witch-bane (rowan), Witch-craft, Witch-ery, Witch's broom, Witch-ing, Witch-ridden, Witch-wife. Be-witch. Bogy, Bogey, a goblin of dread, the devil: Bug-bear, Bog-us, Hum-*bug*. Hag, an ugly old woman, a witch: Hagg-ish, Hag-ridden, Hag-weed, the common broom, a broom-stick. Peccant, sinning: Peccadillo. Puck, a mischievous sprite, goblin: Puck-ish. ? Spook, a ghost, a spectre. Wick-ed, evil, bad, sinful. Wick-edly, Wickedness. The Wick-ed One.

BUZ, PU, PI

Su.—BUZ, PU, PI, Bite, inflame, burn—Poison. Figured as a Serpent. 7527-9, M.5536, B.325, PSL.70. And see *Bur*, *Bu* and *Fi*, Serpent.
Ak.—*Naśāhu*, bite? 739. *Napahu*, inflame, burn. 703. (*Biśu*, bad, wicked. 201).
Eg.—*Bekhen*, deadly (poisonous). 221a. *Bekhenu*, deadly serpents. 221a. ? *Uhi*, *Uhā(t)*, a scorpion. 176a, 179a.
Sk.—*Vish*, to pervade, poison, consuming, be busy. *Bhujag*, a serpent. *Vichiko*, a scorpion. P. *Bish*, poison. IP. *Bichua*, scorpion. IP.
Lat.—*Pestis*, a plague. *Vex-are*, to vex. *Poison*, poison. F.
Co. & Celt.—*Pige*, to prick. Co. *Pystege*, wound. Co.
O.E.—*Puisun*, *Poyson*, poison. *Pest*, a plague. *Pester*, to annoy. *Vexen*, to vex.
E.—Poison, that which infects, impairs, or destroys life: Poison-able, Poison-er, Poison-fang, Poison-gland, Poison-ousness. Pest, a plague: Pest-ilent, Pest-ilential, Pest-er. Vex, to irritate, torment: Vex-ation, Vexatious, Vex-atiously, Vex-atiousness.

BUZ

Su.—BUZ, Voice, Call, cry out, howl. 7569, M.5529, B.325. See *Aka*, Cry, howl.
Ak.—*Habab*, call, cry out, howl. 299. *Malilu*, flute. 549.
Eg.—*Aash* or *Iash*, to call out, howl, the jackal. 25a. *Uaz-na*, a flute, reed pipe.
Sk.—*Vāch*, voice, cry out. *Bak*, speak, speak out. IP.
Gr.—*E-pos*, a word. *Epikos*, a narrative.
Lat.—*Vox*, voice.
Co. & Celt.—*Bauc*, roar. Co. *Vac*, impeached. Co. *Bys*, beseech. Co.
O.E.—*Voys*, *Vois*, voice.
E.—Voice, Voiced, Voice-ful, Voice-less, Voicelessness, Voice-r, Voic-ing. Voc-able, sounded with the voice, a word or name: Voc-abular, Voc-abulary. Voc-al, belong to the voice: Voc-alic, Voc-alize; Voc-alization, Voc-alist, Voc-ular, Voc-al chords, Voc-al music. Voc-ation, calling, occupation, Voc-ational, Voc-ationally. Voc-ative, pertaining to the act of calling: Voc-ative case. Voc-iferate, to cry with a loud voice: Voc-iferous, Voc-iferously. Vouch, to affirm strongly, attest: Vouch-er, Vouch-safe. Vow-el, a single vocal sound and letter representing it. Ad-voc-ate, A-voc-ation, Ad-vow-son, A-vouch, Con-vocation, Con-voke, Equi-vocal, E-voke, In-vocation, In-voke, Irre-voc-able, Pro-voke, Revoke, Re-voc-able. Echo, a reverberated voice or sound. Epic (through the Greek), a narrative of a great event in a lofty style: Epic poem. Hubbub and Whoop (through the Akkad). Beg, seems to come here.

C

A late redundant Greco-Roman letter for G, K and S, awanting in Sumerian, Egyptian and Gothic, etc. See G, K and S.

D

DA, TA

Su.—DA, TA, Hand (human), right hand, arm, side. Pictured by an outstretched right hand as in the Egyptian hieroglyph, or with part of the forearm as well, see pl. II. 6643, 6645, 6647, M.4757, B.294.
Ak.—*Idu*, hand, side, power, force, might. 17.
Eg.—*Da(t)*, Human right hand. 864a, G.12 (172), and ordinary alphabetic letter for D. Its hieroglyph is practically identical with the Sumerian, see plate II. *Ta*, on the one hand. 821a.
Sk.—*Daxa*, right hand, south. *Dos*, arm, forearm. *Dahini*, right hand. IP.
Gr.—*Dexios*, right hand. *Dōron*, palm of hand.
Lat.—*Dexter*, right-hand side.
Goth. & Anc. Br.—*Taihswa*, right-hand, right side. U.

Ger.—*Tappe*, fist.
Co. & Celt.—*Dehou, Dygow*, right-hand side, south. Co. *Dewle*, hands. Co. *Deheu*, right hand. Cy. *Dear*, right-hand side, south. GI. *Dorn*, a hand. Co.Cy., a fist. GI.
O.E.—*Dab*, expert with hand.
E.—Dab, an expert with the hand. Deft, handy : Deft-ly, Deft-ness, A-dept. Dex-ter, right-hand side : Dex-tral, Dex-trality, Dex-trally, Dex-terity, right-handedness, cleverness, Dex-terous, Dex-trous, Dex-terously, Dex-terousness. *Deasil, Deazil*, right handwise, or sun-wise movement for luck. See WPOB. 282-3.

DA, DU

Su.—**DA, DU,** Gift, Offering, tribute. From idea of right hand (*Da*), and pictured by same right-hand sign as foregoing. 6643-4, M.4758, B.294.
Ak.—? *Alāku, Illakku*, offering, tribute. 45.
Eg.—*Da*, give. 864a, 865a. *Da-t*, gift, tribute. 865a. *Du*, give. 868b. *Ta*, to give. 815a. *Danu*, rent, tax. 882b.
Sk.—*Dā*, give, giver. *Dāna*, gift. *Dhā*, to bestow.
Gr.—*Dōs*, a gift. *Dōron*, a present. *Dosis*, a giving.
Lat.—*Do-dare, don-are*, give. *Donum*, gift. *Dotare*, endow. *Dōs*, a dowry, a gift. *Dose*, a dose.
Goth. & Anc. Br.—*Dainn*, inheritance. EI.
Co. & Celt.—*Dain, Danin*, sent. Co.
E.—Don-ate, give, offer as a gift. Don-ary, Don-ation, Don-ative, Don-ator, Don-atory, Don-ee, Don-or. Dose, a giving, a dose : Dos-age, Dos-ed. Dot, an endowment : Dot-al Dot-ation. Dower, a gift for a widow : Dow-ered, Dow-ager. Dowry, gift brought by a wife. Due, that which is to be given or owed : Dues, taxes or tribute, Du-ly. Duty, that which is due : Duty, moral obligation, Duty, taxes or tribute, Du-tiable, Du-ty free, Du-teous, Du-teous-ly, Du-tiful, Du-tifulness.

DA, DU

Su.—**DA, DU,** Do, make, perform. Pictured by a wedge, see pl. II. 5244, 5254, B.227. And see *Du*, to do.
Ak.—*Epeśu*, do, make, execute, practise. 82.
Eg.—*Da*, to cause (to do). 865a. *Daa*, to assist. 865a.
Sk.—*Dhā*, to make, perform, execute.
Gr.—*Ti-thē-mi*, to make (of things).
Goth. & Anc. Br.—*Duge*, to do, help, aid. EI.
Nor.—*Due*, do. DN. *Duga*, do. S.
Ger.—*Thun*, to do.
A-S.—*Dō*, do.
O.E.—*Do*, do.
E.—Do, to perform an action : Do-er, Do-ing, Do-ings, Do-ne, Do-th, Dee-d, Mis-dee-d, A-do. And see *Du*, to do.

DA, DU

Su.—**DA, DU.**—Build, erect, set, place, stand, support, strength, a peg or plug. Pictured by a wedge and by the right hand, see pl. II. 5244, 5248, 5265-9, 6651, B.227 and 294.
Ak.—*Banū*, build. *Ritū*, erect, strengthen. *Śakānu*, set, place, set up. *Iś sikkatu*, a peg, a plug.
Eg.—*Da*, set, place. 864a, 865a. Hiero. as in Sumer, pl. II. *Das*, sit. 868a, 887b.
Sk.—*Dā*, place, set, put. *Dhā*, place, set, hold, support, wear, put on clothes. (*Banao*, prepare, from Akkad. IP.).
Gr.—*De-mō*, to build. *Dō-mos*, a building. Ti-*thē*-mi, to place, set, set up.
Lat.—*Domus*, a house, a home, a temple. *Dom-icilium*, a habitation, a house. ? *Dais*, a seat, throne. F.
Goth. & Anc. Br.—*Dafna*, to thrive well. I.
Nor.—*Dōf*, rest. S.
Ger.—*Dobel*, a plug.
O.E.—*Domicil*, a house, abode.
E.—Domicile, house, abode, home : Dom-estic, Dom-esticate, Dom-estication. Dome, a hemispherical roof. Do, to be fit, suitable, strong, e.g., That will *do*, How-do you *do* ? Don, to put on clothes : Don-ned, Don-ning. Dow-el, a peg or pin of wood or iron.

DA, DU, TA

Su.—**DA, DU, TA,** speak, talk, proclaim. 504, 6643-5, 6648, M.4762, B.294. And see *Dug, Duttu*, to speak.
Ak.—*Dababu*, speak, proclaim, talk. 237. *Qibu, Qabu*, speak, speak aloud, call, cry out, proclaim, command. 904.
Eg.—*Dua*, call, cry out, praise, hymn of praise. 871a, 872b. *Tu*, to talk, speak. 823a.
Sk.—*Da*, to speak.
Gr.—*Daō*, teach.
E.—? Talk. See *Dug, Duttu*, to talk, speak.

DA, TA, DE

Su.—**DA, TA, DE,** suffix of augment and of agentive, locative and ablative cases. 6643-4 6649, 6655-6, B.294, LSG.73 f.
Ak.—*Ana*, to, unto, with, for. *Ina*, in, into, upon, from. *U*, and *Kima*, like, like as, 394.
Eg.—*Tai*, and. 818a. *Tep*, in upon, about, by. 828b. (*Ta* or *T*, as, because, while, during, 815a.
Sk.—*-t, ta* and *tu*, suffix in forming abstract words from root bases.
Gr.—*De*, suffix of motion towards and often added to the names of cities, as Athēnas-*de*, Thēbas-*de*.
Lat.—? *De*, prefix from, away from, down from.
Goth. & Anc. Br.—*-d*, suffix, agentive or locative or location often added to place and other

DAB, TAB

Su.—DAB, TAB, Two, twin, double. 3788, M.2451-3, 2463, B.144.
Ak.—*Sina*, two. 1070.
Eg.—*Ta*, a mark of the dual. 821a. *Senui*, two. 673b. *Sennu*, second. 673b (through the Akkad).
Sk.—*Dvā, Dvi*, two. *Do*, divide. *Do*, two. IP. *Do-āb*, land between two rivers (*āb*).
Gr.—*Duo*, two. *Daiō*, divide.
Lat.—*Duo*, two. *Deux*, two. F. *Due*, two. I. *Dos*, two. S.
Goth. & Anc. Br.—*Tva, Tvei*, two. EI. *Twai*, two. U. *Dwi*, two. L.
Nor.—*To*, two. DN. *Tva, Tu*, two. S. *Dobbelt*, double. DN.
Ger.—*Zwei*, two. *Doppelt*, double.
Co. & Celt.—*Dau, Diu, Denu*, two. Co. *Duy*, two. Cy. *Dā*, two. Gl. *Twa*, two. S.
A-S.—*Twā*, Twain, two.
O.E.—*Twei, Twey*, two.
E.—Two, twain, one and one, double: Two-decker, Two-edged, Two-faced, Two-fold, Two-handed, Two-masted, Two-pence, Two-penny, Two-ply, Two-sided, Two-tongued. Twain, two, twice, Twice-told, Twi-light, Twi-ll, Twi-g, Twi-ne, Twi-st. Twelve, two and ten: Twe-lve-mo, Duo-decimo or 12mo, Twe-lve month, Twe-lve pennyworth, Twe-lve score, Twe-lve tables, The Twe-lve, Twe-lfth, Twe-lfth day, Twe-lfth night. Twe-nty, twice ten: Twe-ntieth, Twe-nty fold, Twe-nty-four, mo., 24mo. Twin, one of two born at one birth: Twin-born, Twin-brother, Twin-sister, Twin-screw, The Twins. Deuce, a card or dice with two spots: Deuce-ace. Div-ide, separation into two parts as in cutting, voting, etc., to part asunder: Div-idable, Divi-ded, Div-idedly, Div-ider, Div-iding, Div-idend, Div-isible, Div-isibility, Div-isor, Div-ision, Div-isional. Double, two-fold, to repeat, turn back: Doub-led, Doub-ling, Doub-le-acting, Doub-le-barrelled, Doub-le bass, Doub-le breasted, Doub-le-dealer, Double-dealing, Doub-le-decker, Doub-le-dyed, Doub-le entry, Doub-le faced, Doub-le facedness, Doub-le first, Doub-le minded, Doub-le quick, Doub-le tongued. Dual, consisting of two: Du-alism, Du-alist, Du-alistic, Du-ality, Dual control. Duel, combat between two: Du-eller, Du-elling, Du-ellist. Duet, composition for two voices or instruments.

Dyad, a pair of units treated as one, Dy-adic. And see WPOB.240, WISD.51.

DAB, DIB, TAB

Su.—DAB, DIB, TAB, Dwelling, surround, fold—a Tent. Pictured by an enclosure or fold with a shepherd's staff. 10,668, 10,670, 10,683, 10,686-9, M.8169, 8178, 8184, B.482. And see *Dib*, dwell.
Ak.—*Kissu*, a dwelling. *Abātu*, bind, tie. 12. *Lamū*, surround. *Kamū, Ramū*, enclosure. *Nabaltu*, living. *Šurbusu*, a fold. *Simāku*, a shrine, abode of the Sun-god, etc. 766.
Eg.—(*Tep, Teba*, a box, chest, coffer. 827b, 832a).
Sk.—(*Dūshya*, a tent). *Ta(m)bu*, a tent. IP.
Gr.—*Dapis, Tapēs*, a rug or carpet (used to make tents or shelters).
Lat.—*Taberna*, a booth, hut, dwelling-place, stall, shop, tavern. *Tabernaculum*, diminutive of *Taberna*, a tent, hut, especially of the augurs. *Tapēta*, drapery, tapestry. *Tapis*, cloth made of wool. *Taverne*, a tavern. F. *Tappeto*, carpet. I.
Nor.—*Tapit*, tapestry in old N. VD.625.
A-S.—*Tæpped*, tapestry.
O.E.—*Tapestrye*, tapestry. *Tauerne*, a tavern.
E.—Tabor, a tented camp among the ancient nomad Scyths, surrounded by their waggons. Tab-ernacle, a tent used by the Romans as a temple for their augurs. And this name was applied by the Roman translators of the O.T. to the *Ōhel moēd* tent for the ark, cp. EB.4862. *Tab*, a "tent" had the Sumerian meaning also of "shrine" for the Sun-god, etc.: Tab-ernacular, Feast of Tab-ernacles. Tav-ern, a tent, booth, hut, or shop for the sale of liquors to travellers: Tav-erner, Tav-erning. Tapis, a carpet, in phrase "on the *tapis*."

DAB, TAB, DIB, TAP

Su.—DAB, TAB, DIB, TAP, Pour out, Lock up, dam, restrain—a Tap. 10,668, 10,670, 10,698, 10,728, M.8176-7, B.482. And see *Dub, Tub*, a tube and tub.
Ak.—*Tabāku*, to pour out. 1142. *Kālu*, hold, contain. *Kalū*, lock up, dam, restrain. 380.
Eg.—*Taf-Taf*, to pour out. 833a. *Tabu*, a vessel for beer and wine. 827b. *Tapait*, drink, victual. 832a.
Lat.—*Tubus*, a pipe.
Goth. & Anc. Br.—*Tappa*, to draw from a cask, to tap. EI. *Tappi*, a tap. I.
Nor.—*Tap*, a tap, a bung. DM. *Tapp*, a tap, a bung. S.
Ger.—*Zapfen*, a bung, a stopper.
A-S.—*Tæppere*, one who taps casks.
O.E.—*Tap*, a spike for a cask. *Tappe*, to tap or draw. T.

E.—Tap, a hole or short pipe in a cask through which liquor is drawn, a plug to stop the hole : Tap-bolt, Tap-house, Tap-per or Tap-ster, Tap-ping, Tap-room, On tap. Tube, a pipe or long hollow cylinder for conveyance of fluids, etc. : Tub-age, Tub-iform, Tub-ing, Tub-ular, Tub-ulate, The Tube.

DADDU

Su.—DADDU, Sign-name for *Da*, Set, place, build, q.v. (6642, B.294)—which word is evidently related to the next following :

DADRU

Su.—DADRU, Established king, King of Justice, Planner of Justice and Mercy. 12,233-4, B.544, PSL.69. And see *Daddu* above.
Ak.—*Śaru kēnu, Śar kitti, Dābib kitti, Dābib damgāti*, established king, etc., etc., as in col. 1.
Eg.—*Dad*, established. G.60, Fig. 14, with uplifted hands supporting a column. *Dad, Dada*, set place. BD.865a. Dad, "Ded," is the name of a god "The Establisher," the so-called "backbone." 892a.
Sk.—*Dhā, Dadhati*, established, protect. *Daddhi*, place, put. *Didhi*, firmness, stability. *Dadhy*, a mythic fire-worshipper who gave his bones to slay the Dragon and establish peace.
Lat.—? *Tutus*, safe.
Goth. & Anc. Br.—*Dād, Dāth*, deed (accomplished), valour. I. (*Tiöd*, tether. I). *Dēds*, deed. U.
Nor.—*Dād*, deed. DN.
Ger.—*That*, deed.
Co. & Celt.—*Dedwh*, law. Co. *Deder*, goodness. Co. *Dedwyddweh*, bliss, happiness. Co.
A-S.—*Deed*, a deed.
O.E.—*Dede*, a thing done. "*Tutelar* god."
E.—Deed, a thing done, established, In-deed, in certainty, In word and deed, Title-deed, Deed-less, Mis-deed. Tutor, a guardian : Tut-orial, Tut-orship, Tuit-ion, In-tuit-ion. Tut-elary, a guardian spirit : Tut-elage, Tut-elar.

DAG

Su.—DAG, Day, Bright, shining, light. Pictured by the rising Sun. M.5741, 5747, 5785, etc., B.337.
Ak.—*Ellu, Ebbu*, bright. *Ūmu*, day. *Nūru*, light. 722.
Eg.—*Ta*, daybreak, "earth-lightening." 815b.
Sk.—*Dakshu*, blazing. *Da(n)s*, shine.
Lat.—*Dies*, a day.
Goth. & Anc. Br.—*Dag*, day. EI. *Daga*, dawn. EI. *Deg-ling*, day-spring or dawn. EI. *Dags*, day. U.
Nor.—*Dag*, day. DNS. *Daggay*, dawn.
Ger.—*Tag*, day. *Elle*, bright, from Akkad. *Tagen*, to dawn.
Co. & Celt.—*De*, day. Co. *Dia*, day. G.
A-S.—*Daeg, Dag*, day. *Dagian*, to dawn.
O.E.—*Dai*, day. *Dawyn*, dawn.
E.—Day, time of sunlight from dawn to sunset. (*N,B.*—the Ancient Egyptians had already dropped out the final *a* from the word) : Day-break, Day-dream, Day-labour, Day-light, Day-long, Day-scholar, Day-school, Day-time, Day-woman, Day-work, Daily, Day-by-day, Day of Doom, Days of grace, Time of day. Dawn, to become day : Dawn-ing, Dawn upon. Daisy or Day's eye.

DAG, TAK

Su.—DAG, TAK, Spread out, stretched out, extend, cover. Pictured by a net. 5529, 5533, M.3869, B.244. See *Sa*, a net, and *Tak*.
Ak.—*Rapadu*, stretch out, lie down, encamp. 979. *Tarasu*, spread out, cover, protect. 1194.
Eg.—*Dakhan*, cover over. 887b.
Sk.—*Dīgho*, long. P. *Dagh*, to reach to. *Sthag*, to cover.
Gr.—*Teg-os*, a roof, a cover.
Lat.—*Teg-ere*, to cover. *De-teg-ere*, to uncover, expose. *Pro-teg-ere*, to cover over, protect. *Toga*, a robe. *Protégé*, a protected person. F.
Goth. & Anc. Br.—*Teygia*, to spread out. EI. *Thak, Thakia*, to thatch or cover.
Nor.—*Dække*, to cover. DN. *Tācka*, to cover. S. *Dæk*, a ship's deck. DN. *Dæck*, a deck. S.
Ger.—*Decken*, to cover. *Deck*, a deck.
Co. & Celt.—*Teghez*, cloaked. Co.
A-S.—*Thæcan*, to thatch.
O.E.—*Thak*, to thatch. *Thacker*, a thatcher. *Protectoar*, protector. *Toge*, covering robe.
E.—Deck, to cover, to furnish with a deck as in a ship : Deck-er, Three-decker, Deck-cargo, Deck-chair, Deck-hand, Deck-house, Deck-load, Deck-passage, Deck-passenger, Quarter-deck, Hurricane-deck, Main-deck. Deck, to cover over with clothes or adornments : Deck-ed, Be-decked, ? Dec-orate. De-tect, to uncover, discover : De-tect-ion, De-tect-ive, De-tect-or. Pro-tect, to cover over, shelter : Pro-tect-ion, Pro-tect-ioned, Pro-tect-ive, Pro-tect-or, Pro-tect-or-ate, Pro-tect-orship. Teg-ument, a covering : Teg-umentary. In-teg-ument. Thatch, a covering for a roof : Thatch-ed, Thatch-er, Thatch-ing. Toga, covering robe for a Roman citizen : Tog-ated, Togs, Tog-gery.

DAG, TAG, TAK

Su.—DAG, TAG, TAK, Stone. 5223, 5229, B.224. And see *Dig*, a wall or dyke.
Ak.—*Abnu*, stone (and cut stone). 8.
Eg.—*Dakhu(t)*, boulders, rough stones. 887b. *Damgi*, stone. 879b.

Sk.—*Da*, mountain. *Dagh*, "rocky mountains" in Upper Mesopotamia, Persia and Asia Minor and Central Asia.
Gr.—*Teichos*, stone wall of a city, fort or fortified post.
Goth. & Anc. Br.—*Drang*, solitary upstanding rock. *Dengja*, to stone or whet a scythe. I.
Nor.—*Dænga*, to stone or whet a scythe.
Co. & Celt.—? *Daze*, a glittering stone from the tin mines. Co.
E.—*Dagh*, name for rocky mountains in Mesopotamia, Persia, Asia Minor and Central Asia.

DAG, TAG, TAK

Su.—**DAG, TAG, TAK**, Dagger, wound, fight, strike (stab). Pictured by a dagger essentially identical with the Egyptian hieroglyph, see pl. II. 3798, B.146.
Ak.—*Mahāṣu*, wound, fight, strike. 522.
Eg.—*Taq*, to cut, to strike. 845a. *Taqas*, to pierce, cut, to stab. 845a. *Daś*, to pierce, blade, sharp point, sword. 889a. G.50, with hieroglyph knife essentially identical with the Sumerian, see plate II. *Das*, to cut up. 867b.
Sk.—*Taksh*, to cut, chisel, split. *Tig*, to be sharp. *Dāo*, sword or knife in Hindustani.
Gr.—*Tenchos*, a tool
Goth. & Anc. Br.—*Takke*, a jag, a tooth. I. *Tang*, blade or spit. EI.
Nor.—*Tak*, *Takke*, a jag, a tooth. DN.
Ger.—*Degen*, a sword.
Co. & Celt.—*Dag*, dagger. Br. *Dagr*, dagger. Co. *Takkia*, to thrust in. Co. *Daigear*, dagger. GI. *Tach*, a nail. Br. *Taca*, a pin, a nail. I. *Tacaid*, a tack. G.
O.E.—*Daggere*, a dagger. *Daggen*, to pierce. *Takke*, a tack.
E.—Dagger, a dirk for stabbing. Tack, a small nail. Tag, a point of metal at the end of a lace. At-tack, to assault, is considered by Sheat and others to be along with At-tach (to take hold), derived from tack, a nail, now seen to be named from *Dag*, dagger. Tang, the spit of a knife, prong of a fork, from Gothic nasalized form of Sumerian.

DAG, TAG, TAK

Su.—**DAG, TAG, TAK**, Take, seize, snatch away, booty, destroy, slaughter. 3793, 3804, M.2746, B.146.
Ak.—*Hatū*, seize, snatch away, overpower. 347. *Śalātu*, spoil, booty. *Tabāhu*, slaughter. 353.
Eg.—*Takk*, to rob, invade. 845a. *Thai*, to seize, carry off, steal. 849a. *Takku*, a robber, marauder, invader. 845b.
Sk.—*Dasyu*, a robber. *Dāku*, *Dākait*, a robber. IP. *Thug*, a murderous robber.
Goth. & Anc. Br.—*Tāk*, to seize, lay hold of.
EI. *Tekia*, take by force, seize, booty. EI. *Tekans*, touch. U.
Nor.—*Tage*, take. DN.
O.E.—*Taken*, to take.
E.—Take, to lay hold of, seize, catch, capture, etc. Tak-er, Take in, Tak-ing, Take-up. Tackle, to attack: Tack-ling, etc. Detach, to take away from: De-tached, De-tachment, etc. Attack, see previous word: *Dag*, *Tak*, a dagger. *Dac-oit* and *Thug*, Indian robbers. ? Touch.

DAL, TAL, TIL

Su.—**DAL, TAL, TIL**, Far away, stretch out—Tall. 67, 2554, 2560, 2567, M.9, B.1, 93.
Ak.—*Nisu*, far away, remove. *Tirsu*, stretching out, extending. 1196.
Sk.—*Tal*, surface, level, measure of length, a span. (*Tara*, across, beyond—(*r* for *l*). (*Dūr*, far).
Gr.—*Tēle*, afar off.
Goth. & Anc. Br.—*Tara*, stretch, spread out. EI. *Til*, till, until, to, too.
Nor.—*Til*, till, too. DN. *Till*, till, too. S.
Co. & Celt.—*Towl*, away. Co. *Tal*, high, lofty, tall. Co.Cy. *Tewlel*, to cast. Co.
O.E.—*Tal*, tall. *Til*, till, until.
E.—Tall, high (stretched out), in stature. Tele-graph, writing or signalling from afar: Tele-phone, Tele-scope. Till, up to, or to the time of: Un-til.

DAM

Su.—**DAM**, Consort, dame or wife, also husband. 11,105, 11,108-9, 11,113, B.500.
Ak.—*Altu*, wife. *Aśśatu*, woman. *Ha'iru*, suitor, consort or mate. *Mutu*, man, consort. 619.
Eg.—*Daima*, bind together. 878b. *Damau*, companies of men. 878b.
Sk.—*Dam* (literally "house") = wife in *Dampati*, "the two masters of the house, husband and wife." MWD.469.
Lat.—*Domina*, lady. *Dominus*, lord. *Dame*, lady. F.
Goth. & Anc. Br.—*Damma*, a dame. I.
Nor.—*Dame*, lady. DN.
Ger.—*Dame*, lady.
Co. & Celt.—*Dama*, mother. Co. *Dimadha*, marriage. Co.
O.E.—*Dam*, *Damme*, a dam.
E.—Dam, a mother, chiefly used of animals. Dame, mistress, lady: Dam-sel, Dame's-school. Bel-dame.

DAMA, DAMU

Su.—**DAMA, DAMU** (*Aś*), The Dame, a title of the mother-goddess *Gula*, "The Dame of the Earth." 6662 and cp. 11,105, 11,108-9, 11,127.

Ak.—*Gula*, the mighty lady and wife of Nergal. 217.
Eg.—*Tami(t)*, the consort of Tam (Tamuz), the first man-god. 834*b*.
Lat.—*Dēmētēr*, the goddess of Agriculture.
E.—The Dame, as title of the Earth goddess Demeter, the goddess of Agriculture.

DAM-TUK-A

Su.—**DAM-TUK-A**, to take a dame or wife = Marry. 11,130, 11,236, MD.333. And see *Tuk*, to take.
Ak.—*Hāru, Khāru*, to marry. 333.
Eg.—*Dahemt*, to marry. 866*a* (literally "to take a woman or wife." Cp. 481*a*).
E.—To "*take* a wife (or dame)" or marry.

DAN

Su.—**DAN.** Strong, powerful, mighty. 6177, 6193-4, B.279.
Ak.—*Dannu*, strong, powerful, mighty. 257. *Dunnu*, strength, might, power. 259.
Eg.—*Danr*, strength. 883*a*.
Sk.—*Dānu*, victor, conqueror.
Gr.—*Dynamis*, power.
Lat.—*Dan-ger*, absolute power. F.
Goth. & Anc. Br.—*Dynt*, a stroke, a blow. EI. *Dynta*, to strike, to dint. I.
Nor.—*Dunt*, a stroke. S.
A-S.—*Dynt*, a blow.
O.E.—*Dunt, Dent, Dint*, a blow.
E.—Dint, strength, force, a blow. Dyn-amic, relating to force, a moving force: Dyn-amics, Dyn-amically, Dyn-amist, Dyn-ameter, Dyn-ametrical, Dyn-amo, Dyn-amometer, Dyne, Dyn-amite, Dyn-amiter.

DAN, TAN

Su.—**DAN, TAN**, Strong lord (human), Lord of all, Bēl. 6177, 6191, 6199, B.279.
Ak.—*Amel kālu*, strong lord—man. *Bēl sa naphari*, Bēl, lord of all.
Eg.—*Dana*, a venerable man. 882*b*, 887*b*. *Dan*, high, distinguished man. 880*a*. *Dani*, title of sun-god Ra. 882*a*. *Tann*, the great god, a very ancient Earth-god. 819*b*, 838*a*, and see Duk-Dun, Lord *Dun*. *Dan-dan*, title of *Āpap*, the serpent of evil. 881*a*. *Tannit*, goddess consort of Tann, 838*a*, and see Di, Lady Diana.
Sk.—*Dāni*, valiant, victor, courageous. *Dānava*, a class of demons, sons of Danu and enemies of the gods.
Gr.—*Dynastēs*, lord, master. *Danu-oi*, title of Greeks.
Lat.—*Dan*, master. F. *Don*, master, lord. S.
Goth. & Anc. Br.—*Dan*, Lord. EI. *Hālf-Dan* or Lord of the half of the world, a title of Thor in the E. *Thegn*, a freeholder, freeman, husbandman, a good man. EI.

Co. & Celt.—*Den, Dyn*, a man. Co. *Din*, worthy. Co. *Dan, Dana*, bold. GI. *Tuatha De Danann*, a famous traditional ruling race in Ireland.
A-S.—? *Thegn*, a lower kind of nobleman.
O.E.—*Thein, Thane, Dan*, master.
E.—Dan, a title of master or sir. Don, a college authority, a Spanish title of nobility: Don-nish, Don-ship. Dynast, a strong ruler establishing a line in his family, or a member of that line: Dyn-astic, Dyn-asty. Thane, a lower class of nobility of the Anglo-Saxons, above mere landowners. Danann, a famous traditional ruling race in Ireland.

DAN

Su.—**DAN**, Cut, tear down, destroy—? Tooth. 6177, 6202, M.4416, B.279.
Ak.—*Nagaru*, cut, tear down, destroy. 720.
Eg.—*Dan, Den*, cut to pieces, split. 881*a*. *Danb*, to gnaw. 882*b*. *Dens*, to cut down. 882*b*. *Dens, Denas*, a title of the tusked hippopotamus. 882*a*, 839*b*.
Sk.—*Dans*, bite. *Dana*, to cut off. *Danta*, a tooth.
Gr.—*Tendō*, to gnaw, to nibble at.
Lat.—*Dens*, a tooth. *Dent*, a tooth. F.
Goth. & Anc. Br.—*Tanna*, to dent. EI. *Tann, Tōn*, a tooth. EI. *Tann-ari*, a tusk-chisel. I. *Tinna*, a flint, a flint-stone. *Tunthus*. tooth. U.
Nor.—*Tand*, tooth. DNS.
Ger.—*Zahn*, tooth.
Co. & Celt.—*Dyn, Tyn*, sharp. Co. *Dan, Dyn*, tooth. Co. *Danta*, to bite. Co. *Ding*, to knock down. S. *Dunt*, to give a blow.
A-S.—*Toth*, a tooth.
O.E.—*Dunt, Dint*, to indent. *Toth*, a tooth.
E.—Dent, to notch or indent, a hollow made by a blow: Dent-ed, a Dunt. Dent-al, relating to teeth: Dent-ate, Dent-iform, Dent-ifrice, Dent-igerous, Dent-iculated, Dent-ine, Den-ist, Dent-istry, Dent-ition, Dent-oid.

DAR, TAR

Su.—**DAR, TAR**, Wound, cut open, tear—Tear, a Dart. Pictured by what seems a dirk or dart, also by a cut twig. 375 f., 3474, 3487-93, M.2234, 2245, B.128.
Ak.—*Mihṣu*, to wound. 524. *Śalaqu*, cut open, tear, tear out. 1047. *Taruku*.
Eg.—*Dar*, to expunge, destroy. 884*a*. *Dār*, to ill-treat forcibly, oppress. 867*a-b*. *Tar, Ter*, to destroy. 822*a*, 840*a*.
Sk.—*Dāra*, tearing up. *Dri*, to tear. *Dara*, cleaving, splitting. *Darana*, cleaving, rending. *Dhur*, injure. *Dar*, to cut. Zend.
Gr.—*Tereō*, to pierce, bore. *Derein*, to flay.
Lat.—*Dard*, a dart. F.
Goth. & Anc. Br.—*Tara*, fight. EI. *Darrad,*

a dart. EI. *Dar*, to ridicule (? wound). I. *Thorn*, a thorn. I. *Thaurnus*, thorn. U. *Dirti*, to flay. L.
Nor.—*Taare*, tear. DN. *Dart*, a dagger. DNS. *Tiorn*, thorn. DN. *Törne*, thorn. S.
Ger.—*Zähre*, tear. *Dorn*, a thorn. G.
Co. & Celt.—*Terry, Tarhi*, to cut. Co. *Tarra, Tardha*, bore, prick. Co. *Tardhar*, a gimlet. Co.
A-S.—*Teren*, to tear. *Daras*, a dart. *Thorn*, a thorn.
O.E.—*Teren*, to tear. *Dart*, a dart. *Teren*, to tear.
E.—Tear, to lacerate, rend : Tear-ing, Torn. Dart, a javelin for throwing, dirk, poniard. Thorn, a sharp spiky spine : Thorn-y, Thorn-less, Thorn-hedge, Black-thorn, Haw-thorn.

DAR, TAR, DARA

Su.—DAR, TAR, DARA, Weave, Variegated cloth, clothing, colour—Drape. 3747, 3482-5, 10,485-6, M.2227-8, B.128. And see *Dar, Dirig*, dress.
Ak.—*Baramu*, weave, especially variegated, coloured threads. 191. *Buruma*, variegated cloth. *Biranu*, a kind of clothing. 1126.
Eg.—*Dar*, a kind of cloth, linen, byssus cloth. 884b. *Daā*, garment, sheet of cloth. 864b, 867a. *Tharu*, to paint, paint colours. 857b. *Tur, Tru*, paint, colour. 825b. *Tar, Ter*, cloth, stuff, garment. 840a. *Thar*, stuff, apparel. 857b.
Sk.—*Drapi*, a mantle, a garment. *Dūrśa*, a garment.
Lat.—*Draper*, to make cloth. F. *Drap*, cloth. F. *Trapo*, cloth. S.
A-S.—*Darn*, a piece, a fragment, patch. Cy. Co., Br.
O.E.—*Drape*, to weave or manufacture cloth. *Derning*, spinning, weaving.
E.—Drape, to cover with cloth, formerly to manufacture cloth : Draper, Drapery. Trap, to clothe or cover with ornaments : Trappings. ? Darn, to mend or patch. ? Drugget, a coarse woollen cloth. ? Drab, colour.

DAR, DIR, TAR, DUR

Su.—DAR, DIR, TAR, DUR, Earth, land, country, territory. 3474, 3488, M.7976, B.128, 481.
Ak.—*Mātu*, earth, land, country, soil. 616. *Aśāśu*, ground.
Eg.—*Darta*, to put oneself on Earth or to land from a boat. 885a. *Ther-thar—Ther-ther*, earth-work, mounds thrown up around a besieged city. 858a. *Ta, Ta(t)*, the earth, ground soil, dirt. 815a. *Turt*, dirt, defilement. 825b.
Sk.—*Dharā*, earth. *Dharitrī*, earth. *Tīra*, a shore, a bank.

Lat.—*Terra*, earth, land. *Territorium*, a domain.
Goth. & Anc. Br.—*Tarra, Terra*, spread out, stretch out. I. *Drit, Drita*, dirt, dirty. EI. (*Jörd*, earth). *Torf*, a turf, sod or peat. I.
Nor.—(*Jord*, earth. DN.). *Torv*, turf. DN. *Torf*, turf. S.
Co. & Celt.—*Doar, Dōr*, earth. Co. *Tēr*, a field. Co. *Tir*, land. Cy.Gl. *Tref*, land annexed to a house. Co. *Ternew*, bank of a river. Co.
A-S.—*Turf*, turf.
O.E.—*Drit*, dirt. *Terestryal*, terrestrial. *Turf*, turf.
E.—Dirt, as earth : Dirt-y. Terra, earth : Terra-cotta, Terra-firma, Terr-ace. Terrestrial, earthy : Terr-ene, Medi-terr-anean. Territory or extent of land : Terri-torial, Terr-itorials. *Terre*, etc., affix in land and place-names : Angle-terre, Finis-terre, Cantire (=Head-land), etc. Turd, dirt, Turf, the surface of land with its grass roots, etc. : The Turf.

DAR, DIR, TAR

Su.—DAR, DIR, TAR, Lock-up, shut, hold back—a Door. 3486, B.128.
Ak.—*Kalū*, lock up, shut up, shut off, hold back. 380.
Eg.—*Taraa*, a door. 822a. *Tiraa*, door, the two leaves of a door. 823a. *Tai(t)*, a door or portal. 819a.
Sk.—*Dvar, Dur*, a door.
Gr.—*Thyra, Thura*, a door.
Lat.—*Fores*, door. *Dore*, door. Old F.
Goth. & Anc. Br.—*Dyr, Dyrr*, a door. EI. *Daur*, a door. U.
Nor.—*Dör*, door. DN. *Dörr*, door. S.
Ger.—*Thor, Thür*, door.
Co. & Celt.—*Daras*, a door. Co.
A-S.—*Duru*, a door.
O.E.—*Dore*, a door.
E.—Door, an entrance gate : Door-bell, Door-keeper, Door-knocker, Door-mat, Door-plate, Door-step, Door-way.

DAR, DARA

Su.—DAR, DARA, Deer-antelope or Goat-antelope, ibex, stone-buck, stag, he-goat. 2947, 2950, M.1870, B.113.
Ak.—*Turahu, Turakhu*, ibex, stone-buck, stag. 1192. *Ailu, Aalu*, stag. 3, 1192.
Eg.—(*Ārt* [? Hart], goat, ibex, gazelle ("deer"), etc. 129a).
Sk.—*Thār*, a wild goat. IP.
Gr.—*Trăgos*, a goat (from Akkad). *Thēr*, a wild beast.
Goth. & Anc. Br.—*Dyr*, a deer, also animal or beast. EI.
Nor.—*Dyr*, an animal or beast. DNS.
Ger.—*Thier*, deer, hind, animal, beast.
A-S.—*Deor-Dior*, wild animal.

O.E.—*Deor*, wild animal, deer, etc.
E.—Deer, an animal of the stag family, also a goat-antelope. In middle English the name was extended to game in general as "small deer." On the deer as a sacred animal of the Sumerians, Phœnicians and Ancient Britons. See WPOB.328 f., 346 f. ? Hart, from Egyptian.

DAR

Su.—DAR, High, lofty, magnate, high officer. 2951 *re* 436, etc., M.1867-9, B.113, and see *Dar*, dare and *Dur*, king, and cp. *Tar*, judge.
Ak.—*Saqū*, high, lofty, grand magnate, high dignitary or officer. 1096-8. *Sāqū*, a general. 1099.
Eg.—*Dar-ina*, lords, nobles. 867b. *Tar, Tara*, honour, renown. 840a. *Tar*, to guide. 848.
Sk.—*Tāra*, high, protector.
Gr.—*Tur-annos*, lord, master.
Lat.—*Tyrr-anus*, lord, master.
Goth. & Anc. Br.—*Dyrd, Tir*, glory, renown. EI.
Co. & Celt.—*Teyrn*, a prince. Co. *Deravas*, lifted up. Co.
O.E.—*Tyran, Tiraunt*, a tyrant.
E.—Tyrant, a despot. And see *Dur*, a tyrant.

DAR, DARA, DŪR, TAUR, TŪR

Su.—DAR, DARA, DŪR, TAUR, TŪR (*Aš* or *An*-), Title of In-Dara, An-Dara or In-Duru, with epithet of *Iggi*, the solar Father-god of the Sumerians, with goat, ibex or stag as his sacred emblem and here pictured by a Deer's head. See WPOB.242 f., 251 f., 286, 320-323 f. 330 f., 334 f. He is also styled here "The Aša or Lord, Father of the Deer," and "Father Induru of the Ships." 2948, 2950 f., 6661, M.1867-8, B.113. And see *An-dara, Asar, Dur, In-Dara, Siqqa*, a Goat, *Tar, Tur*.
Ak.—*Ia, Ea* (*Jah*), god of the waters, etc. 2. And see WPOB.242 f.
Eg.—*Daru*, Light, god. 884b. *Dari*, a god. 884b. *Tharu(t)*, a hawk god. 858a. *Tharta*, a god. 858a. *Dar-ti*, the two eyes of *Ra* the Sun-god. 840a.
Sk.—*Dāru*, a title of Indra (RV. 7, 6, 1). *Indra*, Father-god and holder of the Thunder-bolt.
Gr.—*Dar-danos*, son of Zeus and first traditional king of the Greeks, who were called *Danaoi* or descendant of King *Danaos*, the brother of Aigyptos.
Goth. & Anc. Br.—*Thôr, Dôr, Dur, Attar, Eindride*, with title of *Ygg, Dan*, etc., the deified first king of the Goths in E. On his association with the goat and stag, see WPOB.320 f., 330 f.
Co. & Celt.—? *Dare-den*, lightning. Co. (Thor was given the lightning-bolt).
E.—Thor, Dor, Dur in the *Asa, Ygg* or *Ein-

dride, of the Eddas, the first traditional king of the Goths. On his identity with the Sumerian *Dar, Dur* or *Indara*, see references to WPOB. cited in para. 1; and on his identity as Heria Thor with King Ar-Thur, see WPOB. 195-8, 400; and see *Dur*, re Holy Grail.

DAR, TAR

Su.—DAR, TAR, Advance, go straight, forefront, succeed, noble—Dare.
Ak.—*Ašaru*, advance, go straight, succeed, noble. 120. *Rāšu*, leader, chief, commander, the forefront. 985 f.
Eg.—*Tehār*, brave, distinguished. 841b. *Tehur*, a brave, a soldier. 841b. *Thar*, be strong. 851a. *Tar*, to guide. 840a.
Sk.—*Dhrish*, to dare, venture. *Dhīra*, brave, courageous, resolute. *Dhaurya*, daring.
Gr.—*Tharreō*, to be bold. *Tharr-ein*, daring.
Goth. & Anc. Br.—*Diarf, Dierf*, daring. bold, EI. *Dirfa*, to dare, to defy. EI. *Daursan*, to dare. U.
Nor.—*Driste*, dare. DN.
Co. & Celt.—*Dewr*, valiant. Co. *Daryvas*, discovery. Co. *Daur*, dare. S.
A-S.—*Durran*, to dare.
O.E.—*Dar, Der*, dare.
E.—Dare, to be bold, to venture, be audacious, defy: Dare-devil, Dare-ful, Dar-ing, Daringly.

DARA, DARU

Su.—DARA, DARU, Enveloping rope, fetter, band, swarm of fish—Draw-net. Pictures an enclosure with ribs. 10,483-6, B.48.
Ak.—*Nibittu*, enveloping, fetter, band. 1146. *Ishu*, swarm of fish. 74. *Tubuqtu*, enclosed space. 1146.
Eg.—*Taar*, to bind, fetter. 818b. *Dar*, reap (a harvest). 884b.
Lat.—*Trah-ere*, draw.
Goth. & Anc. Br.—*Dorg*, fishing-tackle. EI. *Draga*, draw, drag. EI. *Drattr*, a draught (of fishes). I.
Nor.—*Draga*, draw. DN.
A-S.—*Dragan*, to draw.
O.E.—*Draht*, draught. *Draga*, draw. *Draughtes*, moves in chess.
E.—Draught, Draft, a drawing of fish, wine, etc. and move in chess or draughts: Draught-net, Draught-engine, Draughts, game: Draught-board, Draughts-man. Draw, to pull along, drawn: Draw-back, Draw-bridge, Draw-ee, Draw-er, Draw-ing, Draw-ing-room, etc. Drag, to draw by force: Drag-net, etc. Drag-on, to compel by force.

DARA, DIRI, DIRIG

Su.—DARA, DIRI, DIRIG, Dressed, be clothed, cover oneself, envelop. 3732, 10,798, B.143, 480. And see *Dar*, to drape.

DARA—DAŚ   SUMER-ARYAN DICTIONARY

Ak.—*Halāpu*, be clothed, cover oneself. 316. *Nibittu*, enveloping garment. 641.
Eg.—*Thar*, to enclose, surround, protect. 851a. *Tai*, to clothe, to dress. 818b.
Lat.—*Dresser*, to dress. Old F.
O.E.—*Dressen*, to dress.
E.—Dress, to cover with clothes, put on clothes : Dress-ed, Dress-ing, Dress-ing-case, Dress-ing-table, Dress-y, Dress-er.

DARA, DIRI, DIRIG, DUR

Su.—**DARA, DIRI, DIRIG, DUR**, Dark, darkness, enveloping, oppress, dread. 3723, 3727, 3733, 3749, 10,486, and 1066, 1072, B.143, 480, PSL.81.
Ak.—*Da'mu*, be dark, envelop. *Adaru*, be dark, fear, sinister. *Halāpu*, hide oneself, be covered. 316. *Erēbu*, be dark. 95. *Zarabu*, oppress. *Aśuśtu*, trouble, sorrow. *Hipū*, ruin. 329.
Sk.—*An-dhera*, darkness. IP.
Gr.—*Drākōn*, a dragon. *Erebos*, the lower world of darkness, from the Akkad *Erebu*, be dark.
Lat.—*Draco*, a dragon. *Erebus*, the lower world of darkness, from the Akkad *Erebu*, be dark.
Goth. & Anc. Br.—*Dōkkr*, dark. EI. *Dreki*, dragon. EI.
Nor.—*Drage*, dragon. DN. *Drake*, dragon. S.
Ger.—*Drache*, a dragon.
Co. & Celt.—*Droc, Droaga*, hurt. Co. *Druic, Dragun*, a dragon. Co.
A-S.—*Deorc*, dark.
O.E.—*Deork*, dark. *Dragun*, a dragon. *Dreden*, fear.
E.—Dark, absence of light, obscure : Dark-en, Dark-ish, Dark-ling, Dark-ly, Dark-ness, Dark-some, Dark-y. The Prince of Darkness (Satan the Serpent-Dragon). Dour, sinister. Drab, a dull colour. Dragon, a fabulous winged serpent of Darkness : Dragon-fly, Dragon's blood, Dragon-et, Dragon-ize, Dragon-ish. Dread, fear : Dread-ful, Dread-fully, Dread-fulness, Dread-less, Dread-lessly. Erebus, title of the Lower World of Darkness, from the Akkad *Erebu*, be dark.

DARDANNU (*Mulu* meś-meś), TARDANNU

Su.—**DARDANNU** (*Mulu* meś-meś), **TARDANNU**, The Dardannu men, Dardanians or Trojans. 359, 406, 6177. And see *Akaia*, Achaian and *Dura*, Troy and Trojan.
Eg.—*Dardaniu*, a Mediterranean people. 867b, 885a. [Dardanians or Trojans.] *Turshau*, a Mediterranean people. 824b. [Tarsians or Tarshish-ians.] *Tarsha*, a foreign land. 822a. (? Tarsus or Tarshish). *Tirku*, a foreign people or tribe. 823a. (? Trojans or Tyrians).
Sk.—*Dārada*, a Scythic (Gothic) tribe in Indian Epics. *Turvaśa* and *Druhyu*, associated Aryan tribes in Vedas.
Gr.—*Dardanoi*, Trojans. *Dōros, Dōrieus*, a Dorian. *Trōos, Trōios*, a Trojan. *Troad*, the country of the Trojans.
Goth. & Anc. Br.—*Thrud*-heim, city of Thōr in the Eddas.
Co. & Celt.—*Thorians*, the east, orient. Co.
E.—Dardanians or Trojans, etc. ? Dorians (the oldest tribe of the Greeks in Ancient Greece and of the Goths in the Gothic Eddas).

DARIA, DURIA, TAUR, DAUR

Su.—**DARIA, DURIA, TAUR, DAUR**, Duration, endure, be lasting, everlasting ages, eternity. 6660, 6695, MD.267. And see *Duria, Duer*, endure.
Ak.—*Dāru, Dūru*, endure, be lasting, far, future, ages, everlasting, eternity. 266-7.
Eg.—*Dara*, time. 884b. *Tar, Ter, Tra, Tri*, time, season. 840a-b.
Sk.—*Dūra*, long in time and space. *Tarhi*, at that time. *Dūr*, far. IP. *Derhi*, long time. IP.
Lat.—*Durrare*, to endure or last. *Ae-ter-nus*, everlasting.
Goth. & Anc. Br.—*Tarra, Terræ*, to stretch, spread out. I. (*Tru, Trygg*, true. EI.), (*Traust*, trust, firmness, confidence. EI.). (*Triggws*, true. U.).
Nor.—(*Tro*, true. DN.). (*Trōst*, DNS.).
A-S.—(*Treowe*, true, established).
O.E.—*Duren*, to endure. *E-ter-nal*, eternal. (*Trewe*, true, firmly established). (*Trust*, trust).
E.—Duration, length of time. Dure, to last or continue : Dur-able, Dur-ableness, Dur-ability Dur-ably, Dur-ing, En-dur-ing. E-ter-nal, everlasting : E-ter-nity. True, certain, firmly established (i.e., enduring), with its compounds and derivatives, Trow, Trust, etc., seem to come here, but see *Dur*, to dwell, abide, and *Dur*, a bond : Truth-ful, Truth-fully, Truth-fulness, Truth-less, Truth-lessness, Truth-teller, Un-truth. Trow, believe to be true. Trust, believe to be true, confiding, credit : Trust-deed, Trust-ee, Trust-eeship, Trust-ful, Trust-fully, Trust-ing, Trust-ingly, Trust-less, Trust-lessness, Trust-worthy, Trust-worthiness, Trust-y, In trust, On trust.

DAŚ

Su.—**DAŚ**, Dog, a servant or slave, submission, subservience. Pictured by the head of a dog. 11,253, M.8642, 8684, B.516.
Ak.—*Kalbu*, a dog, servant, subservience. 384. *Qiddatu*, submission.
Eg.—*Thasm*, a greyhound. 862a. *Thasmt*, a bitch. 862a.
Sk.—*Daś-era*, a biting beast of prey. *Dāsa*, a

slave. *Dasyu*, Non-Aryan aborigines (as "dogs" or slaves).
Goth. & Anc. Br.—*Tik*, a bitch. I.
Nor.—*Dogg*, mastiff. S. *Dogge*, bull-dog. DN.
Ger.—? *Dasch-hund Dogge*, dog.
Co. & Celt.—*Doug*, dog. S.
A-S.—(Absent).
O.E.—*Dogge*, dog.
E.—Dog, domestic quadruped, "the friend of man." Dog-cart, Dog-cheap, Dog-collar, Dogg-ed, Dog-days, Dog-fancier, Dog-fish, Dog-fox, Dog-irons, Dogg-ish, Dogg-ishly, Dog-grass, Dog-kennel, Dog-leech, Dog-letter-(r), Dog-rose, Dog-eared, Dog-tired, Dog-tooth-ornament, Dog-violet, Dog-wood. Dog, term of abuse. Tyke, Tike, a dog, a cur. ? Dast-ard, a cowardly fellow, etc.: Dag, destroy.

DAŚI, DAŚIA

Su.—**DAŚI. DAŚIA,** Title of *Bakuś*, the Corn Spirit, as the resurrecting archangel of Ia (Jah) or Induru, deified as "The man of the Lord Induru." See WPOB. for representations, etc., XV, 243, 338, 354 f., 10,038, 11,250. And see *Dax, Daxas, Duzi, Tax*.
Ak.—*Dias, Daks*, etc., on Phœnician coins. *Res-ep* of late Phœn. inscripts. *Tash-up* of Hittites. *Mero-Dach* of Assyrians. See WPOB.338 f.
Eg.—*Dahi* (or *Dakhi*), the Creator god "Tehuti" or "Toth." 886a. He is represented as Dog (*Daś*)-headed, and is besides "Creator," the god of wisdom, master of spells or "words of power," and judge of the gods. *Ressep*, Syrio-Phœnician Corn and Warrior god of later Egyptians. WPOB.350 f. for picture.
Sk.—*Daxa*, Creator god of plenty and fields. *Das-ra*, an Aświn or "Horse" spirit of the Sun. See WPOB. for representations, etc. 353 f.
Gr.—*Dks, Dzs, Dioc, Theac*, on Greco-Phœnician coins of Phœnicia and Cilicia, with head of Dionysos or Bacchus. See for representations, etc., WPOB.249, 346, 354.
Goth. & Anc. Br.—*Thiazi* or *Dag*, s. of Thor in E., and *Dias, Deas, Tasc* and *Tascio* on pre-Roman coins of Ancient Britain. See representations, etc., in WPOB.338-9, 346, 353 f.
Ger.—*Tuisco*, warrior god of ancient Germans.
Co. & Celt.—*Daz*, revive, preserve, redeem. Co. *Tasc*, angel, spirit, ghost. G.
E.—*Dias* or *Tascio*, solar resurrecting angel of Sumero-Phœnicians on the pre-Roman coins of Ancient Britain. See representations, etc., in WPOB., pp. noted in paras. 1, etc. ? Deuce, a pagan (i.e., according to modern views an Evil) spirit.

DAX, DAKH, TAX

Su.—**DAX, DAKH, TAX,** Haste, help, aid—Dash. This seems related to the root of the name of the solar angel *Daśi* or *Daxa* above. See WISD.71 f., 4534-7, 4539, B.182.
Ak.—*Harnat*, haste. *Narāru*, help, aid. *Risu*, help, assist.
Eg.—? *Tasa*, to visit. 865b. ? *Daā*, to help. 865b.
Sk.—*Tyaj*, to flee, fly away.
Gr.—*Tachus*, swift.
Co. & Celt.—*Daoz, Deugh*, come and go. Co. *Dyg*, bring (? aid). Co.
O.E.—*Daschan*, to rush.
E.—Dash, to hasten, to rush: Dash-ing, Dash-ingly, Dash-er.

DAX, TAX

Su.—**DAX, TAX,** Gather, combine, add, give—Tax. 4535, B.182.
Ak.—*Eṣepu*, gather, combine, and give. 87.
Eg.—*Taās*, to fine. 865b.
Sk.—*Dax*, to increase.
Lat.—*Tax-are*, to rate, appraise. *Taxer*, to tax. F. *Taxe*, a taxation. F.
Co. & Celt.—*Deag*, a tithe. Co.
O.E.—*Tax*, a rate or duty. *Taske*, a task.
E.—Tax, a rate imposed on property, anything imposed, a task: Tax-able, Tax-ation, Income-tax. Tack, to add to, fasten on, sew slightly: Tack-ing. Task, work imposed, a tax: Task-master. Attach, to bind or fasten on to: Attach-able, Attached, Attach-ment.

DAXA, DA-KHA, DA-GANA

Su.—**DAXA, DA-KHA, DA-GANA** (*Aś*), Lord Daxa or Dagana (Tasia—Bacchus), as "Lord of the Feast." 6668. On *xa* and *gan*, syllabic values, see 4032 and 4036 respectively.
Ak.—*Eluluanag*, ? god of music. 47. ("Dagon" of the O.T. See WPOB.354).
Eg.—*Takh*, to drink wine. 887b. *Takhan*, to play music. 887b.
E.—"Dagon," of the Philistines. See WPOB. 354 f.

DE

Su.—**DE,** Pour out (of water), libation, irrigate. 6727, 6731-2, B.297. Associated with *De* from, see following.
Ak.—*Sapāku*, pour out, libate. 1081. *Siqitu*, irrigate.
Eg.—*Tef-tef*, to pour out. 833a.
Lat.—*De*, down.
Goth. & Anc. Br.—*Dy*, a bog. I.
E.—*De-*, "down," prefix in words, e.g., De-clare, De-stroy, De-siccate, De-volve, etc.

DE

Su.—**DE,** In, remove, snatch away (=from away from). 4582, 4601, M.3078, B.185.
Ak.—*Ina*, in *Ana*, unto. *Dipāru*, snatch away, remove. *Emmu*, with.
Lat.—*De*, in, from, away from.

E.—*De-*, "from," "away," prefix in words, e.g.: De-part, De-mise, De-solate, etc.

DE, DI

Su.—**DE, DI,** Shine (as of a furnace, and bronze), be fiery, destroy. A title of Ea as god of the Smiths (Vulcan). Pictured by a furnace, as in Egypt, pl. II. 6715, 6721-3, 6729, B.297. And see *Di*, to shine of sun.

Ak.—*Šād*, shine, be fiery, brilliant. 869. *Abatu*, destroy. 10.

Eg.—*Da*, flame, fervent heat. 864b and G.42. Pictured by a kiln, essentially the same as in the Sumerian hieroglyph. See plate II. *Talu*, or *Taru*, devils, demons, fiends, enemies. 820a. *Tchai*, devil, an enemy of the sun god Ra. 896b.

Sk.—*Da*, burn by fire. *Dava*, burning heat. *Deva*, "god" and sometimes applied to demons.

Gr.—? *Dia-bolos*, devil.

Lat.—*Dia-bolus*, devil. *De-mon*, a demon, coined by Christian ecclesiasts from Greek *Daimēn*, God, the Deity, a good genius and given by them an evil sense.

Goth. & Anc. Br.—*Dio-full*, devil. EI. *Ty(r)*, enemy of Thor in E.

Nor.—*Dje-vul*, devil. DN.

Ger.—*Teu-fel*, devil.

Co. & Celt.—*Diaul*, fiend, devil. Co. *Diabol*, devil. I. *Deil*, devil. S.

A-S.—*Deō-fol*, *Deō-ful*, the devil. *Tiw*, god of Tuesday.

O.E.—*Deuil*, *Deouel*, devil.

E.—Devil (coined from *Diabolus*), an evil spirit: Devil-ish, Devil-ishly, Devil-ishness, Devil-ry, Dia-bolic, Dia-bolical. Demon, an evil spirit: Demon-iac; Demon-iacal, Demon-iacally, Demon-olatry, Demon-ology.

DEL

Su.—**DEL,** Cutting, a cutting tool (graving or writing, etc.)—Delve. Pictured by an angular cutting tool. 7748-50, M.5731-2, B.336. And cp. *Dul*, a hole, hollow and *Til*, to pierce.

Ak.—*Itquru*, cutting. *Itqurtu*, a cutting tool, an edge, a rim. 129.

Eg.—*Dalf*, to write, inlay, inscriptions. 884b. *Dalf*, writing, inscriptions, documents. 885a. *Duan*, hollows. 872a.

Sk.—(*Darī*, a hollow, a dell).

Gr.—*Del-toō*, write on tablets. *Del-oō*, make manifest, make known.

Lat.—*Telum*, a dart, a dagger.

Goth. & Anc. Br.—*Telja*, cut or hew. EI. *Deila*,, to divide or deal, share. EI. *Deili*, marks (cuttings). *Dal*, a dale, dell. EIU. *Dail*, a portion or deal. U.

Nor.—*Dela Dele*, divide, deal out. *Dal*, a dale. DNS.

Ger.—*Telb*, dig. *Thal*, a dale.

Co. & Celt.—*Tellys*, holed. Co. *Dally*, to make a hole. Co. *Dealwa*, an image (graven). Co. *Dealb*, image (? graven). I. *Dela*, written history. I. *Dowl*, a design. Co. *Dol*, a dale. Co., Cy. *Dal*, *Dail*, dale. I.

A-S.—*Delf*, dig. *Dael*, a deal or division. *Dæl*, a dale.

O.E.—*Delue*, delve. *Deel*, deal or share. *Delle*, a dale.

E.—Delve, to dig with a spade: Delv-er, Delv-ing. Dale, a cleft or hollow between hills, a vale: Dales-man. Dale, suffix in place-names, e.g.: Aire-dale, Annan-dale, Clydes-dale, Dove-dale, in Peak district, Lons-dale, Wear-dale. Dell, a dale or cleft, and-Del, affix in place-names as Arun-del. Deal, to divide out, allot, a "cutting" or share: Deal-er, Deal-ing, Double-dealing, Dole, The Dole. ? Doll, Idol, a graven or cut image and see *Bid*, image. Tool, an instrument for cutting, etc.

DI

Su.—**DI,** Shine, shine with splendour as the sun and stars, cause to shine—Divine. 2550, 2564, B.93. And see *Dag*, shine, day.

Ak.—*Nabātu*, shine with splendour, as day, stars, etc., cause to shine. 635. (*Diparu*, a torch. 264, LSG.209).

Eg.—*Dap*, *Dep*, shine. 876a.

Sk.—*Dī*, shine. *Div*, heaven, sky. *Dyaus*, sky-god. *Dīp*, a live blaze, a lamp. *Deva*, a god.

Gr.—*Dios* or *Dif-os*, Zeus. *Theos*, God, a god. *Daimōn*, God the Deity, a good genius, fate.

Lat.—*Dies*, day (as the shining). *Deus*, a god.

Goth. & Anc. Br.—*Dīar*, *Tivar*, gods and priests. EI. *Tivi*, a god. EI.

Co. & Celt.—*Deu*, *Du*, god. Co. *Dyu*, god. Cy. *Dia*, god. GI.

O.E.—*Deitè*, deity. *Diuine*, a divine.

E.—Div-ine, godly, sacred: Div-inely, Div-inity, Div-ination, Div-inator or Div-iner, Div-ining-rod. Deity, the divinity, god-head: Dei-fy, Dei-form, De-ism, De-ist. Day, see *Dag*, shine of the sun.

DI, DU

Su.—**DI, DU,** Speak, to teach, see *Dug*, to speak, to teach.

DI, DĪ, DIMA

Su.—**DI, DĪ, DIMA,** Judgment, justice, law-suit, decision. Pictured by a circle or lozenge divided into two equal halves, i.e., literally, a "decision." 9518, 9525-6 and cp. *Di-ma*, 9556. And see *Dan*, judge, *Dimma* edict and *Sa-tar*, decide.

Ak.—*Dīnu*, *Denu*, judgment, justice, decision, law-suit. 259.

Eg.—*Di*, to plead. 868a.

Sk.—*Diś*, to decide. *Di*, right. *Dhī*, knowledge, prayer, thought. *Dhamma*, law. P.
Gr.—*Dikē*, justice. *Them-is*, law.
Goth. & Anc. Br.—*Dōm*, judgment, doom, a court of judgment, a law-court. EI. *Domo*, judgment. U.
Nor.—*Dom*, judgment, decision, sentence. DN. *Dommer*, a judge, umpire.
Co. & Celt.—? *Diogel*, certainty. Co.
A-S.—*Tihian*, to judge. *Tihan*, to convict. *Dōm*, judgment. *Demān*, to give judgment.
O.E.—*Deem*, to judge.
E.—Die, as lot or cast of judgment. Deem, to judge, to think : Deem-ster, one who pronounces judgment in the Isle of Man. Doom, judgment : Doom-ed, Dooms-day, Doomsday-book, Crack of Doom.

DI
Su.—DI (-*kud*, *An*-), Lady, *Di*, - the - Judge or decreer—Diana.
Ak.—*Tanit*, the great goddess of the Carthaginian Phœnicians. *Il(at)*, *Daiānu* (*Kud*=*Šamu*, decree. Br.381).
Eg.—*Tannit*, *Tennit*, The Earth-Mother goddess. 838*a*.
Sk.—*Danu*, mother of giants.
Gr.—*Diōnē*, daughter of Zeus.
Lat.—*Diāna*, oracular goddess.
Co. & Celt.—*Dianass*, chaste. Co.
O.E.—*Diana*, the goddess Diana.
E.—Diana, the great tutelary oracular goddess of the Ephesians, and of the Ancient Britons, and whose temple was on Ludgate Hill. See WPOB.45, 64, 184. *Tanit*, a dialectic form of Diana the great tutelary goddess of the later Phœnicians of Carthage, who is invariably invoked before Bel in the inscriptions.

DIB
Su.—DIB, Dwell, enclose, hold, retain. Pictured by an enclosure containing a battle-axe or sceptre. 10,686, M.8176, B.482.
Ak.—*Kiṣṣu*, dwelling. *Kalū*, hold, contain, retain, persons and things. 380.
Eg.—*Deb(t)*, a settlement, inhabited district. 873*b*. *Di*, remain. 868*a*.
Sk.—*Dīpo*, resting-place, an island. P. *Dvipa*. S.
Goth. & Anc. Br.—*Dvelia*, dwell, tarry, abide. EI.
Nor.—*Dvāljas*, to dwell. S. *Dvaele*, linger.
A-S.—*Dwellan*, to delay.
O.E.—*Dwellen*, to delay.
E.—Dwell, to abide, linger : Dwell-er, Dwell-ing.

DIE, DI-E, DĒ
Su.—DIE, DI-E, DĒ, Perish, destroy. Pictured by a fiery furnace. 6721, B.297.
Ak.—*Abātu*, to perish, destroy. 11.
Eg.—*Duai*, death, destruction. 872*a*. *Dua-t*, "*Tuat*," "Land of the Dead." 871*b*.
Sk.—*Dī*, perish, decay.
Goth. & Anc. Br.—*Deyia*, die. EI. *Daud*, dead. EI. *Diw*, die. U. *Dauths*, dead. U.
Nor.—*Diwa*, *Döe*, die. DN. *Död*, dead. DNS.
Ger.—*Tod*, death.
A-S.—*Die*. (Absent in A-S. where the word is *Steorfan*, to die). Dead.
O.E.—*Dyen*, *Dien*, to die. Dead.
E.—Die, to perish, to lose life : Dy-ing. Dead, deprived of life : Dead-ly, Dead-liness, Dead-en, Dead-ness, Dead-alive, Dead-beat, Dead-drunk, dead-letter, Dead-level, Deadlock, Dead-march, Dead-reckoning, Dead-set, Dead-shot, Dead-wall, Dead-water, Deadweight. Death, state of being dead : Deathbed, Death-blow, Death-duties, Death-rate, Death-trap, Death-wound, etc.

DIG, BAD
Su.—DIG, BAD, Wall, strike down, heap up, be high—a Dike, Dig, Ditch. Pictures a walled enclosure. 4386, M.2909, 2913, B.171. And see *Dag*, a stone, and *Duk*, dig.
Ak.—*Duru*, a wall. *Saqū*, be high. *Kamāru*, strike down, overthrow, cover, heap up. 397.
Eg.—(*Debi*), a plinth, pedestal. 875*a*).
Gr.—*Teichos*, a wall or rampart.
Lat.—*Dig-uer*, to dike, to dam. F.
Goth. & Anc. Br.—*Diki*, a dike, a ditch. EI. *Dig*, deep of sound or tune. I.
Nor.—*Dige*, a ditch, to dig. DN. *Dike*, *Dika*, ditch, dig a ditch. S.
Ger.—*Teich*, a pond.
Co. & Celt.—*Dike*, a wall, as fence. IS. ? *Disc-ar*, break down. Co.
A-S.—*Dis*, a dike, a ditch. *Dician*, to make a dike or ditch.
O.E.—*Diche*, a dike, a trench. *Diggen*, to dig.
E.—Dike, Dyke, a wall, an embankment heaped up to keep out inundation, etc., a trench or ditch in throwing up an embankment. Ditch, a trench dug in the ground : Ditch-er. Dig, see *Duk*, dig.

DIKH, DIX
Su.—DIKH, DIX, Tablet, clay tablet, writing, document. Pictured by a tablet or seal. 3923, 3926, 3935, M.2954, 2600, B.157.
Ak.—*Tuppu*, tablet, clay tablet, writing, document. 262. *Kanāku*, a seal.
Eg.—*Thi*, a scribe. 852*b*. *Thau*, writing document. 849*a*.
Sk.—*Likh*, to write (L for D). *Lik-na*, to write. IP.
Lat.—(*Documentum*, example, pattern, proof).
Goth. & Anc. Br.—*Tigl*, a tile. *Teikna*, to mark, denote, draw, a drawing. EI. *Tākn*, a token. *Tāikns*, a token, a sign. U.
Nor.—*Tigl*, a tile. DN. *Tegn*, token. DN. *Tecken*. S.

Ger.—*Zeichen,* a mark.
A-S.—*Tacen,* a token.
O.E.—*Token,* token.
E.—Tick-et, a bill, marked card, a token: Tick-eted, Ticket-collector. Token, a mark, a sign inscribed, voucher, a coin. Be-token. Document, written or inscribed records: Docu-mental, Docu-mentary. Dock-et, a label, ticket, see *Dag,* dagger, cut.

DIM, TI

Su.—DIM, TI, Tie, bind, hold fast, retain, a rope or cable. 2737, 2739, 2741, B.107.
Ak.—*Harāśu,* bind, hold fast. 341. *Timmu,* rope, cable. 1166. *Pihu,* locked. 794. *Qisru,* a knot (tie). LSG.210.
Eg.—*Dema,* tie, bind, gather together. 878b. *Dema,* conflux, confluence. 878b. *Temi,* join together. 836a. *Temu,* parts of a net. 835b. *Them,* a bandlet, tiara. 855a. *Thi,* a tie, a band. 852b.
Sk.—*Dāman,* a rope, a garland. *Tāj,* a crown. Pers.
Gr.—*Dei, Deō,* bind.
Goth. & Anc. Br.—*Taum,* a rein, bridle, a team. EI. *Damm,* a dam. I. *Tuihan,* to tow. U.
Nor.—*Tōmma,* rein, bridle. DN. *Dæmme,* to dam. DN.
Ger.—*Zaum,* rein. *Damm,* a dike.
Co. & Celt.—*Dimedh,* marriage (=? tie). Co.
A-S.—*Tygan,* to tie. *Dam, Dom,* a dam. (Old Frisian).
O.E.—*Teye,* a tie. *Tizen,* to tie. *Dam,* a dam.
E.—Tie, to bind with cord, to fasten with a ligature: Tie-d, Ty-ing. Tie-beam, Tie-rod, Marriage tie, Neck-tie, Play off a Tie. Team, a harnessing together: Team-ed, Team-ster, Team-wise. Tow, originally a rope for towing, the coarse flax of hemp, the act of towing: Tow-ed, Tow-ing, Tow-age, Tow-boat, Tow-ing-net, Tow-path, Tow-line, Tow-y, like Tow. Dam, embankment to retain water: Dam-med, Dam-ming, *dam,* suffix in place-names, and see *Dim,* to build.

DIM

Su.—DIM, Pillar, post, column, bolt, bar, log, a mast—Timber. Pictured by a shaped post. 2738-40, 4252, M.1795, B.107-168.
Ak.—*Dimmu,* pillar, post. 252. *Dimtu,* pillar. *Makutu,* mast, pillar. *Markasu,* a bolt, railing. 588.
Eg.—*Demi,* a stick, staff. 879b. *Dem,* cut through. 878a. *Temsu,* wooden objects. 837b.
Gr.—*Temnō,* cut off.
Lat.—*Temo,* a pole.
Goth. & Anc. Br.—*Timbr,* timber. EI. *Timrjan,* to build. U.
Nor.—*Tōmmer,* timber. DN. *Timmer,* timber. S.

Ger.—*Zimmer,* to timber, to square.
A-S.—*Timber.*
O.E.—*Timber,* building logs.
E.—Timber, dressed wood for building: Timber-ed; Timber-ing.

DIM

Su.—DIM, Build, of houses, etc., erect, create. 9112, 9118, B.395. And see *Dimmena,* a temple platform.
Ak.—*Banū,* build, build houses, erect, construct, create. 173. *Epešu,* build, of houses, etc., make. 82.
Eg.—*Dem, Dam,* enclosure. 878b. *Demaā,* a fortress. 878b. *Dema, Demi,* a town, a village. 879b. *Thema,* a throne. 855a.
Sk.—*Dam,* a house. *Dhama(m),* a dwelling.
Gr.—*Demō,* build. *Domos,* a house, a building.
Lat.—*Domus,* a house, a temple. *Dome,* a town house, guild-hall. OF. *Dôme.* F. *Duomo,* a dome, a chief church. I.
Ger.—*Dom,* dome, cathedral.
Co. & Celt.—*Ti,* a house. Co.
O.E.—*Dome,* a town-house, guild-hall, etc.
E.—Dome, a building (poetic), a cupola, cathedral: Dom-al, Dom-ed. Domestic, belonging to a house: Dom-estically, Dom-esticate, Dom-estication, Dom-esticity, Dom-estics, Dom-estic economy. Domicile, a house or abode: Dom-iciled, Dom-iciliary.

DIM

Su.—DIM (*As-*), Lord Induru or Ia (*Jah*) as The Creator. 9117, B.395.
Ak.—*Il Ea,* god. Ea or Ia.
Eg.—*Tem, Temu,* the Creator of heaven and earth. 834. *Demaā-at,* title of Horus, the sun-god as "The Fortress Father." 878b. *Tem Ra,* the sun-god of day and night. 834b.
Sk.—*Dama,* son of *Dara,* the Creator.
Gr.—*Daimōn,* God, the Deity, a good genius, fate.
Lat.—*Dominus,* the Lord in Christian ecclesiastic literature.
E.—Dominical, belonging to the Lord, Lord's day: Dominical letter. Daimon, a good genius.

DIM

Su.—DIM, Ruler, great lordly man, conquer, subdue—Tame. 1166, 1172, M.658, 6864, 11,190, B.60, 395. And see *Dimmer,* the doomer or judge.
Ak.—*Amel idinnu,* officer. *Śurbū,* great powerful lord. *Salātu,* rule. *Kabābu,* subdue.
Eg.—*Tems,* to direct, a course. 837a. *Themaā,* a hero, warrior. 855a. *Temui,* estates, land. 835b.
Sk.—*Dam,* to tame, conquer, subdue.
Gr.—*Damaō,* to tame, subdue.
Lat.—*Dominus,* lord, master. *Tem-perator,* one

who governs. *Tempero*, to control, be temperate. *Dom-āre*, to tame. *Domaine*, estate. OF. *Dom*, a lord. (Port.)
Goth. & Anc. Br.—*Tam, Tema*, to tame. EI. *Ga-tanjan*, to tame. U.
Nor.—*Tam*, to tame. DNS. *Dominere*, to domineer. DN. *Domæne*, crown-land, domain. DN.
Ger.—*Zahm*, tame.
Co. & Celt.—*Dām*, learned man. I.
A-S.—*Tam*, tame.
O.E.—*Tame*, tame. *Dominacion*, domination. *Temprian*, to temper.
E.—Tame, to conquer, subdue, reclaim: Tamable, Tame-less, Tame-ly, Tame-ness, Tam-er. Dom, a ruler, a lord. Dominate, to be lord over, to govern: Dom-ination, Dom-inator Dom-inance, Dom-inancy, Dom-inantly Pre-dom-inance, Pre-dom-inantly, Domineer Dom-ineering. Dom-inion, lordship, control: Dom-inion Day: and -dom, suffix in King-dom, Official-dom, Bumble-dom, etc. Dom-inie, a school-master (Scot.). Domain, estate, territory, crown-land: Dem-ain, Dem-esne. Temper to practise on, interfere with. Temper, to control, moderate: Temp-erament, Temp-eramental, Temp-erate, Temp-erateness, Temp-erature. Dis-temp-er, In-temp-erance, In-temp-erate. Temerity, rashness.

DIM

Su.—DIM, Overwhelm, crushed down, cut-Doom. 360, 1168, B.12, 60. And see *Dima*, *Dimmu*, judgment.
Ak.—*Sanāqu*, overwhelm, crush down, oppressed. 771.
Eg.—*Tems*, a decree of doom. 837a. *Dem, Dam*, cutting, killing. 878a. *Dema*, dead. 879a. *Tem*, to die, perish, to come to an end. 834b. 835a. *Temm, Temiu*, the dead, the damned. 835b. *Themes*, a condemned person. 855b. *Dem, Dam*, the Serpent of Evil (*Apap*). 878a.
Sk.—*Tam*, to choke. *Tāma*, distress, anxiety. *Tāmasa*, a demon causing disease.
Gr.—*Temnō*, cut off.
Lat.—*Damnum*, loss, damage. *Demo*, to take away. *Temere*, by chance, fortuitously. *Timor*, fear. *Dommage*, damage. F. *Timide*, timorous.
Goth. & Anc. Br.—*Dōm*, doom. EI.
Nor.—*Domme-dag*, doomsday. DN.
Co. & Celt.—*Damprys*, to condemn. Co.
A-S.—*Dom*, doom.
O.E.—*Damnen, Dampnen, Demnen*, to condemn. *Tymerous, Tymeros*, timorous.
E.—Doom, condemnation, ruin, destiny (evil): Doom-ed, Dooms-day, Crack of Doom. On Doom, judgment, see *Dimmu*, judgment. Damn, to condemn, to doom to eternal punishment, an oath, a curse: Damn-able, Damn-ably, Damn-ation, Damn-atory, Damn-ed, Damn-ing, Con-demn, Con-temn, Con-demnation, Con-dem-ned. Timid, afraid, fearful: Tim-idly, In-tim-idate. Timorous, full of fear: Tim-orously, Tim-orousness. Damage, hurt, injury, loss: Dam-ageable, Dam-aged.

DIM, DIMMA

Su.—DIM, DIMMA, Weak in body and mind, frail, weakling. 4253, 4255, B.168.
Ak.—*Ulālu*, weak in body and mind, frail. 47.
Eg.—? *Demam*, grovel. 879a. ? *Dem*, a worm. 879a.
Sk.—*Tāmasa*, dark, ignorant. stupid.
Gr.—('*Alaos*, blind, from Akkad).
Goth. & Anc. Br.—*Dimm*, dim, dark. EI. *Dimia*, dimness. I.
Nor.—*Dimma*, fog. S. *Dimmig*, foggy. S.
Co. & Celt.—*Teim*, dim. I.
A-S.—*Dim*, dim.
O.E.—*Dim*, dim.
E.—Dim, weak in sight, obscure, dusky, dark: Dim-ly, Dim-ness, Be-dim.

DIM

Su.—DIM, People, offspring. 1167, 2742, 9114-5, M.663, B.60, 107, 395.
Ak.—*Binutu, Bunnanu*, offspring, creation. *Umatu* (*Ummalu*), people, multitude. 64. *Tarbū*, offspring. 1190.
Eg.—*Temu, Temmu*, people, mankind. 834a. *Deman*, companies of men. 878b. *Demain*, townspeople, villagers. 879b. *Demdui*, people. 880a. *Temhu, Tamhu*, Libyans. 837a.
Sk.—*Tamil* or *Dramida*, aboriginal people of S. India. ? *Ādmi*, man. IP.
Gr.—*Dēmos*, people, also country district. *Demas*, the living body of man.
Goth. & Anc. Br.—*Taum*, offspring.
Co. & Celt.—(*Tiz*, people. Co.).
E.—Demos, the people. Demo-cracy, government by the people: Demo-crat, Demo-cratic, Demo-cratically, Demo-cratist: Endemic, Epi-demic. Demi-urge, Creator of the world and its people of the Gnostics.

DIMA, DĪ-MA

Su.—DIMA, DĪ-MA, judgment. 9556. See *Di*, judgment and *Dim*, doom.
E.—? Duma, imperial Russian Parliament.

DIMMA, DIMMEIR

Su.—DIMMA, DIMMEIR, Lord or king as the Doomer or Judge. 4254, 4257.
Ak.—*Šarru*, king, lord.
Lat.—*Duum-vir*, a magistrate.
Goth. & Anc. Br.—*Dōmari, Domandi*, a judge. EI.
Nor.—*Dommer*, a judge. DN. *Domare*, a judge. S.

DIMMENA

Su.—DIMMENA, Temple foundation, temple, platform, corner-stone. 7684, 7710, M.5681, B.330.
Ak.—*Tēmānnu*, temple foundation, temple platform, a corner-stone. 1170.
Eg.—*Dehmu(t)*, *Tehmu(t)*, entrance? chamber? 885a.
Gr.—*Temenos*, the precincts of a temple, piece of land sacred to a god, piece of land "cut off" and allotted for any purpose.
Lat.—*Temulum*, old Latin for *Templum*, a temple.
A-S.—*Templ*, *Tempel*, a temple.
O.E.—*Temple*, a temple.
E.—Temple, a fane, edifice in honour of a deity or for religious worship: Templ-ar, Knight Temp-lar, Good Templ-ars, Inner Temple, Temple Bar.

DIMMIR

Su.—DIMMIR, God as the Doomer or Judge. 421.
Ak.—*Ilu*, god.
Eg.—*Dimer(t)*, Heaven, the Sky. 867b. *Demur*, title of Osiris? 878a.
Lat.—? *Dimanche*, Sun-day, the Lord's day. F.

DIMMU

Su.—DIMMU, Command, order, decree, decision, message, report, judgment in general. Pictured by a head with projecting tongue. 735-6. And see *Di* and *Dima*, judgment.
Ak.—*Tēmu*, command, order, decree, decision, message, judgment in general. 356. *Šipru*, a report, answer by message or letter. 1090.
Eg.—*Dem*, to proclaim, to proclaim a name or title. 877b.
Sk.—*Dhammo*, Law, Scriptures. P. *Dharma*. S.
Goth. & Anc. Br.—*Dōm*, *Dæma*, decision, judgment. EI. *Domjan*, to judge. U.
Nor.—*Dom*, decision, judgment. DNS.
Co. & Celt.—*Dremas*, just. Co.
A-S.—*Dēman*, to decide, to judge.
O.E.—*Deem*, judge, think.
E.—Deem, to judge, to think, suppose. See *Di*, *Dima*, judgment. ? Theme, a subject for thinking, discussion or report.

DIM-SAR

Su.—DIM-SAR, Durable record or writing, edict, or obelisk. 12,254, PSL.80.
Ak.—*Nabiu*, he who writes on an obelisk. PSL.80.
Eg.—*Dem*, to cut an inscription. 878a. *Tem*, *Temi*, inscribe, cut. 836a. *Themes(t)*, document. 855b. *Themu*, writing. 858a. *Temmut*, writings, documents. 836a.
Sk.—*Dhammo-thambho*, pillar of the law. P. *Dharma-stambha*. S.

Gr.—(*Temnō*, to cut or draw a line).
E.—Dom-bok or Dooms-day Book.

DINGIR

Su.—DINGIR, Star, the shining bright one, the flickering—? Twinkling. 432, M.346, B.13.
Ak.—*Kakabu*, a star. *Kababu*, flicker. 378. *Ellu*, bright, shining. 40.
Eg.—(*Dua neter*, the star of the god. 871a).
Goth. & Anc. Br.—*Tungl*, a star, a luminary (later, the moon). I.
Nor.—*Tungel*, the moon. S.
Ger.—*Tungal*, a star, luminary. OG.
A-S.—*Tungel*, *Tuncgel*, a star. *Twinclian*, to twinkle or shine faintly.
O.E.—*Twinklen*? to twinkle, of light.
E.—Twinkle, to shine with a quivering light like the stars (*l* for *r* of the Sumerian): in a Twinkling. Latterly the word was confused with Wink, to blink.

DIRI, DIRIG

Su.—DIRI, DIRIG, Dark. 3718. See *Dara*, dark.

DIRIG

Su.—DIRIG, Bend, bow down, running, dark, despoiled—a Dwarf. 3733, M.2421, 2430, 2434, B.143.
Ak.—*Sahuhu*, bend, bow down. *Hipu*, broken, ruined. *Nagarruru*, running. *Nasallula*, despoiled. 739.
Eg.—*Dirga*, a dwarf. 868b.
Sk.—*Dhŭrv*, to bend, allied to *Dwev*, to injure, hurt, and *Dur*, bad, wicked. *Dhvaras*, a female evil spirit or elf.
Gr.—(*Thouros*, raging).
Goth. & Anc. Br.—*Dverg*, a dwarf. EI.
Nor.—*Dvarg*, a dwarf. DNS.
Ger.—*Zwerg*, a dwarf.
Co. & Celt.—*Urf*, a stunted child. S.
A-S.—*Dweorg*, *Dwerg*, a dwarf.
O.E.—*Dwerghes*, dwarfs.
E.—Dwarf, a small deformed man: Dwarf-ish, Dwarf-ishness.

DIS, DIIS, ANA

Su.—DIS, DIIS, ANA, One. Pictured by a vertical stroke. 10,062, B.439. See *Ana*, one.
Ak.—*Isten*, one.
Sk.—*Deśa*, one, a point, a spot, also a province, a country.
Lat.—? *Dis*, apart.

DIŚ, DIIS

Su.—DIŚ, DIIS, God, *Ia* (*Jah*) or *Induru* (*Indra*), as The One God. Pictured by a vertical stroke. 10,062, 10,068, B.439.
Ak.—*Il*, *Ea*, god. *Ia* or *Induru*.
Sk.—*Dyaus*, god of the sky, the sky.
Gr.—*Dis*, Zeus. *Theos*, god.

Lat.—*Deus*, god. *Dius-pater, Dius-piter*, Jupiter or Father. *Ju* or *Dius*.
Co. & Celt.—? *Dich*, powerful. Co.
E.—Theos, God, see *Di*, to shine.

DU, DA

Su.—DU, DA, Do, make, perform. See *Da*, to do.

DU, DA

Su.—DU, DA, Build, erect, set, stand. See *Da*, to build.

DU

Su.—DU, Dwell, habitation, earthwork, mound. See *Dul, Dun* and *Dur*, dwell.

DU, DA, TA

Su.—DU, DA, TA, Speak, talk, see *Da, Duk, Duttu*, to speak.

DU

Su.—DU, Due, taxes, collect, appropriate, fit, becoming. 9134-5, 9161, B.396.
Ak.—*Asita*, taxes, export taxes. 88. *Asamu*, of it, appropriate, becoming. 75. *Puhhuru*, collect, gather.
Eg.—*Denu, Tenu*, due rent taxes. 838a, 882b. *Tama*, fitting, seemly. 819a. *Tut*, collect, gather, assemble. 826a
Sk.—*Deya*, due, fit proper, to be given or paid (as debt, wages, taxes, etc.).
Lat.—*Deb-ere*, to owe, to be due. *Dû, Due*, due, owed, part of *Devoir*. F. *Dovere*, duty. I.
O.E.—*Dewe*, debt, due. *Duelich*, duly. *Dette*, debt.
E.—Due, owed as a debt, tax or tribute : Dues, Due-ful. Duly, fit, appropriate. Duty, that which is due in taxes : Du-tiable, Du-tied, Du-ty free. Duty, obligatory service : Du-teous, Du-teously, Du-tiful, Du-tifully, Du-tifulness. Debt, a sum due : Deb-tor, Deb-it, Deb-enture, In-deb-tedness.

DU, GIN

Su.—DU, GIN, Go, come, reach, go gradually. Pictured by a foot. 4860, 4871, B.207.
Ak.—*Alaku*, go, come, reach, go gradually.
Eg.—*Da*, to pass away. 864b. *Deben*, to go about, to wander round. 875a. *Du*, sandals. 864a.
Sk.—*Du*, to go.
Gr.—*Duō*, to come over, to enter.
Co. & Celt.—*Dos, Dhov, Deugh*, come. Co.
E.—Dawdle, to go gradually, slowly : Daw-dler.

DU, TU

Su.—DU, TU, Thou. 4877, M.3330, B.207. And see *Zu*, thou.
Ak.—*Atta*, thou. 126.
Eg.—*Thu*, thou. 852b. *Ta*, thou, thee. 815a. *Tha*, thine, thee. 848a.

Sk.—*Tvam*, thou.
Gr.—*Tu*, Su, thou.
Lat.—*Tu*, thou.
Goth. & Anc. Br.—*Thu*, thou. EIU.
Nor.—*Du*, thou. DNS.
Ger.—*Du*, thou.
Co. & Celt.—*Di*, thou. Co. *Dhy*, thy. Co. *Ti*, thou. Cy. *Tu*, thou. G.
A-S.—*Du*, thou.
O.E.—*Thou*, thou.
E.—Thou, 2nd pers. pronoun : Thy, Thine.

DUAER, DUAURU

Su.—DUAER, DUAURU (*Uku-*), The Duaer or Duauru nation—(?) Tyrians or Turians.
Ak.—*Ni-iš da-ād-mī*.
Eg.—*Tur, Thaaur*, "a district in Syria, site unknown." 1055a, 1058a. (? Tyre). *Zair, Zar, Tchair*, Tyre. 1063b.
Sk.—*Tritsu*, an Aryan clan, allies of the *Bhara-tas*, and sailors in the Vedas.
Gr.—*Turos*, Tyre. *Turi-oi*, Tyrians. *Turrēnos*, an Etruscan.
Lat.—*Tyrus*, Tyre. *Tyrii*, Tyrians, also Carthaginians. *Tyrrheni*, Etruscans.
E.—Tyre, the famous Phœnician city in Phœnicia: Tyrian purple, Tyrian cynosure, the constellation of Ursa Minor, a favourite guide of the Phœnician sailors of Tyre, Tyrrhenian or Etruscan Sea. Tyrone, and other place-names.

DUB, TUB

Su.—DUB, TUB, Tablet, writing document, surround, store up, platform—a table. Pictured as a tablet. 3927-8, 3931, 3935, B.157. *Dub-šar* or scribe.
Ak.—*Dabr*, a document (tablet). P. *Duppu, Tuppu*, a tablet, clay (inscribed), tablet, writing, document. 262. *Šapāku*, store up. 1081. *Tapšuhtu*, platform. LSG.211.
Eg.—*Daba(t)*, a table of offerings. 874b. *Dab(t)*, a block, a tile. 874a. *Dabi*, discharge (receipt) for debt. 874b. *Tab, Teb*, on, upon. 828a. *Thupar*, a scribe, copyist, secretary. 853a.
Lat.—*Tabula*, a plank, board, a table, a gaming board, tablet for writing, a painting, tablet of the Long register, account-book. *Tabella*, a small tablet.
Goth. & Anc. Br.—*Tafl*, a table for game of draughts and chess, any square board. EI.
Nor.—*Tabel*, table. DN.
Ger.—*Tafel*, a table.
Co. & Celt.—? *Daffar*, furniture. Co.
O.E.—*Table*, table.
E.—Table, a flat board, a board with legs, an article of furniture, board for games of draughts, chess, etc. : Table-beer, Table-book, Table-cloth, Table-cover, Table-d'hôte, Table-ful, Table-land, Table-leaf, Table-linen, Table-money, Table-rapping, Tables (back-

gammon). Table-spoon, Table-spoonful, Table-talk, Table-turning, Table-ware, Table-wise, the Lord's Table. Tableau, a pictorial representation : Tableau vivant. Tablet, a small flat surface, a surface on which something is written : Tabl-ature, Tabl-oid, En-tabl-ature Tablet of the mind, Tabula rasa. Tabular, of the form of or pertaining to tables : Tab-ula, a writing tablet, a legal record, Tab-ularize, Tab-ulate, Tab-ulation, Tab-ling, forming columns of tables, Tab-le book. Tab-le-work (setting up columns of tables in type).

DUB, TUB, TUP

Su.—DUB, TUB, TUP, Heap up, pile up—Top. 3931-3, B.157.
Ak.—*Tabāku*, pile up, heap up. 1142. *Šapāku*, heap up of dust, etc. 1081.
Eg.—*Tap, Tep*, high ground. 828a. *Tap, Teb*, the top of anything. 828a. *Tapiu*, the tops of the masts of a ship. 828a. *Tap, Teb*, a horn. 873a. *Thu*? mount up. 853b.
Sk.—*Thupa*, a tope, a conical heap, pile or mound of earth or masonry erected over relics or as a cenotaph. P. *Stūpa*. S.
Gr.—*Tumbos*, a burial mound, a burrow, a tomb
Lat.—(*Tumulus*, a mound of earth).
Goth. & Anc. Br.—*Topp*, top, crest, a tuft.
Nor.—*Top*, top, crest, tuft. DN. *Topp*. S.
Ger.—*Zopf*, top of a tree, etc., a tuft.
Co. & Celt.—*Top*, top, crest. Cy. *Topach*, having a crest or tuft. G. *Tap*, top. S. *Topi*, to gore with horns. Cy. (Cp. Egyptian, para. 3).
A-S.—*Top*, top.
O.E.—*Top*, top. *Toumbe*, a tomb.
E.—Top, the summit, highest point : Top-most, Top-coat, Top-draining, Top-dress, Top-gallant (cp. Egyptian, para. 3), Top-heavy, Top-knot, Top-less, Top-man, Top-mast, Top-per (one who excels), Top-ping, Top-pingly, Top-proud, Top-sail, Top-side, Top-soil, Top-stone. Tip, the top or point of anything small : Tip-top. Tip, to tilt : Tip-ple, Tip-sy. ? Tomb, a burial mound : Tomb-stone. *Tope*, a Buddhist tumulus. Topple, to tumble over from the top : fall down.

DUB, TUB

Su.—DUB, TUB, Pour out, libation, overflow—Tube. 3929, M.2625, B.157.
Ak.—*Sarāqu*, pour out.
Eg.—*Tef-Tef, Thef-Thef*, to pour out water, etc. 833a, 854b. *The-tef*, to pour out by drops, to sprinkle. 862b. *Dep, Dap*, to exude. 876b.
Sk.—*Dhav*, to flow.
Lat., Goth. & Anc. Br., Nor., Ger., Co. & Celt. and A-S.—For details see *Dab, Tap*, a Tap, a tube.
O.E.—*Tubbe*, a tub.
E.—Tube, see *Dab, Tap*, a tube. Dew, moisture deposited from air, cognate with Egyptian *Dep*, to exude, and see *Dug*, overflow.

DUB, TUB

Su.—DUB, TUB, Enclose, encompass, surround, catch, hold—Tub. 3927, 3930, B.157.
Ak.—*Lamū*, enclose, surround, encompass. *Ṣibū*, catch, hold.
Eg.—*Dapu, Dabh*, pot, vessel, vase. 876a, 877a. *Daf*, pot, urn, vessel. 877b. 874b. *Dab*, wall up. 873b. *Tabu*, vessel for beer or wine. 827b.
Gr.—*Dapas*, a beaker.
Lat.—(*Tubus*, a pipe).
Goth. & Anc. Br.—*Dapi*, a pool.
Ger.—*Tubbe*, a tub.
Co. & Celt.—*Dippa*, a pit. Co. *Dub*, a pool of water. S.
E.—Tub, an open vessel, a cask : Tub-by, Tub-ful. ? Toby, a kind of beer-mug. ? Top-er, an excessive drinker. And see *Dub*, tube.

DUB

Su.—DUB, Smite, strike, strike dead, kill. 7029, 7032, B.309.
Ak.—*Napāṣu*, smite, smash, shatter, kill, strike dead. 708.
Eg.—*Dab-Dab*, stab, kill. 876b. *Tabha*, storm-god, a serpent, fiend. 826a.
Sk.—*Dyu*, to go against. *Tūfān*, a hurricane. IP.
Gr.—*Tupos*, a blow. *Typhōn*, storm, giant.
Lat.—*Tuer*, to kill, to slay. F.
Goth. & Anc. Br.—*Dubba*, to strike. EI. *Drappa*, to drub. EI. (*Tauf*, sorcery. I.).
Nor.—*Dubba*, strike. DNS.
Ger.—*Tupfen*, to touch.
Co. & Celt.—*Dova*, to subdue. Co. *Deave*, to strike, smash.
A-S.—*Dubban*, to strike, to dub.
O.E.—*Dubbe*, strike, to dub. *Drepe*, beat, slay, kill.
E.—Dub, to strike, to strike the shoulder with the flat of a sword in conferring Knighthood : Dub-bing. Tub, the striking surface of a steam-hammer. ? Drub, to beat or thrash, from allied Gothic *drappa*, to drub. ? Typhon, a whirlwind, hurricane.

DUG, DUK, DUG-XI

Su.—DUG, DUK, DUG-XI, Dish, pot, bowl—Dish or Jug. Pictured by a drinking-bowl or jug with a spout. 5891-3, 8223, B.264. And see *Dug-Namtar* (MD.43) and *Dur*, a magic bowl and *Gar*, a jar.
Ak.—*Kanna*, a vessel for water, wine, etc., a "can." 406. *Kup-uttu*, a bowl ("cup."). *Kar-patu*, a pot, jug. 440.

Eg.—*Des, Das*, a pot, vessel, jug. 883*a*. *Dukh*, to drink. 887*b*. *Kabu*, a measure. 786*b*. Pictured by a cup or pot—from the Akkad.
Sk.—*Dagshē*, a pot. IP.
Gr.—*Dochē*, a receptacle.
Lat.—*Discus*, a plate.
Goth. & Anc. Br.—*Deig-la, Digull*, a stone bowl, a crucible. EI. *Disk*, a plate. I. *Dŏkk*, a dock, a pool. I.
Nor.—*Diske*, a dish. DN. *Digel*, a crucible. DN. *Dok*, a dock or ships' basin. DN.
Ger.—*Tugel*, a crucible. *Docke*, a dock.
A-S.—*Disc*, a plate, dish, table.
O.E.—*Disch*, a dish. *Iugge, Jugge*, a jug.
E.—Dish, a vessel on which food is served, a bowl, plate, jug, etc.; Dish-cloth, Dish-cover, Dish-ful, Dish-ing, Dish-water, Dish up. Disc, Disk, a round plate, a counter, the face of a celestial body, Disc-al, Solar disc. Dock, a basin for ships: Dock-er, Dock-master, Dock-yard, Dry-dock, Graving-dock, Floating-dock, Wet-dock. ? Jug, a kind of pitcher for liquors.

DUG

Su.—DUG, Pour water, inundate—Douse. 8232, B.353.
Ak.—*Rihū*, pour water, inundate. 957.
Eg.—*Desh-Desh*, flow out, overspread of waters. 889*a*.
Lat.—*Ductus*, a leading, a canal. *Docciare*, to flow. I. *Douche*, a shower-bath from Italian. F.
Goth. & Anc. Br.—*Deigja*, wetness, dampness. I. *Dyka*, to dive. S. *Dögg*, dew. EI.
Nor.—*Dukke*, to plunge. DN. *Dug*, dew. DN. *Dagg*, dew. S.
Co. & Celt.—*Diog*. flow. Co. *Dook*, duck or plunge into water. S.
A-S.—*Deaw*, dew.
O.E.—*Douz, Douce*, douse. *Deau, Dyau*, dew.
E.—Douse, Dowse, to drench or splash with or plunge into water. Douche, a shower-bath. Duck, plunge or dive into water, soused, Duck-ing. Duct, a channel for flowing water, etc.: Aqua-duct, etc. Dew, see *Dub*, pour out.

DUG, DUK

Su.—DUG, DUK, Leader, supreme prince, the impeller or drawer by the bar or sceptre—Duke. Pictured by the hat or cap of a leader. 11,231, 11,235, B.515.
Ak.—*Asāridu*, leader, supreme prince. 121. *Amela bar sududu*, drawer or impeller by the bar or sceptre. Cp. 1014.
Eg.—*Thaso*, captain, general. 860*b*. *Thesu*, commander, captain, general. 860*a*. *Thesas*, chief lord, master. 862*a*. *Tchaas*, to command, be lord and master. 896*a*.
Sk.—*Drish*, to show the way.
Gr.—(*Diakonos*, a servant, a messenger, a minister of the church in the Christian era).
Lat.—*Dux*, a leader. *Duc-ere*, to lead. *Doge*, duke in Italian provincial. *Ducato*, a duchy. I. (*Diaconus*, a deacon). *Educare*, to bring out, lead out, educate.
Goth. & Anc. Br.—*Tigu*, prince, lord. EI. *Tiggi*, a king. I. *Tigin*, highness. I. *Duga*, to help and show prowess. EI. *Dygd, Dugandi*, doughtiness, valour. EI.
Nor.—*Dygtig*, capable, doughty. DN. *Duga*, show prowess. S. *Dygd*, doughtiness. S.
Ger.—*Her-zog*, a duke.
Co. & Celt.—*Dug*, a general. Co. *Duvog*, great grandfather. Co. (*Diagon*, deacon. Co.).
A-S.—*Toga*, a leader. *Dyhtig, Dugud*, doughty. *Dugan*, to be strong.
O.E.—*Duc, Duk*, a duke. *Douzti, Duhti*, doughty. (*Daken*, a deacon). *Toggen*, to tug.
E.—Duke, a leader, the highest order of nobility next below prince, on the Continent a sovereign prince: Duch-y, Duke-dom, Duk-ery, Duke-ship, Duk-eries, Duch-ess, Duc-al coronet (see Sumerian sign). Duke of Cornwall, first Brito-Phœnician duke in Britain, c.1103 B.C. See WPOB.154, 160-170, 214 f., 404 f. (Deacon, a subordinate order of clergy: Arch-deacon, Deacon-ry, Deacon-ship). Doge, duke in Italian provincial. Doughty, valiant, strong: Dough-tily, Dough-tiness. Ducat, a gold coin of the duchy of Venice, etc. Duct, to lead, lead out: Duct-ile, Duct-ility, Con-duct, Con-duct-ion, Con-duct-or, De-duct, De-duct-ion, De-duct-or, Ad-duce, Con-duce, De-duce, E-duce, In-duce, etc. Dux, a leader, the head boy in a school. Educate, to lead out, to train. See *Dug*, to teach. Tug, to draw, pull, drag along: Tug-ging, Tug-boat, Steam-tug, Tug-of-war.

DUG, DU, DI

Su.—DUG, DU, DI, Speak, command, call, cry out. Pictured by a head with protruding tongue. 505, 527-8, 531-2, 11,238, 11,241, B.15, 515. And see *Da, Duttu*, to speak and *Kir*, to cry out.
Ak.—*Qibū*, speak, command. 904. *Qabū*, speech word. 904. *Babālu*, speech, word, saying. *Zamāru*, cry out, sing. 284.
Eg.—*Tu*, to speak. 823*a*. *Thes*, speech, saying. 860*b*. *Thesasiu*, words, speeches, formulæ. 862*a*.
Sk.—*Diś*, to tell, command, order, speak. *Dhak*, exclamation of wrath.
Lat.—*Dic-ere*, to say, tell. *Dic-are*, to proclaim. *Dic-tatus*, dictated.
Goth. & Anc. Br.—*Tja*, to tell. EI. *Ga-teihan*, to tell. U.
Ger.—*Zeihen*, to accuse.
Co. & Celt.—*Dychan*, to jeer. Cy.
O.E.—*Dict*, an order, a rule. *Diction*, speech. *Decre*, decree.

E.—Dictate, to tell another what to say or write, to command : Dict-a, Dict-ation, Dict-ator, Dict-atorial, Dict-atorship, Dict-atory, Dict-um. Diction, a saying or speaking, manner of speaking or expressing : Dictionary, Bene-dict-ion, Contra-dict-ion, Male-dict-ion. Dick (slang for) fine words. Decree, an order, decision, law : Inter-dict, Inter-dict-ion, Edict, a proclamation, command : E-dic-tal. Babble, from Akkad, *Babālu*. Gibe and Quibble, from Akkad, *Qibu*.

DUG

Su.—DUG, Meditate, be wise, discourse—Teach. 522, 527, 529, 549, 8229.
Ak.—*Atmū*, discourse, pronounce. 131 and LSG.211. *Erēsu*, be wise, sensible, decide. 106. *Dabābu*, proclaim, plan, meditate. LSG.266. *Namqu*, be wise. *Tamū*, tell, relate. 1165.
Eg.—*Degg*, examine, see scrutinize. 819a. *Degaa*, a seer, wise man. 891a. *Tehasa*, a wise or learned man. 900a. *Thi*, a learned man. 852b. *Thes*, to compose a statement to arrange words in logical sequence. 860b. *Thesu*, law-makers. 860b.
Sk.—*Diś*, to teach, point out, to show.
Gr.—*Deik-numi*, show, point out. *Dokein*, to think. *Thesis*, a proposition.
Lat.—*Doc-ere*, to teach, instruct. *Disc-ere*, to learn.
Goth. & Anc. Br.—*Dikta*, to compose poetry. I.
Co. & Celt.—*Diskys*, taught, learned. Co.
A-S.—*Tæcean*, to teach.
O.E.—*Techen*, to teach.
E.—Doctor, a learned man, a teacher, a physician ; Doc-torate, Doc-torship. Doc-trine, a thing taught, a belief, Doc-trinal. Dogma, an opinion taught by authority, Dog-matic, Dog-matical, Dog-matize, Dog-matizer, Dog-matism, Dog-matist. Didactic, fitted or intended to teach : Di-dac-tically, Di-dac-tics. E-ducate, to teach, to train up : E-duc-able, E-duc-ation, E-duc-ational, E-duc-ationally, E-duc-ationist, E-duc-ative, E-duc-ator. Indicate, to point out, give reasons : In-dic-ative, In-dic-atory, In-dic-t, In-dic-table, In-dic-tment. Teach, to impart instruction or knowledge : Teach-able, Teach-er, Teach-ing, Teach-less. Thesis, an essay on a theme or proposition, see Egyptian, *Thes*, para. 3.

DUG

Su.—DUG, Sweet, agreeable, good, pleasing—Douce.
Ak.—*Tābu*, sweet, agreeable, pleasing, good. 349.
Eg.—*Degg(t)*, appearance. 891a.
Sk.—*Tejas*, dignity.
Gr.—*Dug-ma*, seeming good.

Lat.—*Decus*, grace, ornament, esteem, honour, virtue. *Dec-ōrum*, seemliness. *Dec-ere*, to befit. *Dig-nus*, worthy. *Douce*, sweet, mild. F. *Decent*, seemly.
Goth. & Anc. Br.—*Dygg*, good, worthy, faithful. El. *Dygth*, virtue, probity. I.
Nor.—*Dyd*, virtue. DN.
Ger.—*Tugen*, virtue, good quality. *Tēg*, pleasant, honest, fair. Co.
Co. & Celt.—*Douce*, sweet, sober. S.
A-S.—*Dugan*, to be virtuous, good, honourable, noble.
O.E.—*Dow*, to be good. *Dignetee*, dignity.
E.—Douce, sweet of manner, agreeable, pleasing : Douce-ly, Douc-eur, something intended to please, a present or bribe. Decent, becoming, modest : Dec-ently, Dec-ency. Decorum, seemliness : Dec-orous, Dec-orously. Dignity, worth, rank : Dig-nitary, Dig-nify, Dig-nified.

DUK

Su.—DUK, Leader, see *Dug*, leader, duke.

DUK, DU-UK, DUN

Su.—DUK, DU-UK, DUN, Dig in the earth, open a canal. Pictures what appears to be a spade or shovel. 9864, 9868-70, B.427. On *Uk*, alternative value of second syllable, cp. 5912 with 9864 and WISD.62. And see *Dig*, a ditch.
Ak.—*Harāru*, to dig. 334. *Hirū*, *śa arṣiti*, dig in the earth. 341. *Ditu śa nāri*, open of a canal. 335.
Eg.—*Deg*, *Dega*, to plant. 867b, 891b. *Degi*, gardens. 891b. *Den*, to dig a canal. 881b.
Goth. & Anc. Br.—*Dīk*, *Diki*, a ditch, a dike. I. *Digans*, made of earth. U.
Nor.—*Dige*, to dig. DN. *Diha*, to dig a ditch. S.
Ger.—*Teich*, a ditch, a dyke or dike.
A-S.—*Dician*, to make a ditch or dike or dyke.
O.E.—*Diggen*, to dig.
E.—*Dig*, to turn up the earth, cultivate with a spade, excavate : Dig-gable, Dig-ger, Dig-gings, Dig in, Dug. And see *Dig*, a ditch, dyke.

DUK (Aś-) DUK-AG, DUK-AKA (Aś-) or DUN (Aś-)

Su.—DUK (Aś-) DUK-AG, DUK-AKA (Aś-) or DUN (Aś-), a variant title of Bakus or Bacchus or Dionysos as "The Lord Digger of the Earth." 9867, 9873, B.427. And see *Bakuś*, *Daxa*, *Dun*, and previous note on *Duk*, synonym of *Dun*.
Ak.—*Il Bau*.
Eg.—*Daqq*, title of a god. 890b. *Das aaku*, a singing god. 888a. (*Tanath* or *Tanit*, goddess of later Phœnicians of Carthage). *Dakh*, the vine. 887b. *Dakhu*, grain. 885b. *Deq* grain and fruit. 890b. *Tann* or *Dann*, a very ancient Earth-God. 819b, 838a, 881. *Tannit*.

Tanut, *Danit*, consort of *Tann* or *Dann*, 819b, 838a.
Sk.—*Daksha* or *Daxa*, the creative god, is represented standing in a field of crops. See illustration in WPOB.353.
Gr.—*Dionysos* (or Bacchus), as patron of the fields and cultivation.
Lat.—*Dionysius*, earth god of plenty and cultivation.
E.—*Tascio* or *Dasi* (or *Dionysius*), of Pre-Roman Briton coins as "The Lord Digger of the Earth." See WPOB.338 f. ? *Tanit* (Diana), goddess of the Phœnicians at Carthage. See *Dan*.

DUL, DU

Su.—DUL, DU, Dwell, dwelling, cave, cover, hole, protect. Pictured by a fortified enclosure. 9578-80, 9582, 9588, B.417. And see *Dun*, dwell and *Til*, dwell.
Ak.—*Katāmu*, cover, protect, conceal, closed door. 457. *Asābu*, dwell. *Subtu*, dwelling, habitation. 1008. *Tilu*, hill, heap or mound of ruins. 1160.
Eg.—*Tel-Tel*, *Ter-ter*, strong place, fort. 840a.
Sk.—*Ālaya*, an abode. *Dih*, habitations. IP.
Goth. & Anc. Br.—*Dvelja*, to dwell, tarry, abide. EI. *Dul*, concealment. I.
Nor.—*Dvæle*, to dwell. DN. *Dvāljas*, to dwell. S.
Co. & Celt.—*Telhar*, a palace. Co. *Tellou*, land taxes. Co.
O.E.—*Dwellen*, to linger, delay.
E.—Dwell, to abide in a place, to inhabit, reside, remain : Dwell-er, Dwell-ing, Dwelling-house, Dwell-ing-place. Dally, delay.

DUN, DU

Su.—DUN, DU, Fortify, gather, assembly of inhabitants, earthwork, mound, enclosure, cave, cover, protect, dwell—a Town. Pictured by same sign as foregoing, of which its name is a synonym. 9577, 9580, 9583-5, B.417.
Ak.—*Pahāru*, fortify, strengthen, gather, assembly of inhabitants. 796. *Mulū*, earthwork, mound. 544. *Dū*, habitation, enclosure. *Katāmu*, cover, protect. *Tilu*, *Tillu*, hill, mound. *Nigiṣṣu*, a cave. 643.
Eg.—*Den(t)*, abode. 881b. *Dennu*, a government building (a fort ?). 881b. *Dena*, *Denat*, embankment, dike, barrage. 882a. *Ten*, *Then*, raise up, exalt. 837b, 856a. *Tun*, to stretch out. 872b. *Tenzai*, a sanctuary. 839b. *Then(t)*, abode, sanctuary. 856a. *Ten*, the hole (den) of a serpent. 837a. *Thenemu*, dens, caves. 857a. *Dennu*, *Tennu(t)*, many, great number (? assembly). 838a, 882b. (*Demi*, a town, a village. 836b, 879b).
Sk.—*Dhanu*, a sandbank. (*Tan*, to extend, spread out).
Gr.—(*Teins*, to stretch out, extend). (*Teichos*, a city wall). (*Moles*, a great heap a pier from Akkad *Mulū*, earthwork, para. 3). (*Mole*, a pier, embankment or causeway, from Akkad. F.).
Goth. & Anc. Br.—*Tūn*, a fenced-in enclosure, in which a house is built. A farm-house with its buildings, a homestead, a dwelling. I.
Nor.—*Tūn*, fenced enclosure of dwelling, in Old N.
Co. & Celt.—*Doun*, town. Co. *Din*, *Tin*, fortified hill. Co. *Dinas*, a town. Cy. *Din*, a hill-fort. Cy. *Dun*, *Dinn*, fort, fortified, hill. Gl. *Towyn*, the turfy downs. Co. *Toon*, *Toun*, town. S.
A-S.—*Tūn*, a town. *Denn*, a cave, a sleeping-place. *Dūn*, a hill.
O.E.—*Toun*, a town. *Den*, a cave, a den. *Donjon*, keep tower of a castle. *Denizen*, an inhabitant. (*Mole*, a pier, from Akkad *Mulū*, para. 2).
E.—Town, a large village formerly fortified, inhabitants of towns : Town-clerk, Town-council, Town-councillor, Town-crier, Town-hall, Towns-folk, Towns-man, Towns-people, Town-ship, Town-y. -Town, ton, and tun, suffixes in place-names : Adding-ton, Arre-ton, Ash-ton, Bils-ton, Bridling-ton, Cadding-ton, Cathers-ton, Chitting-ton, etc., etc. Den, a cave, a sleeping-place, lair of a wild beast, a private retreat for work. -den, suffix in place-names : Britten-den, Chitten-den, Cotten-den, etc., etc. Denizen, an inhabitant. Downs, lowhills in S. of England. Dun, a fortified hill or mound and *Dun* or *Don*, prefix in place-names : Dun-bar, Dun-barton, Dun-edin (ancient name of Edin-burgh), Don-caster, etc., etc., and -*don*, suffix in place-names : Lon-don, the Augusto-dunum of the Romans (and see WPOB.407 f.) : Abing-don, etc., etc. Dune, a low sandhill. Dungeon, the keep or chief tower in a castle, a cell underground, a prison. Mole, a pier, embankment, causey or breakwater, from Akkad, *Mulū*, para. 2.

DUN

Su.—DUN, Dig, a variant of *Duk*, dig, q.v. 9864, B.427. And cp. *Dan*, to cut.
Eg.—*Den*, to dig a canal. 881b. *Den*, *Denn*, to cut, cleave, split. 881a. *Den*, a field. 881b. *Dena Deniu*, fields. 882a. *Ten*, *Tenn*, the earth, ground. 838a. *Tenu* a dike or ditch. 838b.
A-S.—*Denu*, a valley.
E.—Dene, a small valley, an artificial hollow in excavations for chalk in Kent and Essex : Dene-hole and -*dene*, suffix in place-names.

DUR, DŪR, TAUR, TŪR

Su.—DUR, DŪR, TAUR, TŪR (*Aś-* or *An-*) or Lord *Dur* or *Tur*, the title of Andara, Induru or Indara, or Thor, the first king of the Goths in the Eddas. 6661. And see *Andara, Dar,* or *Tŭr* and *Duran,* titles of Indara or Thor. And see WPOB.243, 251, 286-7, 316 f., 318, 320, 331, 344, etc.

Ak., Eg., Sk., Gr., Lat., Goth. & Anc. Br., Nor., Ger., Co. & Celt., A-S., O.E.—For details in these languages, see *Dăr, Tŭr,* Indara or Thor.

E.—Thor, first king of the Goths in the Eddas, and see evidence for his identity with the Sumerian *Dar, Dŭr* or *Tŭr* or *In-dara* in WPOB., cited in para. 1. Thurs-day or Thor's-day, named after Thor, the first king of the Goths.

DUR, DURU

Su.—DUR, DURU, Water as "The Shining One" (?), cp. PSL.9. A synonym for *A* or *Ā,* water, flowing water. Pictured by wavelets of water, essentially identical with the Water-sign in Egyptian. 11,319-20, 11,335 and CIWA.ii, 43, 30c, B.481, and *Dur,* a marsh. LSG.212. And see *A, Badur* or *Baduru* and *Me,* water.

Ak.—*Labāku, Narabu*—the meanings of both of which are yet unknown, but the latter is probably cognate with *Năr, Năru,* a river, a stream. 721. *Ibbā,* shining (4), is an ideographic value of this sign.

Eg.—*Iăr,* river, as "The Shining One." 142b. *Taru, Teru, Tru,* a stream, a river. 840b. *Atar, Ataru, Atru,* river, stream. 99a. (cp. Greek, *'Udor,* water). *Thari,* to sprinkle, to moisten. 857b. [The ordinary Egyptian word for Water is *Mu* from the Akkad, *Mu* water, corresponding to the Sumerian synonym *Me*].

Sk.—*Dara, Dhārā,* a stream or current of water, a flood. *Drū,* flowing. *Drapsa,* a drop. *Darya,* river, sea. IP. (And see WISD.11 f.). *Tarai,* a swamp at the foot of the Himalayas.

Gr.—*'Udŏr, Udatos,* water, water of rivers, etc. *Dosos,* pure water (especially dew and tears).

Goth. & Anc. Br.—*Ăr,* river. EI. *Vatr,* water, rarely in E. (where *Ā, Ăr*=river, stream and *Vatn*=water). *Driupa,* to drop or drip. EI. *Tiŏrn Tjorn,* a tarn, pool or lake. EI. *Wato,* water. U. *Thrŏ,* a water trough. I.

Nor.—*Vatre,* water. DN. *Tjŏrn,* a tarn. *Tărn,* tarn, pool. S. *Dryppe,* to drop or drip. DN.

Ger.—(*Wasser,* water).

Co. & Celt.—*Dour, Durra,* water. Co. *Durva,* watery. Co. *Dewerryau,* drops. Co. *Dwr,* water. Cy. *Dur,* water. Gl. *Drook,* to drench. S.

A-S.—*Wæter,* water.

O.E.—*Water,* water. *Tern,* a small lake or pool.

E.—Water, the elemental fluid in seas, rivers, lakes and in tears, etc. : Water-barrel, Water-biscuit, Water-boat, Water-borne, Water-bottle, Water-butt, Water-cart, Water-closet, Water-colour, Water-course, Water-craft, Water-cress, Water-cure, Water-drain, Water-drop, Watered, Water-engine, Water-fall, Water-flow, Water-fowl, Water-glass, Watering-can, Water-ing-place, Water-trough Water-less, Water-level, Water-lily, Water-line, Water-logged, Water-man, Water-melon, Water-mill, Water-parting or W-shed, Water-pipe, Water-pot, Water-power, Water-proof, Water-rat, Water-shed, Water-spaniel, Water-spout, Water-supply, Water-tank, Water-tight, Water-wheel, Water-works, Water-y, etc. And see WPOB.324, WISD.11. *Dur, Der, Dore,* etc., in river names : *Durra,* in Cornwall ; *Dour,* in Kent, Fife, Aberdeen ; *Dore,* in Hereford ; *Duir,* in Lanark ; *Thur,* in Norfolk ; *Doro,* in Queen's Co. and Dublin ; *Dairan,* Carnarvon ; *Durar* and *Deargan,* Argyle, several ; *Dover, Der-*went, in Cumberland, Yorks and Derbysh. and Durham ; *Der-*wen, Denbigh ; *Dar-*ent, Kent ; *Dart,* Devon, etc. The suffix, *-der* or *dur,* in many river-names ; Cal-*der,* of which there are over a dozen ; A-*dder,* several ; A-*dur,* in Sussex ; A-*dar,* in Mayo ; Lo-*dore,* etc., see TWP.209 f. *Drook,* drench, be drenched. S. *Drop,* a small quantity of water or other fluid : *Drip. Dropsy,* abnormal collection of "water" or serous fluid in the body : *Dropsical. Drown,* death by immersion in water : *Drown-ing. Drunk,* over drinking, and *Drinks, Drink-ing. Hydro,* series of names from Greek *'Udor* or *Hydor,* "water" : Hydr-ant, Hydr-ation, Hydr-aulic, Hydraulics, Hydr-aulic cement, Hydr-aulic-press, Hydr-aulic-ram, Hydro-carbon, Hydro-dynamics, Hydro-gen, Hydro-pathic, Hydro-phobic, Hydro-statics, Hydr-ous, etc. *Tarn,* a small lake or pool.

DUR, TUR

Su.—DUR, TUR, The Magic Stone Divining Bowl or Cauldron of Indur, The Holy Grail of the Sumerians, styled, "The Bowl of complete Vision and Revelation." It is frequently referred to in Sumerian litanies, and is called "The Split or shattered Bowl of the Seers," indicating its archaic age and vicissitudes, and as "The Lost Bowl," with Lamentations for its loss and prayers for its return. It is pictured in its word-sign as a bowl or jar containing inside the sign for "shattered" (*Mahāṣu,* 3611, B.227). 3329-30 and 2113, 7403, M.2108-14, B.122. And see *Dug-nam-tar,* a magic bowl.

Ak.—*Abnu-nătu,* the split stone bowl. 8, 742. *Inu,* the eye, see. *Amăru,* behold, perceive.

59. *Napharu*, wholly, all. 707. *Kaluma*, reveal. 587. *Riksu*, a ban, a charm. 965. *Ezimtu*, lamentations. 26.

Eg.—*Tir-ushebt*, a magical vase or pot or cup of a Fire-god (*Usheb*), cp. 823b, 186a. *Der*, *Ter*, vase or pot. 884a. *Therb*, a pot or vessel. 851b. *Terr*, *Tuhar*, an oven or furnace. 840a, 841b. *Terp*, make, make offering, pour out, libation. 884b. *Der*, *Ter*, to produce, drive out, expel, destroy. 840a, 841a. *Ter-ti*, the two eyeballs of Ra. 840a.

Sk.—*Tark*, divination. (*Drona*, a wooden vessel or bucket for the Soma or ambrosia).

Gr.—*Teras*, omen, portent. *Terazo*, to interpret portents and omens. In Septaugint the Chaldean divining fetish is generally spelt *Therapein* for the Hebrew *Teraph-im*, is probably from Heb. *Tervmh*, an oblation.

Lat.—(*Cra-ter*, a bowl).

Goth. & Anc. Br.—*Hver*, the Magic stone, divining bowl of Iörd (Ur) captured by Heria Thor, from the weirds of Jörd, which was also shattered. *Dar*, charm, fascination. EI. *Dyrd*, a miracle. I. *Tiörvi*, a charmer, a wizard. I.

Co. & Celt.—*Tern*, an oven, a furnace (cauldron). Co. *Torkhan*, a fire. Co. *Tar-rutan*, a phantasm, a whim. Co. *Darlow*, to brew. Co. *Druw*, a Druid. Co. *Derwydd*, a Druid. Cy. *Draoi*, *Druidh*, a magician, sorcerer. GI.

A-S.—*Dry*, a magician.

O.E.—*Druyds*, Druids. (*Greal*, grail, a corruption from Low Latin). *Cratella*, from *Cra-ter*, a bowl : but it now seems possibly related to the Greek, *Kratailcōs*, " stony."

E.—The *Tur* or *Dur*, Magic Stone Bowl or Holy Grail of In-Dur or King Heria Thor (Ar-Thur), which appears to be the inscribed votive stone bowl of the Sumerian priest-king Udug, see under *Azu Sib*. The *Teraph* or *Teraph-im* : Chaldean and Amorite divination fetish of Laban of *Ur*, stolen from him by his daughter Rachel for Jacob (Gen. 31, 19-35) was probably one of these *Tur* bowls, see under Egypt and Greek. It was also in David's house (1 Sam. 19, 13-16), rendered in English as idol, and it was extensively consulted for divination by Israelites, down to time of Hosea (in 8th cent. B.C.), who declared it to be essential to the religious observance of the Jews, and in its absence their religions would cease (Hosea, 3-4). Druid, a magician or sorcerer, priest of the lunar cult aborigines of Albion, as ? priest of the *Dur*, magic bowl or cauldron of the Chaldees.

DUR, TUR

Su.—DUR, TUR, Turn, turn round, return, restore, change, driveback. 3329, M.2114, B.122.

Ak.—*Turru*, *Tāru*, turn, return, come back, restore, give back, change, lock up, drive back. 1189, 1185.

Eg.—*Tur*, to turn from. 825b.

Sk.—*Dhūrv*, to bend.

Gr.—*Tornu-ein*, to turn. *Tro-pos*, a turn.

Lat.—*Torn-āre*, to turn. *Turn-us*, a turn. *Tourn-er*, to turn. F. *Tour*, a turn, around, compass, a bout, a walk. F.

Goth. & Anc. Br.—*Turna*, to turn. I. *Turnera*, a tourney. I.

Nor.—*Tur*, a trip, an excursion. DN. *Trind*, *Trindt*, round, around. DNS.

Ger.—*Turnen*, to turn.

Co. & Celt.—*Tro*, a turn. Co. *Troi*, turn. Cy.

A-S.—*Tyrnan*, to turn. *Trendel*, a ring, a circle, a hoop.

O.E.—*Turnen*, *Tournen*, to turn. *Tour*, to tour.

E.—Turn, to revolve, whirl around, cause to revolve : Turn-about, Turn-back, Turn-coat, Turn-cock, Turn-down, Turn-er, Turn-ery, Turn-ing, Turn-ing lathe, Turn-ing point, Turn-ing tool, Turn-key, Turn-over, Turn-pike, Turn-pike road, Turn-screw, Turn-spit, Turn-stile, Turn-table, Turn-up, Turn-away, Turn-back, Turn-down, Turn-in, Turn off, Turn on, Turn-out, Turn-over, Turn-round, Turn up, Turn upon, Good turn, Ill turn, Take turns. Tour, going round, a circuit : Tour-ist. Tournament, a turn at a game, a bout : Tourney. Tourniquet, a turning, twisting instrument to control bleeding. Trend, to turn or bend away. Trope, a word or expression turned from its proper sense for irony or metaphor. Tropic, one of the two circles in the celestial sphere, on each side of the equator, where the Sun apparently *turns* : Tro-pical, Tro-pically. Trendil, a hoop. Trundle. ? Drive, to urge on ; Drove.

DUR, TUR

Su.—DUR, TUR, Bond, band, rope, tie—Truss. 10,538-9, M.2113, B.122, 481. And see *Dare*, a band or fetter and *Dur*, a tent.

Ak.—*Riksu*, a bond, band, bandage, rope, tie. 965. *Markasu*, a rope, cord, band, tie, lock, bolt.

Eg.—*Ter*, a bandlet. 840a. *Dara(t)*, a bandlet. 884b. *Theru(t)*, a bandlet, a fetter. 858a.

Sk.—*Dora-ka*, a rope. *Dhur*, a yoke.

Lat.—*Tor-tus*, twisted. *Tor-quere*, to twist. *Tor-mentum*, a slinging instrument, an instrument of torture. *Tor-ciare*, twist wrap, tie ; fast. I. *Tor-cis*, a torch. I.

Goth. & Anc. Br.—*Thyr*, bondsman. EI. *Thræll*, a bondsman, serf, a slave. EI. *Tortis*, a torch. I.

Nor.—*Træl*, a bondsman, serf, slave. DN. *Trāl*, a serf. S.

Co. & Celt.—*Dasire*, a bondage. I. *Traust*, a beam. Co.

O.E.—*Trussen*, to bind. *Torture*, a wringing pain. *Trist, Tryst*, a bond or pledge to meet.

E.—Truss, to bind up, fasten: Truss-beam, Truss-ing. Traces, drawing straps. Thrall, a bondsman, serf, slave: Thral-dom, En-thral, En-thral-ment. ? Torch, a light from *twisted* tow or rags dipped in pitch, etc., a flambeau: Torch-bearer, Torch-dance, Torch-light. Torment, torture, anguish, with idea of twisting (?) and see *Dur*, to turn. Torque, a twisting, a necklace of twisted rings: Tor-quate, and see *Dur*, turn. Tortuous, twisted, and see *Dur, Tur*, turn. Tress, a curl or lock of hair, and see *Dur, Tur*, to turn. ? Troth, truth, fidelity, bond, compact: Be-troth, see also Truth, under *Daria*, endure. Trousseau, a bundle, a package. Truce, a temporary bond or agreement between belligerents. Tryst, a bond or pledge to meet.

DUR, TUR, DURU

Su.—DUR, TUR, DURU, Established, settle, stay, sit, dwell, enclosure, a tent, wall, be high, fortress—a Tower. *Dur*, was a prefix of walled cities in Ancient Mesopotamia, e.g., *Dur Bâbili* or Babylon. *Dur Nippuri* or Nipur (Br.8408-9), the chief city of the Sun worship and the site of Udug's votive stone bowl. 10,498-9, 10,523, 10,545, 10,580, M.7981, B.481.

Ak.—*Asâbu*, settle, stay, sit, dwell, establish. 112 f. *Durru, Dûru*, wall, fence, fortress, castle. 267. *Zaratu*, a tent. 298. *Nasu*, be high, lofty. 732.

Eg.—*Thar*, enclose, surround. 851a. *Thar*, be fortified, protected, strong. 851a. *Ter-Ter*, a foot. 840a. *Thar-t*, a fortress, a walled enclosure. 851a. *Ter-t*, stairs. 841b.

Sk.—*Dhruva*, fixed, firm. *Dhruva*, a mountain. *Durga*, a fort, a stronghold.

Gr.—*Tursis*, a tower.

Lat.—*Turris*, a tower. (*Tur-ba*, a crowd of people, a swarm).

Goth. & Anc. Br.—*Turn*, a tower. I. *Torga*, a mart, a market. EI. *Tōra*, to live, to linger. I. (*Tor*, hard. I.). *Thorp*, a village. EI. *Thaurp*, a village. U.

Nor.—*Taarn*, a tower. DN.

Ger.—*Thurm*, a tower. *Dorf*, a village.

Co. & Celt.—*Tūr, Tor*, a tower, a high place. Co. *Drey, Tre*, a walled town, a city. Co. *Trege*, to dwell. Co. *Drē, Trev*, a village, a house. Co. *Tre*, a dwelling. Cy. *Twr*, a town. Cy. *Torr*, a tower, lofty hill. G. *Tor*, a castle. I. *Dreyas*, tarried. Co. *Thor*, durance, confinement. S(JD).

A-S.—*Tur, Torr*, a tower, a fort. *Træf*, a tent. *Thorp*, a village.

O.E.—*Tower*, a tower. *Thorp*, a village.

E.—Tower, a lofty building, a fort, to be lofty: Tower-ed, Tower-ing, Tower-y, Tur-ret, Tur-reted. Tor, a tower-like rock, especially in hill-names in Devon and Derbyshire. Tarry, dwell, stay, linger, loiter. -*Thorp*, -*Thorpe*, -*Trop* and -*Dorf*, suffix in place-names: Al-thorp, Bishop-thorpe, Copmans-thorp, Il-thorp, Wils-trop, Dussel-dorf, etc., etc., see TWP.165 f. *Tre-*, "Town" or "Dwelling," prefix on Cornish and Welsh place and personal names. Tre-degar, etc., and in the old adage:

"By *Tre*, Pol and Pen
You may know the Cornish men."

For this *Tre*, "town" prefix or affix in place-names elsewhere in Britain than in Cornwall and Wales, and on the Continent, Treves, etc., see TWD.240. Dur-ance, confinement within walls, imprisonment: Duress. Durance, lasting, enduring: established, permanent: Durable, Dur-ableness, Dur-ability, Dur-ably Dur-ation.

DUR, TUR

Su.—DUR, TUR, Prince, king, the great, lofty.—Tyrant. 10,576, M.7992, B.481. *Dur-max* or *Tur-max*=mighty king, wherein *max*=mighty, see *Max, Makh*, mighty.

Ak.—*Rubû*, a prince, a king. the great, lofty, 945. *Sarru*, king.

Eg.—*Tu*, the king. 823a. *Dar-ina*, lords, nobles. 867b. *Tar, Tara*, honour, renown. 840a.

Gr.—*Tur-annos*, lord, master, absolute sovereign, later a tyrant, a usurper.

Lat.—*Tyrr-anus*, lord, master. *Tyran*, a tyrant F.

Goth. & Anc. Br.—*Drottinn*, lord, master. EI. *Dyrd, Tir*, glory, renown. EI.

Co. & Celt.—*Teyrn*, a prince. Co.

A-S.—*Tir*, glory.

O.E.—*Tiraunt*, a tyrant.

E.—Tyrant, absolute monarch, a despot: Tyr-annic, Tyrannical, Tyr-annically, Tyr-annous, Tyr-anny.

DURA

Su.—DURA ('*Ukû*), "The *Dura*, nation, host," presumably identical with "The *Akaia* nation of *Dura*, city-land"—The Dorians of Troy. 5915, CIWA.IV.12, 19 and 28, 23a. And see *Akaia* and *Dardannu*.

Ak.—*Kissatnisi*, the host or multitudinous nation. *Tirit Kissat nisi*, or the mother nation of *Tirit*, as applied to the *Akaians* of *Dura* city.

Eg.—*Dardaniu*, a Mediterranean people. 885a.

Sk.—*Dārada*, a Scythic (Gothic) tribe in Epics. *Turvasu* and allied *Druhyu*, two of the five tribes of the Aryans in the Vedas. *Darva* or *Dara* clan in *Saki*-land with Sumerian seals, see WISD.94 f.

Gr.—*Trōos, Trōios,* a Trojan. *Troia, Troiē,* Troy.
Lat.—*Trōs, Troius, Trojanus,* a Trojan. *Troja,* city of Troy. *Tri-novantes* or *Tri-noantes,* or people of New Troy as a name for early Londoners. (See WPOB.407 f.).
Goth. & Anc. Br.—*Thrud*-heim, the home of Thor in the Eddas. *Troe-Noey,* or "New Troy," name for London in Norse Sagas. (See WPOB.407 f.).
Co. & Celt.—*Thorians,* the east or orient. Co.
E.—Troy, the famous Aryan city in Ionia. Trojan or Dorian, native of Troy. "New Troy," the name traditionally given by King Brutus about 1100 B.C. to his new city on the site of London, is confirmed by the Roman name of *Tri-noantes* or *Tri-novantes* for the people of that neighbourhood, and by the Norse Saga name of Troe-Noey apparently for London. See WPOB.156 f., 175, 407 f.

DURA

Su.—**DURA,** Draw together, draught animals—Drive. Pictured by the Horse and Ass sign. (211), plus the sign *Dura,* draw together, side, beside, "and" (412). 4996, 9456, PSL.91. And see *Dura,* a fetter, *Dur,* to turn, drive back, and *Dur,* a rope.
Ak.—*Agalu,* swift footed, horse, ass, bullock, willing to obey. 14.
Eg.—*Tur,* to turn from. 825b. *Tur,* part of a waggon. 825b. (? Traces or drawing-straps). *Zaāri,* to drive away. 896b.
Sk.—*Dhur,* a yoke, and figuratively the pole of the carriage and the load or burden. *Dhri,* bear, carry.
Goth. & Anc. Br.—*Draga,* to draw, pull. EI. *Drātti,* pulling a draught. I. *Drifa,* to drive. EI. *Dragan,* draw. U.
Nor.—*Drage,* draw, pull. DN. *Draga,* draw. S. *Drǎg,* a sledge or dray. S. Drive, drive. DN. *Drif-va,* drive. S.
Ger.—*Trieben,* drive.
Co. & Celt.—*Dhora,* bring. Co.
A-S.—*Dragan,* to draw. *Drifan,* to drive.
O.E.—*Drag, Draze, Drawe,* to draw. *Driuen,* to drive.
E.—Draw, to pull along or drag, draw lines, etc. : Draw-able, Draw-back, Draw-bridge, Draw-er, Draw-ing, Draw-ing-board, Draw-ing master, Draw-ing paper, Draw-ing pencil, Draw-net, Draw a blank, Draw it mild, Draw off, Draw on, Draw out, Draw rein, Draw up, Over-drawn, etc. Drag, to draw by force : Drag-net. Drag, a mail-coach. Drain, to draw off. Draught, act of drawing, draw out : Draughts, Draft-board, Draught-y, Draf-ty, Draf-tiness. Dray, a low cart for heavy goods : Dray-horse. Drive, to urge on : Driv-er, Driv-ing, Drif-t, Drover, Drove, a drive of cattle.

DUR-ABBA

Su.—**DUR-ABBA,** Sea or Ocean as "The House of the Waters." 11,474 and see *Abba, Agia,* ocean. *Dur,* water and *Mer, Muru,* the sea or "watery space." The Sumerian and Akkad names of the chief seas are (cp. MD. 1175) : *D. rapastu,* "The Great Sea," or Mediterranean. *D. Saplitu,* "The Lower Sea of Sunrise or the East," The Persian Gulf and Indian Ocean. *D. elenitu* or *ša šalam šamši,* "The Upper Sea of Sunset or the Western Sea," Mediterranean. *D. Saplitu šu eret šamši,* "The Western Lower Sea" or Red Sea. *D. ša mat Amurri,* "Sea of the Land of the Amorites," The Levant. *D. ša mat Khatti,* "Sea of the Land of the Khatti or Hittites," the N.E. of the Mediterranean. *D. ša šulmi šamši adi mat Mušri,* "The Sea of the Land of Egypt," The Libyan Sea of the Mediterranean. *D. ša mat Nairi,* Lake Van. *D. ša Napax šamši,* Caspian. *D. ša šulmi Šamši,* The Black Sea or Euxine (see *Agia*).
Ak.—*Tāmtu, Tām-du,* the ocean. 1173.
Eg.—*Uazur,* the sea, ocean, "The Great Green Water," the Mediterranean. 151a.
Sk.—*Samu-dra,* the ocean. *Darya,* the sea. IP. and see WISD.11 f.
E.—*Darya,* Indo-Persian name for the Sea or Ocean, and the source of the name. *Daro,* in the name "Mohenjo-Daro," the modern name of the site of the Great Sumerian seaport city of about 3100 B.C. on the Indus, yielding many inscribed Sumerian seals figured and deciphered in WISD.

DURAN, TURAN

Su.—**DURAN, TURAN** (*An*-), Lord Bēl of the (Magic) Bowl (*Dur*), a title of Induru. The Lord of the Land (En-Sakh). Pictured by the Magic Bowl with the addition of -*an* and the prefix "Lord" (*An*), 3331 and see *Dar, Dur* and *Dūr, Tur,* Induru or Thor.
Ak.—*Bēl ša,* The Lord of the Jar. (*ša*).
Eg.—(*Taher-sta-nef,* a title of Osiris. 816b. —*Tahar*=oven or furnace, a term in the Gothic for the magic bowl as a cauldron).
Sk.—*Dūr,* the deity of Life (*Prāna*).
Goth. & Anc. Br.—*Durinn,* a title of King Thor or Sig, the capturer of the magic stone bowl or cauldron in the E.
E.—*Durinn,* title of King Thor in the Gothic Eddas.

DURIA, DUUR, TAUR

Su.—**DURIA, DUUR, TAUR,** Duration, endure, everlasting. 6660, 6695. See *Daria, Dūr,* duration, endure, everlasting.
Ak.—*Darū,* endure, everlasting. 266 f.
Eg., Sk., Gr., Lat., Goth. & Anc. Br., Nor., Ger.,

Co. & Celt., A-S. and O.E.—See details in these languages under *Daria, Dŭr,* endure.

E.—Dure, enduring, everlasting, true, trust, etc. See *Daria, Dur,* Dure, endure.

DUTTU, DŬTTU, DU

Su.—DUTTU, DŬTTU, DU, Talker, one who speaks or proclaims, brings messages or reports, a plotter—a Tout. Picured by two, human heads with projecting tongue, i.e., two persons talking together. 506, 570, 572-3 and cp. 559, B.15, doubled. And see *Kir Kir,* a crier.

Ak.—*Dabibu,* a talker. 239. *Dabābu,* speak, proclaim, plot, intrigue, bring message or report. 237-9.

Eg.—*Tu,* to speak. 823a. *Theftenn,* a messenger 854b. *Tchedd,* to speak, to say. 913a. *Thest,* a plot, crafty design. 860b.

Sk.—*Dūta,* a messenger. *Dhutio,* crafty, subtle, cheat, deceiver. P. (Sanskrit, *Dhūrti*).

Goth. & Anc. Br.—*Tauta,* to mutter. I. *Taut,* to manage a person. I. *Teyda,* an abusive person, vile, wicked. EI.

Co. & Celt.—*Teaut,* the tongue (Armoric). *Theveth,* a curse. Co. *Tithia,* to hiss. Co. *Tretury,* treachery. Co. *Tod,* a fox. S.

A-S.—*Teōthan, Tihtan,* to solicit, allure, entice, draw-on, persuade, provoke, accuse. *Theotun,* to howl.

E.—Tout, to canvass, as a messenger, for custom, to solicit unscrupulously for profit: Tout-er, Tout-ing. Toady, a mean servile flattery, sycophant, hanger on: Toady-er, Toady-ism.

E

E.—changing dialectically or inflectively to A and I.

E letter is absent in Egyptian alphabetic script, which is written without vowels except *a, ā, i* and *u,* the short vowel *a* (arbitrarily rendered by Egyptologists, *e*) being inherent in every consonant as in retrograde Phœnician, Sanskrit, etc.

E

Su.—E, Water, reservoir, irrigation canal, ditch. Pictured by angular irrigation canal. 5842-4, B.263. And see *A,* water and *Eku,* lake, irrigation canal.

Ak.—*Mu,* water. *Iku,* reservoir, lake, water, ditch. 33.

Eg.—*Ā,* a dam, dike or ditch. 106a. *U,* a kind of well or spring in the Great Oasis. 144a. *Uau,* a water conduit. 145a.

Sk.—*E,* n. of Vishnu, the Sun of the Waters. (See WISD.82 f., 86 f., 128 f.).

Lat.—*Eau,* water. F.

O.E.—*Eye,* etc., river-names.

E.—*Eau,* "Water," in Eau-de-Cologne, Eau-de-Nîl, Eau-de-Vie, etc., from the French. *E, Ey* and *Eye, Wye* and *Yeo,* river-names.

E

Su.—E, Great, high, full grown. Also used as a verbal prefix or infix. 5845-6, B.263.

Ak.—*Rabū,* great. *Sadū,* high. *Supū,* full grown. 1079 and LSG.212.

Eg.—*Ā,* a great one, chief. 107a. *Āā,* great, mighty, great person. 106a. *Ā,* to grow, wax (of the moon). 107a. *An,* full, totality. 2b.

Goth. & Anc. Br.—*Ei, Ey, Æ,* ever, eternity, everlasting. EI.

Co. & Celt.—*E,* verbal prefix in Co., e.g., *Dew, e-wyr,* God knows.

A-S.—(? *Ge-* verbal prefix).

O.E.—*Eye,* a brood.

E.—E=great, in E-normous or great, beyond normal: Enormously. *E-,* intensive prefix in words, e.g.: E-squire, E-special, E-scutcheon, E-state.

E

Su.—E, Speak, cry out, exclaim. 5843, M.4157, PSL.93, B.263.

Ak.—*Qabū, Qibu,* speak, cry out, proclaim, announce. 902.

Eg.—*Ā, Ai,* to speak, cry out. 106a.

Sk.—*E !* interjection of recollection, addressing censure or contempt.

Gr.—*Ea !* exclamation of wonder or displeasure.

A-S.—*Ea !* interjection of surprise.

O.E.—*Ey !* interjection of surprise. *Aye,* yes.

E.—Eh ! interjection of surprise. Aye, yea, yes.

E

Su.—E, House (? contraction for *Es,* house, q.v.). 6238, B.281.

Ak.—*Bitu,* house.

Eg.—*Ā(t), Āā(t),* a house. 106a, 107a. *Ai,* a house. 32a.

E

Su.—E, Rise, go out, go forth, of the Sun—the Dawn in the East. Also causative to cause, to go. Pictured by the Sun and a Foot as sunrise, the coming forth of the Sun. 7873, and see *Eussi, Ezi,* "the East" and *Eri,* going forth.

Ak.—*Aṣu,* rise, go forth (of the Sun), go out, cause to go forth. 84. *Elū,* to go up. 41.

Eg.—*Ai, Au,* to go. 30a, 31a. *Aia,* to go away. 144a. *Ahez,* to dawn. 77a. *Aab-t,* the east. 18b.
Sk.—*E,* to go near, to enter. *Eva,* going, moving. *Ush,* the dawn.
Gr.—*Eaō,* let go. *Iōeimi,* to go. *Eōs,* the dawn.
Lat.—*Eo,* to go. *E, Ex,* out of form. *Ēōs,* the dawn.
Co. & Celt.—*A,* out of. Co.
E.—Eoan, relating to the dawn. East, and see *Eussi, Ezi,* the east. *E-,* prefix, "out from." in words: E-dict, E-ducate, E-ffect, E-ject, E-mend, E-merge, E-rupt, E-vade, E-volution, etc., etc., etc., and see *Exi,* go forth.

E

Su.—*E,* Take away, curse—privative. 7882.
Ak.—*Niśu,* take away, curse. 733-6.
Eg.—*Aāh,* to hold back, restrain. 30a. *Au,* to cut off. 31b. *Ua,* to drive away. 145a. *Ua, Uai,* to destroy. 145a.
Sk.—*A,* privative.
Goth. & Anc. Br.—*E, Ei, Eg.,* negative prefix, not. EI. *Æfe,* never. EI.
Nor.—*Ei,* not. DN. *Eg,* nor. S.
E.—Eh! execration. *Ex-,* privative in Ex-army, Ex-emperor, Ex-king, Ex-mayor, Ex-provost, etc.

E

Su.—*E,* Here, unto, to—and used as a prefix 5847, B.263.
Ak.—*Ana,* unto, here. Cp. LSG.224.
Eg.—*Ā, Āā,* here. 107a.
Sk.—*E, Eta,* to go or come near.
Lat.—*Ea,* there. *Eo,* thither, that place.
E.—? Here.

EDIN, ETIN

Su.—EDIN, ETIN, Plain, field, desert. Pictured by what are considered to be a network of irrigation canals and marsh land, see figs in WISD.35 f. 4526, B.181.
Ak.—*Edinu,* plain, field, desert. 21.
Eg.—*Aten, Iten,* ground, earth, farm. 13b, 99a. *Aaut, Jaut,* waste land. 16b. *Atenu* or *Jtenu,* rebels, fiends. 99b.
Sk.—*Edin, Otin,* title of Sindh, desert of Lower Indus, on Sumerian seals, etc. See WISD. 7, 27 f., 33, 49, 57, 102 f.
Goth. & Anc. Br.—*Audn,* wilderness, desert. EI. *Eydi,* waste, desert. EI. *Auths,* wilderness, desert. U. *Jötun,* or *Iötun,* giant enemies to Thor-Adam in the Eddas or Edenites.
Ger.—*Öden, Ode,* waste, wilderness.
Co. & Celt.—(*Uun,* the downs. Co.).
E.—Aden, name presumably cognate with Chaldean *Edinu,* a desert. The abode of the *Jötuns* or *Iötuns,* malignant "giants" of the desert in the Eddas or "Garden of Eden."

EDIN, ETIN

Su.—EDIN, ETIN, Lofty temple, house, high place. Historical Sumerian shrines in Mesopotamia, c.3100 B.C. See details in WISD.35 f. Pictured by same sign as foregoing. Name is supposed to be probably compounded of *E,* "water" and *din* or *tin,* "life" or Water of Life. PSL.95, 4527-29, M.3048, B.181. And see *Ru, Rum,* sacred place.
Ak.—*Sirum* lofty of temple, etc., and an epithet of the goddess Isthar, etc. 889. *Bitu,* temple, house. *Bumātu,* high place. 172. *Bamāti (Du),* epithet of goddess Zagga (? Ishtar). 172.
Eg.—? *Aden, Aten, Aaten,* "disc of the Sun." 26b, 27b, 98b. The cult of the Pharaoh Aken Aten. *Uden,* an altar. *Udeni,* a shrine at Memphis.
Sk.—*Edin,* a historical Sumerian Sun Temple of an oracle priestess in Indus Valley, c. 3050 B.C., with inscribed seals, see WISD.33 f.
Goth. & Anc. Br.—*Jötun-heim* or home of the *Jötuns* in *Iord* (Ur), the seat of the Serpent-priestess of the oracular Magic Bowl captured by Thor in the Eddas.
E.—*Jötun-heim,* the home of the malign enemies of Thor, with shrine of the oracular Serpent-priestess Jörmun of the Magic Bowl and Tree of Knowledge in the Gothic Eddas. ? The Garden of *Eden* of the Semitic legend.

EGA, EGURA

Su.—EGA, EGURA, Dark or Black water (*A-gi*), high tide, flood-water. 11,593. On *gur* syllable, cp. 6105, and see *Agia,* flood-water, *Eku* and *Esa,* forest stream.
Ak.—*Agū,* high water, flood, current. 13. Apparently connected with *Agū,* full orb of moon, with reference to tides. Cp. 13.
Eg.—*Ag,* stream, flood. 95b. *Aaki,* flood. 22a. *Aukh,* flood. 31a. *Uazur,* the ocean. 151a.
Sk.—*Uksh,* to sprinkle.
Gr.—*Ōke-anos,* the ocean. *Axe-nos,* the Euxine Sea.
Lat.—*Aqua,* water, the sea. *Euxine,* the Black Sea.
Goth. & Anc. Br.—*Ægir,* the ocean. E. *Ægir, Ægi,* ocean. I. *Ekin,* a stream flowing from the basin of the Gel lake (*Hver-gel-mir*), in the Eddas.
Nor.—*Ukana,* water. L.
Co. & Celt.—*Isge,* water. Co. *Eigian,* ocean. Cy. *Ach, Oich,* water. G. *Usig,* water, river. G. *Aiger,* ocean. GI.
A-S.—*Eg, Egor, Eagor,* the sea, water, sea-stream.
O.E.—*Eagre,* flood.
E.—Aqua, water, Aqua-tic, etc., Ocean, Ocean-ic, etc. Eux-ine or Black Sea. Ægean Sea, be-

tween Asia Minor and Greece. Eagre, tidal bore. And see *Agia*, ocean.

EGI

Su.—EGI, 1st pers. pron. I. (Through its ideograph). 10,501, 10,522.
Ak.—*Onak*. I. P.(BP14). *Anaku*. I. 70.
Eg.—*A* or *Ja*, 1st pers, pron. I, me, my. 15*a*. *Anukkhu*, I, myself. 60*b*. (from the Akkad).
Sk.—*Aha(m)*, I. *Aza(m)*, I. Z.
Gr.—*Egō*, I.
Lat.—*Ego*, I. *Je*, I. F.
Goth. & Anc. Br.—*Eg, Ek*, I. EI. *Ik*, I. U.
Nor.—*Jeg*, I. DN. *Jag*. S.
Ger.—*Ich*, I.
Co. & Celt.—*Agan*, ours. Co. *I*, I. Cy.
A-S.—*Ic*. I.
O.E.—*Ik, Ich*, I.
E.—I, 1st pers. pron. Ego, "I": Ego-ism, Ego-ist, Ego-istic, Ego-tism, Ego-tist, Ego-tistic, Ego-tistically.

EGIR

Su.—EGIR, Backwards, future (forwards), behind, after, far off—Vagrant. Pictured by a headless human body walking away. 4999, 5001. And see *Er*, to go, to wander.
Ak.—*Arku*, backwards, behind, after, future. 100. *Arkatu*, back, also future, far off. 101.
Eg.—*Ju, Au*, backwards. 30*b*. *Jua, Aua*, to travel. 32*a*. *Asa, Uz*, to travel. 83*a*, 192*b*.
Lat.—*Uagor, Uageri*, to wander. *Uagus*, wandering. *Vaguer*. F. *Vagare*, to wander, roam. I.
Goth. & Anc. Br.—*Vagr*, to go and come on the way, roam. EI. *Vegna*, to proceed. EI.
Nor.—*Usikker*, vague. DN.
Co. & Celt.—*Udzhe*, afterwards. Co. *Ais*, back, backwards. GI.
O.E.—*Vague*, to wander.
E.—Vagary, a wandering. Vagrant, a wanderer: Vagr-ancy, Vag-abond, Vag-ue, Vag-uely, Extra-vag-ance, Extra-vag-ant, Extra-vagantly.

EKU

Su.—EKU, Lake, irrigation canal, ditch. 5838, 5841. And see E, water, *Ega*, tidal water, and *Esu*, stream.
Ak.—*Iku*, lake, ditch, canal. 33.
Eg., Sk., Gr., Lat., Goth. & Anc. Br., Nor. and Ger.—See details under *Ega*, flood-water.
Co. & Celt.—*Ik, Ick, Yk*, common suffix of creek names in Cornwall, e.g., Pordin-ik, Pradn-ik, Portyss-ik.
E.—Aqua, water, see above, *Ega*, flood-water.

EL, IL

Su.—EL, IL, Shine, be bright, splendour, pure. Pictured by the Moon and the sign for female, implying that the shining Moon was considered to be female. 1172 f., B.507. And see *Ar*, to shine.
Ak.—*Ellu*, shining bright, splendour, pure. 41. *Abābu*, bright, clean, pure. 5.
Eg.—*Hel, Her*, a furnace. 499*b*. *Ul, Ur*, flame, fire. 174*a*. *Ul, Ur*, the grave. 174*b*.
Sk.—*Ul*, to burn. *Ulasa*, shining, bright, splendid. *Ulkū*, fire, falling from heaven, to set on fire, a torch. *Āli*, pure.
Gr.—'*Elē*-, the light or heat of the Sun. '*Eibē*, the Sun's warmth, warmth of fire. *Helios*, the Sun.
Goth. & Anc. Br.—*Yl*, warmth of the Sun and fire. EI. *Jōl*, winter solstice festival or return of the sunshine about 23rd Dec. *Eld*, fire. EI. *Elda*, to light a fire. EI. *Heilag*, holy, sacred. EI. *Hel*, hell, death. EI. *Val-hōl*, "Val-halla," the abode of Wodan's dead. *Halja*, hell. U.
Nor.—*Ild*, fire. DN. *Öld*, fire. S. *Hellig*, holy. DN. *Helig*, holy. S. *Hel-vede*, hell.
Ger.—*Hell*, bright, clear.
Co. & Celt.—*Heol*, the Sun. Br. *Houl*, the Sun. Co. *El, Ail*, an angel. Co. *Joul*, the Devil. Co.
A-S.—*Helle*, clear, bright. *Hælg*, light. *Æl, Æld*, fire. *Hælig*, holy. *Hell*, the grave, the tomb.
O.E.—*Halo*, a halo. *Yule*, Christmas. *Holi*, holy. *Helle*, hell.
E.—Halo, a luminous ring round the Sun or Moon, and around heads of Saints: Halation, in photography. Helios, the Sun: Helio-graph, Helio-grapher, Helio-graphy, Helio-gravure, Helio-latry, Helio-logy, Heliometer, Helio-scope, Helio-stat, Helio-trope, Helio-type, Hel-ium. Yule, the great Ancient Briton and Gothic festival of the winter solstice or return of the sunshine about 23rd Dec., which was transferred by Christianity to Christmas. Yule-log or Yule-stock, the log for the Yule fire. Hallow, to make pure or holy: Hallow-e'en, evening of All Saints' Day, Hallow-mass, the festival of All Saints on 1st Nov. Holy, pure, sacred, Holi-ness, Holy Grail, Holy Rood, Holy Thursday, Holywater, Holy writ, Holy city, Holy communion, Holy Land, Holy orders, Holy places, Holy quest (for the Grail), Holy war; and see *Alal*, whole. Hell, Hades, the underground place of the dead or Lower World of the ancients, or the place of evil spirits and everlasting torment of the wicked by fire in Christianity: Hell-fire, Hell-cat, Hell-hound, Hell-ish, Valhalla. St Elmo's Fire.

EL, IL

Su.—EL, IL, Jubilate, rejoice, cry out—Holiday. 11,174, B.507.
Ak.—*Alulu*, rejoice, jubilate, cry aloud. 46.
Eg.—*Helta, Herta*, a feast or festival. 449*b*.

SUMER-ARYAN DICTIONARY

Hali, Hari, to please or gratify the heart. 442.

Sk.—*Elā,* pastime, merriment. *Elāya,* to be merry. *Hōlō,* a chief festival of the Hindus. *Ullas,* to sport, play, be merry. *Ululi,* a cry of exultation and joy. *Halahalā,* a cry of applause.

Gr.—*Eilapinē,* a feast. *Heleleu,* a loud cry. *Ulan,* to howl.

Lat.—*Ulul-are,* to howl (from the Akkad). *Joli,* gay, jolly. F.

Goth. & Anc. Br.—*Helg,* a feast, a holiday, revel, EI. *Hœla, Hœla,* to praise. I. *Yla,* to howl, to make a noise, chiefly of animals. EI.

Co. & Celt.—*Halan,* calends, the 1st day of the month. Co.

A-S.—*Hil-song,* a drum.

O.E.—*Ioli, Ioly,* jolly.

E.—Holiday, a festival day, day of amusement or idleness: The Holidays. Jolly, gay, merry, revelling: Joll-ity, Joll-iness. Hail! exclamation of meeting or praise: Alleluiah! from the Akkad. Halloa, Hallo! stop, wait: Halloo, Halloo-baloo, Howl, Yowl, Yell, chiefly of animals.

ELA

Su.—*ELA,* Deep Sea, flood, a well. Pictured by Water sign + "steep" or "deep." (*Kala* or *Astu*). 11,534, 11,537-8, PSL.98.

Ak.—*Milu,* flood, high tide, water, deep sea. 544. *Inu,* a well. 66.

Eg.—*Uli, Uri,* flood, a mass of water. 174b. *Hal, Har,* a pond, lake, sheet of water. 442a.

Sk.—*Āli,* a ditch. *Hala,* water.

Gr.—*'Als* or *Hals,* the sea. *Hab-Kuōn* or sea-dog, also king-fisher of deep-sea blue.

Goth. & Anc. Br.—*Äll, Hyl,* a narrow channel or hole in sea or in a river. EI. *Alda,* a wave in calm weather. EI. *Velle,* to surge or well up, to boil. EI.

Nor.—*Vaeld,* a spring.

Ger.—*Welle,* a wave, a surge.

Co. & Celt.—*Olen,* salt. BrI. *Helu,* brine. Co. *Haloin, Halein,* salt. Co. *Haloiner,* a salter. Co. *Hel,* a marsh, a river. Co.

A-S.—*Weallan,* to surge or well up.

O.E.—*Welle,* a well or spring. *Halcyon,* serene (of days).

E.—Hal-cyon or "sea-dog" or king-fisher: Hal-cyon days, or serene days. Halo-gen, a term originally for substances produced from Sea-salt: Hal-oid, like Sea salt. Hole, a cavity, see *Hal,* or excavation. Well, to surge up, a spring or fountain or spring of water: Well-boring, Well-bucket, Well-curb, Well-head, Well-spring, Wells, a spa name.

ELA-MU, TUM

Su.—*ELA-MU, TUM,* Mount, rise, go up, be high—Hill, Alp. Pictured by a flying insect with extended wings giving idea of "mount up, be high," see representations in WISD.81, 89, 92, 9009, 9013-4, B.387. And see *Al, Il,* high, lofty.

Ak.—*Elū,* mount, be high, rise, go up (of hills, etc.). 41. *Elamu,* high. 47.

Eg.—*Hel, Her, Hal,* a mountain. 442a, 449b. *Hel, Her,* lofty. 450a.

Sk.—*Īla,* the earth.

Lat.—*Al-ius,* high, deep. *Al-pēs,* the Alps. *Ala,* a wing.

Goth. & Anc. Br.—*Hall,* a hill, a slope, a boulder. EI. *Hallus,* a rock. U.

Co. & Celt.—*Ehual,* high. Co. *Als, Aules,* a cliff, ascent. Co. *Hāl,* a hill. Co. *Ail,* a rock. I. *Allt,* cliff. Cy. *Alt,* height, a cliff. I. *Ailt,* high. GI. *Alp,* high mountain. G.

A-S.—*Alpis,* the Alps.

E.—Alp, high mountain, by phonetic interchange of *p* for *m*: Alps, Alp-ine, Alp-inist Alp-enstock. Elam, or "The high-lands," a province of Persia bordering the S.E. of Mesopotamia. Hill, from the Akkad, *Elū* or Sumerian *Al* and *Il,* high.

ELIM, ILIM

Su.—*ELIM, ILIM,* Leader of the herd, a he-goat or stag, ram or bull, a title of Lord Bēl or Zax (Zeus, Indara or Thor), of whom those animals are symbols. See WPOB.251, 334 f., for representations from Sumerian and Phœnician seals and Gothic monuments. Pictured by head of a stag or ram. 8882-7 B.374, PSL.99.

Ak.—*Ditanu,* a leader, a he-goat, ram or bull. 271. *Bēl,* the Lord Zax [Zeus]. *Kibtu,* exalted. *Sarru,* king.

Eg.—*Ail,* a stag. 2a.

Sk.—*Aila,* title of "King Purū of the Sun (-cult)." See *Bur,* title of King Thor.

Gr.—*'Alkē,* kind of antelope. *'Ellos,* a young deer.

Goth. & Anc. Br.—*Bil,* title of Thor in E. *Elg,* an elk. I.

Nor.—*Elg,* elk. S.

A-S.—*Eolh,* an elk.

O.E.—*Elk,* elk.

E.—Bil, title of Thor in the Gothic Eddas and his He-goat symbol. See WPOB. refs. in para. 1. ? "Billy," title of a he-goat. ? "Ilim" source of "William," re Bil. Elk or Eland, the arctic stag.

EME

Su.—*EME,* Tongue, language, mouth. Pictured by a mouth containing a tongue. 835-6, B.34, PSL.99.

71

Ak.—*Lisānu,* a tongue, language, tongues or nation. 499. *Pū,* mouth, issue from mouth, words, tongue. 787.
Eg.—? *Am,* understand. 6a.
Sk.—*Aum! Ōm!* sacred, mystic syllable of assent, "the root of speech." *Im,* particle of affirmation.
Gr.—*Oimē,* a tale, a poem. (*Amen,* verily).
Lat.—*Omen,* a prognostication. (*Lingua,* a tongue from Akkad, *Lisānu* ?).
Goth. & Anc. Br.—*Emia, Emya, Ymia,* to howl. EI. *Ōm,* voice. EI. *Ōma,* to resound. E.
Co. & Celt.—*Amane,* a kiss (*re* mouth). Co. *Umhm!* exclamation of assent. S.
O.E.—*Hem! Ahem! Hem! Amen!* verily, exclamation of assent. (*Puke,* to vomit, from Akkad, *pū,* the mouth ?).
E.—*Ahem! Hem!* a half-coughed interjection to call attention, or introductory to speaking: Hem-ming, to Hem and Haw. Amen, word of assent. Yammer, to mutter or whimper. Puke, Spit, Spue, to vomit, from the Akkad *Pū,* a mouth. ? Lingual, Language from the Akkad *Lisānu,* a tongue nasalized.

ĒN, ĒNI, IN, INI

Su.—*ĒN, ĒNI, IN, INI,* Lord, king, the high one, noble, applied to god, kings and priests. Pictured by a high-backed chair or throne (as the enthroned). See representation in WISD.57, 2807-8, 2810, 2813, 2816, B.112. And see *Anna,* lord, king.
Ak.—*Bēlu,* lord. *Elū,* be high. 41. *Ēnu,* lord. 67. *Šārru,* king.
Eg.—*Ansu,* a king. 63a. *Ānz,* a king. 128b. *Āuz-mer,* ancient title of chiefs, governors. 128b.
Sk.—*Indo,* lord, king, chief, in Pali. *Indra, Endra,* in Sanskrit.
Gr.—*Anax,* lord, a king, applied to gods, esp. Apollo, the Sun-god, also to earthly kings, lords and chief officers of State.
Goth. & Anc. Br.—*Yngl-*ing or *Yngl-*clan, an ancestral clan of Thor or Ottar in the Eddas, from whom the kings of Norway claim descent.
Co. & Celt.—*Enchin-ethel,* a giant. Co.
A-S.—*Ent,* a giant. (*Engle, Angle,* the Angles).
E.—*Yngl* clan (or *Yngl-ing*) of the Gothic Eddas, an ancestral ruling clan of King Thor in the Eddas, from which the kings of Norway claim descent in the Yngling Saga. ? *Yngl,* an ancestral Gothic clan of the Angles, *re* the Ingae-vones of Tacitus. See WPOB. 186 f. ? *Anak,* title of the Amorites in Phœnicio-Palestine in the Old Testament. ? *Inca,* title of the ancient priest-kings in the dead cities of Peru.

EN

Su.—*EN,* Enchantment, Incantation, exorcism. Pictured by a Star within the crescent Moon. 10,857, B.491. And see *An,* negative prefix.
Ak.—*Siptu,* incantation, exorcism. 1095.
Eg.—*An, Yn,* turn back, drive away, repel. 57b.
Sk.—*Ene,* rescue from evil, misfortune and sin.
Gr.—(*An,* negative prefix). (*Ainos,* dread, terrible). (*Anti-*, against, hostile).
Goth. & Anc. Br.—*Ōn,* hope. EI. (*And-,* against, hostile. EI.).
Co. & Celt.—(*Un, An,* negative prefix. GI.).
A-S.—(*And-,* negative prefix, "against").
E.—En-chantment, Incantation or exorcism by Stars and Moon, ∴ "white" magic spells. (? Endor, witch).

EN, IN

Su.—*EN, IN,* And, with, together with, unto, until. 2809, B.112.
Ak.—*Adi,* and, with, unto, to, until, as long as. 17.
Eg.—*Anah,* and. 32b. *An, Yn, In,* to, so that. 56a. *Yn, an,* carry [=unto]. G.16.
Sk.—*Ann, Anti,* to, in the presence of, near.
Gr.—*En,* moreover, upon, among, within, near, at. *Anti,* before, over against.
Lat.—*Ante,* before (over against).
Goth. & Anc. Br.—*Enda,* and, even, moreover (=and). EI. *En,* but, than. EI.
Ger.—*Und,* and.
A-S.—*Ond, And,* and.
O.E.—*An, And,* if.
E.—And, copulative conjunction, together, with.

EN-DUR-RA

Su.—*EN-DUR-RA,* Endura of the Flood, a variant title of Induru, Indara or the Gothic Eindri(d) title of Thor. 2900.

ENE

Su.—*ENE,* 3rd personal independent pronouns He, she, it; and also "this, that." 5866, P.102.
Ak.—*Šu,* he, she, it, this, that. 992 f.
Sk.—*Ena,* pronoun, basis for 3rd pers. pronoun. P. and S.
Goth. & Anc. Br.—*Hann, Hon, Hūn,* he, she. EI. *Inn, Hinn,* the article "the." EI.
Co. & Celt.—*En, E, Hane-ih,* he. Co. *En,* the for "an." Co. *Ene,* they. Co.
E.—? *Any,* indefinite pronoun, some one. The indefinite form of "one." See *Ana,* one: Anyone, Anything.

ENE

Su.—*ENE* Plural suffix of nouns. LSG.82.
Eg.—Vestiges in Egyptian, e.g., *Y, I, En,* we. (ME.16).

SUMER-ARYAN DICTIONARY

Ger.— *-en*, plural suffix.
E.— *-en*, plural suffix, e.g., in Ox, Ox-en; Child, Children; Man, Men, Woman, Women.

ER, ERI, IR

Su.—**ER, ERI, IR**, Hurry, go swiftly, hasten, bring swiftly, take swiftly, a sling. Pictures a Sling with stones, and thus essentially identical with Egyptian hiero., see pl. III. 5379-81, 5385, 5390, B.229. And see *Ar, Ara*, to hurry.
Ak.—*Alāk hamṭu*, go swiftly, hasten. 321. *Tabulu hamṭu*, bring quickly. *Irru*, a sling. 93.
Eg.— *Yr, Ar*, a sling. G., figs. 41, 43. Pictured by a sling essentially identical with the Sumerian, see pl. III. *Yri, Ari*. to visit, 65a. *Yr, Ar*, to, towards. 65a.
Sk.—*Ara*, swift, going. *Ir*, to go. *Er*, to bring near. *Ri*, to go. *Arvant*.
Lat.—*Ire*, to go, wander.
Goth. & Anc. Br.—*Ör, Örr*, swift, an arrow. EI. *Hurr*, a whirring noise (as of a sling stone). EI. *Ärr*, a messenger. EI. *Ern*, brisk. EI. *Airus*, a messenger. U.
Nor.— *Hurra*, to whirl round, to swing round. S. *Hurr*, hurry. S. *Hurre*, to hum, to buzz [as a sling stone]. DN.
Co. & Celt.—*Ire*, progress. GI.
A-S.—*Earh*, swift.
O.E.—*Horien*, to hurry. *Eyre*, a journey, a circuit.
E.—Hurry, to hasten, urge on. See also *Ara*, to hurry. Hurri-cane, swift driving storm: Hurri-cane-deck. Hurl, to throw, to whirl: Hurl-ed, Hurl-er, Hurl-ing, Hurl-ey, Hurly-Burly. Urge, to impel, drive on, press forward: Urg-ency, Urgent, Urg-ently. Whir, Whirl, rapid turning, rapid revolution or curving: whirl-er, whirl-igig, whirl-ing, whirl-pool, whirl-wind.

ER, ERI

Su.—**ER, ERI**, Seize, bind, fetter, rob, against. Pictured by the foregoing Sling Sign. 5384-6, 5392, B.229. And see *Ari*, Hurry.
Ak.—*Ana*, against, unto. 64. *Kamū*, seize, bind, lead, capture. 392. *Habatu*, rob, plunder, carry away. 303.
Eg.—*Hurā*, to rob, plunder. 473a. *Hurā*, "robber," a name of a devil. 473a.
Gr.—(*Euro-s*, the tempestuous S.E. wind).
Lat.—*Heurt-er*, to run against. F. *Urt-are*, to hit or dash against. I.
Goth. & Anc. Br.—*Aer*, furious. EI. *Jara*, war, battle. EI.
Co. & Celt.—*Hyrddu*, to impel, butt, ram. Cy.
O.E.—*Hirten*, to dash against, to injure.
E.—Hurt, to cause damage bodily or wound the feelings: Hurt-er, Hurt-ful, Hurt-fully, Hurt-fulness, Un-hurt. Hurtle, to dash against. And see *Ari*, harry.

ER

Su.—**ER**, Her, hers, pron. possessive and objective of She. M.3719, B.229.
Ak.—*Shā*, she, her, hers (also, he, his). 992.
Eg.—*Sa*, a woman (also a man) (from Akkad). 583a.
Sk.—*Sa*, she (from Akkad).
A-S.—*Hire*, her.
O.E.—*Here, Hire*, her.
E.—Her, pron. possessive and objective of She—see WPOB.412. She, from the Akkad, *Shā*, she.

ER, ERI, URU

Su.—**ER, ERI, URU**, City, fortified city. 889, B.39. See *Uru*, city.
Ak.—*Ālu*, fortified city. 38.

ERIDU

Su.—**ERIDU** (-*Ga*), Paradise-city of the Chaldeans, and centre of the Lunar cult of the Mother-goddess Ishtar and her son Tammuz, and of Ea as the god of the sea. Supposed to be at the modern Abu Shahrein in the Lower delta of Mesopotamia. It is defined in 2649 as "The City of Heaven (*Du*, 8233)" or "The City of the Flood (*Dug*, 8232)." 2645, 2649, 8219, B.353. And see *Arata*, the Earth.
Ak.—*Eridu*. 98.
Goth. & Anc. Br.—*Jörd, Iörd* or *Iörth*, the Earth, and especially the home of the matriarch Serpent-priestess. *Jörd, Frigg* or *Gol*, the wife of Wodan, the enemy of Thor in the Eddas.
E.—*Jörd* or *Iörd*, the home of the matriarch Serpent-priestess, *Jörd, Frigg* or *Gol*, the wife of Wodan and arch-enemy of King Thor and his solar cult in the Eddas.

ERIM

Su.—**ERIM**, Enemy and the Sea as Chaos—the original enemy in the Babylonian cosmology. Pictures a Fire-torch and the Bow sign presumably indicating the Enemy as The Archer of Fire-bolts. 4603-4, 4608 and cp. M.845 for "Bow." PSL.105. And see *Ari*, enemy.
Ak.—*Aibu*, enemy. 4. *Tamtim*, the sea or chaos. 1173.
Eg.—*Heru* (or *Kheru*), enemy. 561a. *Hermuti*, a form of *Apap*, the great Serpent enemy. 562b.
Sk.—*Aryman*, the Devil as the Enemy. *Ahriman*, as the devil or enemy in the Sun-worship of Zoroaster. Z.
Lat.— *Vermis*, a worm.
Goth. & Anc. Br.—*Orm*, the great Serpent or

"Worm," the She-Devil of Midgerd in the Eddas.
A-S.—*Earm, Airn,* miserable. *Irminge,* wretchedly. *Irming-sul, Armen-sula,* a Saxon idol. *Irming-strœt,* Erming Street.
O.E.—*Orme,* the great Serpent of the Deep.
E.—*Ahriman* or "Old Harry," the Devil as the Enemy. And see *Ari,* enemy. *Erming* Street, one of the so-called Roman roads, seems named after a "Saxon" idol of a presumably malignant deity or devil *Irming-sul* (*sul* in A-S.="plough"), and in part of its course it is called "The Devil's causeway." *Harm,* injury and its comps. See *Ar,* enemy.

ERIM, ZAB

Su.—**ERIM, ZAB,** Army, soldier, warrior. Pictured by the Lightning sign. 8139, 8170, B.347. And see *Zab,* soldier.
Ak.—*Sābū,* soldier, warrior. 851. *Ummānu,* men, people, army. 58. *Pahāru,* assemble, collect, of men. 795.
Eg.—*Zaba,* soldiers, a host, an army. 897b. from the Akkad *Sābū,* or Sumerian synonym, *Zab,* soldier.
Sk.—*Sipāhī* or "Sepoy," a soldier. IP.—From the Akkad, *Sābū.*
Lat.—*Arm-are,* to arm, to furnish with weapons (*Arma*). *Spahi,* Algerian horse-soldier. F.—From Akkad, *Sābū.*
Goth. & Anc. Br.—*Hermod,* a mail-armoured prince in the Eddas.
O.E.—*Armee,* an army.
E.—Army, a large body of men armed for war: Army-corps, Army-list. Armada, an armed fleet. Arms, Fire-arms, Arm-our, Arm-ory. Armistice, a short suspension of hostilities. *Sepoy,* an Indian and Persian soldier, and *Spahi,* Algerian horse-soldier, from the Akkad *Sābū* or Sumerian synonym *Zab,* a soldier like the Egyptian. ? *Homo,* man and Human and their compounds, from the Akkad, *Ummānu,* men, people.

ERIN

Su.—**ERIN,** Cedar-tree. It is styled by the Assyrians "Darling of the great gods," "The tree of the enclosure" (*Giš-Immaru*—a name also applied to the Date-palm) and by other titles. Neither the Cedar nor Cypress is native to Mesopotamia. 10,803-4, M.8308, MD.103, B.486.
Ak.—*Erinu,* Cedar-tree. 103.
Eg.—(*Heriaa-dadd,* sacred tree. 496a).
Sk.—(*Hari-dru,* the sacred cedar or Deo-dār—"Tree of the gods." *Pinus deodara*).
Goth. & Anc. Br.—*Iārn, Jārn,* a tree or grove of such trees at the well of the weird of Urd, the Serpent-priestess Jörd and her Magic Bowl or cauldron.
E.—*Iārn,* tree and grove at the site of the well of the weird of Urd and her Magic Bowl, in the Eddas. The Cypress probably derived its n. from *Cypris,* a title of Venus.

ERU

Su.—**ERU,** Woman, maid-servant, slave. 3658-60, 3675-6, B.134.
Ak.—*Amat,* maid. PBP.13. *Amtu,* maid, maid-servant, slave. 62. *Zimištu,* a woman. *Abdu,* a servant. 5.
Eg.—*Hamt,* a woman, a wife (? from Akkad, *Amtu*). 481a.
Sk.—*Hūrī,* nymph of paradise. IP.
Gr.—*Erōs,* love.
Goth. & Anc. Br.—*Hōra,* courtesan. EI.
Co. & Celt.—*Hōr, Hora, Hoar,* a miss, a sister. Co.
O.E.—*Hore,* harlot.
E.—Whore, har-lot. Houri, nymph of paradise. Ero-tic, amorous.

ERU, ERŪA

Su.—**ERU, ERŪA** (*Aš-* or *An*), The Lady Erūa, styled The Shining goddess, The Progenitress, a title of the queen-consort of Bēl (and later of Mar-duk). She is also called *Laxamun* (1014), i.e., *Laxmī* or *Lakshmī,* the goddess of Prosperity of the Sanskrit. 5855-6, B.448.
Ak.—*Zarpanitu,* the shining goddess, the progenitress. 295, 894.
Eg.—*Heri(t),* goddess of Heaven, a form of Nut. 469a.
Sk.—*Hārītī,* a n. of the mother-goddess, in Buddhist literature. *Laxmī* or *Lakshmī,* goddess of Luck and Prosperity, from her other Sumerian synonym.
Gr.—*Hēra,* queen of Heaven and w. of Zeus.
E.—*Hēra,* the Roman Juno, wife of Zeus or Jupiter and queen of Heaven, and meaning of the name as given by the Sumerians who coined it. *Laxmi* or *Lakshmī,* Indian goddess of Good Luck, from her other Sumerian synonym.

EŚ

Su.—**EŚ,** House, a habitation, a temple. 3817, 6238, with value *Eš,* cp. 3817, B.147. And see WPOB.74, 412. Pict. as in Egypt, pl. III.
Ak.—*Es,* house. P. (See WPOB.74 f.). *Bātu,* a house, habitation, a temple. 202.
Eg.—*Hez,* a house. 523. *Ys, As,* abode, room, palace. 79b., 81b. Hiero. as in Sumer, pl. III.
Sk.—*Vāsa,* a house, abode.
Gr.—(*Oikos,* a house).
Goth. & Anc. Br.—*Hŭs,* house. EI. *Hus,* house. U.
Nor.—*Hus,* house. DNS.
Ger.—*Haus,* house.
Co. & Celt.—*Hoose,* house. S.

A-S.—*Hās*, house.
O.E.—*Hūs*, a house.
E.—House, a building for dwelling in: Housing, House-agent, House-boat, House-breaker, House-breaking, House-duty, House-factor, House-flag, House-fly, House-hold, House-holder, House-keeper, House-less, House-maid, House-surgeon, House-physician, House-warming, House-wife, Huss-if, House-hold word, House-hold gods, House-hold troops.

EŚ

Su.—EŚ, plural suffix of verbs, etc., literally = Much, double, repeat. The plural sign is pictured by three crescents or three strokes. 9984, 9995, 11,897, B.432, 539, LSG.225, and see *Ene*. N.B.—The three crescent signs here are identical in value with three strokes. See WPOB.243 f. and for representation of the signs and their equivalency, WISD.89 f.
Ak.—*Ma'duti*, much. *Salalti*, three (i.e., a plural number). *Śunu*, them, cognate with *Śanū*, a second, double, repeat. 1066 f.
Gr.— *-es*, plural suffix.
Lat.— *-es*, plural suffix.
A-S.—*as* or *s*, plural suffix.
O.E.—*es* or *s*, plural suffix.
E.— *-es* and *s*, plural suffix. ? *Us*, the objective case of *I* plural or *we*.

EŚ

Su.—EŚ, adverbial suffix as, like as, as much as. 10,001, B.432.
Ak.— *-iś*=*kīma*, adverbial suffix, as, like as, as much as. 109.
Eg.—*As*, to wit, that is (="as"). 79*b*.
Goth. & Anc. Br.— *-es* "as" relative pronoun and adverbial suffix in older MSS. of E.
O.E.—*As*, *Als*, as.
E.—As, relative pronoun, with sense of that, e.g., "Take the box *as* stands in the fire-place." As, conj. and adverb that is, to wit, like as, as many as, as for example.

EŚA

Su.—EŚA, Water of the Forest. 11,581, PSL.95. And see *Ega*, Dark water.
Eg.—*As*(*t*), running water. 9*b*. *Ig*, a stream, a flood. 95*b*.
Gr.—? *Isca* or *Isca-mauder*, river of Troy.
Lat.—*Isca*, n. of several rivers and towns in Britain.
Goth. & Anc. Br.—*Isca*, n. for *Esk*, rivers in Britain as recorded by the Romans. *Veisa*, a pool of stagnant water. I.
Co. & Celt.—*Isge*, water. Co. *Usig*, water. G.
O.E.—*Esk*, *Ex*, etc., river-names.
E.—Esk, Ex, Axe and Ouse, river-names in Britain. See WPOB.173 f., 198, 208.

EŚHA

Su.—EŚHA (*Aś-* or *An-*), A title of the goddess Ishtar as "Lady of the House of the Fishes" or Ocean. See *Aś* and *Eussa*.

ETIL

Su.—ETIL, Lord, ruler, regent, king. Pictured by a spear or arrow-head as sceptre. 1506 and Haupt. B.70.
Ak.—*Etillu*, lord, ruler, regent, king. 130.
Eg.—*Yti*, *Yt*, king, sovereign, suzerain prince. 97*a*.
Goth. & Anc. Br.—*Œthl*, *Othal*, *Œdl*, *Ŏdal*, prince, noble. EI. *Ethli*, noble birth. EI. *Ŏthal*, *Ŏdal*, patrimony in landed property of prince or nobles held from king free of duty. I. and Norway. *Ŏthl-ing* or *Ŏthl* clan, the clan of King Thor in Eddas allied to the Yngl-ings.
Nor.—*Ædel*, *Œdel*, noble. DN.
Ger.—*Edel*, *Adel*, noble, nobility.
Co. & Celt.—*Adletha*, a soldier. Co.
A-S.—*Æthele*, a noble. *Ethele*, ruler, governor. *Edel*, patrimony. *Æthel-ing*, the son of a king, a prince, heir-apparent, one of the royal blood, a nobleman next in rank to the king.
E.—Ethel-ing, an Anglo-Saxon crown-prince or premier, noble. *Odal* (transposed by legal Latinists into "Allodium"), freehold landed estate held not subject to any feudal superior, having been originally *royal* or crown land. Edel-weiss or "Noble-white," a high alpine plant. *Athel*, *Attle*, *Adel*, etc., in place-names: Athel-ney, or "Royal or Nobles' island," in Somersetshire, the reputed residence of King Alfred, Attle-bury in Norfolkshire, Adel, Addle-stone, Adeles-trop, Audley, Edale, Otley, Watl-ington, etc. Watl-ing Street or Royal road, an Ancient Briton Pre-Roman road. See WPOB.182 f., 191 f., 198; 205 f., 399 f., 409.

EUSSI, EIZI

Su.—EUSSI, EIZI, Seeing, the going forth of Daylight—the Dawn or East. Pictured by the Sun and a Foot and a Fire-torch. 7894-5. And see *E*, The going forth of the Sun and *Ussa*, to burn, to shine. The Dawn goddess was called by the Sumerians *Aida* (7886 and cp. 7929), i.e., the Mother-goddess Ishtar.
Ak.—*Bar-du* ("Vaśdu"), defined as *Uru-bara aṣū* or "Daylight, behold the going forth." *Paru Śame-i*, the bursting through the sky of glory. (Cp. *I*=glory, M.2630).
Eg.—*Yhez*, *Ahez*, to dawn (of the Sun). 77*a*. (*Ya-bt*, the East. 18*b*., wherein the letter *b* is the Foot hieroglyph. And this Egyptian "East" hieroglyph pictures a torch, cp. GH.p.61). *Astariat*, *Asthareth*, *Asthert*, the goddess Ashtireth, Astarte or Ishtar. 136*b*.
Sk.— *Ushas*, the dawn. *Ej*, to shine.

Gr.—*Ēōs*, the dawn, and the personified goddess of the Dawn, the sister of Helios, the Sun.
Goth. & Anc. Br.—*Aust*, the East.
Nor.—*Öst*, east. DN. *Östan*, east. S. *Ausz-ra*, the East. L.
Ger.—*Ost*, east.
Co. & Celt.—*Astor, Ach*, issue, bring forth. Co.
A-S.—*Eāst*, east. *Eāstore*, n. of a Saxon goddess whose festival was at the Vernal Equinox (Easter).
O.E.—*Est*, east.
E.—East, the quarter of Sunrise: East-end, East-ern, East-erly, East-ernmost, East-land, East-ward, The East. Easter, the Vernal Equinox, now a Christian spring festival commemorating the rising of Christ, but formerly it was the festival of the goddess *Eāstore* (Ishtar), the pagan Saxon goddess of Reproduction, of the Dawn and the Morning Star (Venus), which was held at the Vernal Equinox, about 21st March—the ancient New Year of the Agricultural calendar of Ancient Britain, as with the Sumerians. This New Year old style (or Easter) continued in England till 1752, when the New Year was changed by Act of Parliament to 1st January in accordance with the Gregorian calendar. Ishtar (Astarte), Mother-goddess of the Dawn, etc. See *Aś*, Lady *Aś* or *Ash*.

EWIR
Su.—**EWIR**, Vessel for water, wine, etc.—a Ewer. Pictured by a jar with a spout and handle. M.3477, B.217. And note that the alphabetic letter *W* is used in the Sumerian spelling of this word.
Ak.—*Kanna*, a vessel for water, wine, etc. 406.
Eg.—*Yrr*, a wine-jar. 72a. *Yrrp(t)*, a wine-cup. 72b.
Gr.—? *Arutēr*, a cup or ladle for taking up liquids.

Lat.—*Urna*, a vase, urn. *Verre*, a drinking-glass, a wine-glass. F.
Goth. & Anc. Br.—*Hver*, a wine or drinking vessel. EI.
O.E.—*Ewer*, a water-jug.
E.—*Ewer*, a water-jug. ? Urn, a rounded vessel or vase having a foot, a water-vessel: Tea-urn. Can, a vessel, from the Akkad *Kannu*, a vessel for water, wine, etc.

EXI, EKHI
Su.—**EI, EKHI**, Exit, going out or forth, product, offshoot, offspring. B.6611-13, PSL.97. And see *E*, rise, go out.
Ak.—*Situ*, exit, march out, departure, product, offspring. 898. *Tarbūtu*, offspring. 1190.
Eg.—*Aq(t)*, exit. 138b. *Ys, As*, make haste (from ?). 9b, 82b.
Sk.—*Ech*, go, hasten.
Gr.—*Ek, Ex*, out, from out of, off, away.
Lat.—*Ex*, out of, from. *Ex-eo*, to go out. *Issue*, to go out of. F. *Oster*, to remove. F.
Goth. & Anc. Br.—*Yis, Œs, Asi*, hasten. EI. *Ausu*, to sprinkle. EI.
Ger.—*Aus*, out, out of.
Co. & Celt.—*Aus*, out. Co. *Ach*, issue, offspring, root of a tree. Co.
O.E.—*Exit*, exit. *Issue*, issue.
E.—Exit, outgoing, departure: Exeunt. Issue, to go, flow or come out, progeny, product: Issu-able, Issu-er, Issue-less, At issue, General issue, Special issue, Immaterial issue, Material issue, etc., Isthmus. Oust, to eject, expel. *Ex-, Ec-*, and *Es-*, very numerous prefixes in words: Ec-centric, Ec-clesiastic, Ec-lectic, Ec-lipse, Ec-logue, Ec-stasy and Es-cape, Es-cheat, Es-chew, Es-cort, Es-planade, etc., Ex-act, Ex-aggerate, Ex-alt, Ex-amine, Ex-ample, Ex-cavate, Ex-ceed, Ex-cel, Ex-odus, etc., etc. And see *E-*, prefix "out."

F

This letter is found in most Aryan alphabets, but has not been previously recognized in Sumerian where the sign in question has been rendered *Pi*. The evidence for its *F* value in Sumerian is detailed in my work on *The Aryan Origin of the Alphabet*. Only a few of the more obvious *F* Sumerian root-words are cited here.

FI, PI, SIR
Su.—**FI, PI, SIR**, Serpent, bite, burn, afflict, a rope—Viper, Fiend. Pictures a Viper with two horns. 7506-7, 7523, 7529, 7536, M.5536, B.325. And cp. 5524 (B.242) and PSL.270, where the definition *ga-pi* is rendered "the one who causes lamentation." Its *Sir*, synonym evidently=*Sir*, serpent. 7638-9.
Ak.—*Naśāhu*, bite. *Sarāpu*, burn. *Sanāqu*, afflict *Murkas*, a rope. (*Siru*, serpent, snake. 891).
Eg.—*Fi, Fy*, the snake, Cerastes. G.25. Pictured by a two-horned viper. *Fai*, a mythological serpent. 259b. *Fau*, a serpent or worm. 23b, 259b. *If, Vf, Af*, a viper, a serpent. 43b. *Hefa(t)*, a viper. 479b. *Fāu*, evil, wicked. 260a. *Fi!* to feel disgust. 258a.
Sk.—*Phani*, a serpent. ? *Visha*, poison.

Gr.—*Ophis*, a serpent, a snake.
Lat.—*Vipera*, a viper. L. and I. *Vipère*, a viper. F. *Vilis*, vile. ? *Virus*, poison. *Fée*, an elf or fairy. F.
Goth. & Anc. Br.—*Feig*, a fey or one fated to die. EI. *Fiăndi*, a hater, an enemy. EI. *Fijands*, a fiend. U.
Nor.—*Vieg*, a fey. DN. *Fiende*, a hater, an enemy. DNS.
Ger.—*Feind*, a fiend.
Co. & Celt.—*Wyber*, a serpent. Co.
A-S.—*Fiŏnd, Feŏnd*, a hater, enemy. *Fæge*, doomed to die.
O.E.—*Uivera*, a viper, a snake. *Fend*, an enemy, a hater. *Fy! Fie!* exclamation of disgust.
E.—Viper, a poisonous snake of the *Viperidæ* or Adder family : Vip-erine, Vip-erish, Vip-erous. Fey, an elf, a fairy in its bad sense. *Fey*, doomed to die. ? Fie ! exclamation of disgust (see the Egyptian, para. 3). Fiend, an enemy, a hater, the Devil, Fiend-ish, Fiend-ishness. Venom, poison, spite, malice, see *Bana*, hostile. Vile, evil, hateful, Vil-ifier Vil-ify. *Virus*, poison : Vir-ulently, Vir-ulent. *Wy-vern*, in heraldry, a kind of flying serpent or two-legged dragon.

FID, BID, BIAD, PID

Su.—**FID, BID, BIAD, PID,** See, perceive, consider or believe—Faith, View. Pictured by an Eye. 9258, B.406. On *Bid* or *Biad*, value, cp. 9257, 5119 and 103. And see *Bid*, *Bad, Si*, see, perceive.
Ak.—*Amaru*, see, behold, declare, consider. 59. *Si*, see *Idu*, know, perceive. 17.
Eg.—*Petr*, to see, look, reveal, declare. 253*b*, 254*a*. *Petr-iu*, those who have sight, those who see. 254*a*.
Sk.—*Vid*, to know. *Viśvas*, faith.
Gr.—*Fidō*, old Greek for *Eidō*, to see, to know. *Peith-ein*, persuade.
Lat.—*Vid-ere*, to see, know, perceive, consider. *Fides*, faith. *Ved-ere*, to view. I. *Fede*, faith. *Vue*, view. F.
Goth. & Anc. Br.—*Vita*, to see, know, understand. *Vit*, wit, understanding, opinion. *Witan*, to see, to know.
Nor.—*Vide*, know. DN. *Vidne*, witness. DNS.
Ger.—*Wissen*, knowledge.
Co. & Celt.—*Fyth*, faith. Co. *Fidir*, know, consider. GI.
A-S.—*Wittan*, to know, understand, consider.
O.E.—*Feith, Feyth*, faith. *Wit*, understanding. *Wot*, know.
E.—Faith, belief, trust in others and in what is considered to be the Truth : Faith-ful, Faith-fulness, Faith-healing, Faith-less, Faith-less-ness, Faith-worthy, The Faith-ful. View, a seeing, belief : View-able, View-er, View-finder, View-less, View-y, Re-view, etc. Wit, to know.

FIL, PIL, BIL, PI

Su.—**FIL, PIL, BIL, PI**, Flame, blaze, burn, Pictured by a Fire-torch. 4566, 4575-6, 4589. M.3100, 3136, B.185-6. See *Bil, Pil*, Blaze, flame and *Pir*, Fire.
Ak.—*La'bu*, flame. 465. *Nablu*, flame, fire, glow. 637. *Qalū*, burn. 912.
Eg.—*Pā'h*, flame, fire, spark. 234*a*.
Sk.—*Bahula*, fire.
Gr.—*Phlegō*, to flame, blaze up, kindle. *Phlegma*, a flame, fire, heat. *Phlox*, flame.
Lat.—*Flamma*, flame. L. and I. *Feu*, fire. F. *Flagr-āre*, to burn.
Goth. & Anc. Br.—*Bāl*, a flame and a pyre. EI. *Blys*, a torch. EI.
Nor.—*Flara*, to blaze. DN. *Flasa*, to blaze. S. *Blus*, a torch. DN.
Ger.—*Flamme*, flame, blaze.
Co. & Celt.—*Bil, Bel, Beal*, fire. Co. *Beal-time*, fires, lighted to Beltus. Co. *Bêl*, fire, festival. GIS. *Bleeze*, blaze. S.
O.E.—*Flame*, a flame. *Flayre*, a flare.
E.—Flame, a blaze : Flam-ing, Flam-beau, In-flame, In-flamm-able, In-flamm-ation, In-flamm-atory, Flam-ingo, a flame-coloured bird, Flam-en, a priest of ancient Rome for burnt offerings. Flag-rant, glar-ing, glow-ing, Flag-rance, Flag-rancy. Flare, to blaze up, burn brightly : Flar-ing, Flar-ingly. Flash, to blaze up suddenly : Flash-ily, Flash-ing, Flash-iness, Flash-y. Phlogiston, a supposititious element formerly imagined to cause flame and fire, from Gr. *Phlegō*, to flame. Blaze, see *Bil*, to blaze, boil.

FIR, PIR, BIR, BAR

Su.—**FIR, PIR, BIR, BAR**, Fire, burn, bright, light, shining. Pictured by the crossed Fire-stick, by the Sun and by Lightning. 1724, 1744-5, 1810, 7764, 7798, 8141, 8147, M.998, 5747, 5758, B.77 (Fire-sticks), 337 (Sun) and 347 (Lightning). On the Crossed Fire-sticks for fire-production by friction with description and signs. See WPOB.271, 291 f.
Ak.—*Nūru*, fire, light. *Bararu*, shine. *Birratu, Ellu*, brightness. *Titaltu*, flame. *Urru*, light.
Eg.—*Pā'h*, fire, flame, spark. 234*a*. *Bar*, shine, sunrise. 242*a*. *Bar-ga*, give light. 204*b*.
Sk.—*Barhis*, fire, bright, splendour. *Bhraj*, bright. *Pra-jaś*, shine, illumine.
Gr.—*Pyr*, fire. *Phr-ygō*, roast, fry.
Lat.—*Fer-uare*, be hot, glow. *Fer-vor*, heat, raging heat. *For-nax*, a furnace, oven. *Fri-re*, to fry. F.
Goth. & Anc. Br.—*Fyre, Fŭrr*, fire. EI. *Biart*, bright. EI. *Varm*, warm. EI. *Biarmi*, beaming. I. *Baer*, hearth. I. *Friŏ*, fry. EI. *Bairths*, bright. U.

Nor.—*Fyr*, fire. DNS. *Varm*, warm. DNS. *Frō*, fry. DNS.
Ger.—*Fauer*, fire. *Warm*, warm.
Co. & Celt.—*Forn*, oven, furnace. Co. *Fria, Fryā*, fry. Co. *Frio*, fry. Cy. *Par-et*, baked. Co. *Brwd*, warm. Cy.
A-S.—*Fyr, Fir, Fyryne*, a fire. *Wearm*, warm.
O.E.—*Fyr*, fire. *Bright*, bright. *Warm*, warm. *Frie*, fry.
E.—Fire, light and heat of flame or burning: Fier-y, Fire-alarm, Fire-arms, Fire-brand, Fire-brick, Fire-brigade, Fire-bucket, Fire-clay, Fire-damp, Fire-eater, Fire-engine, Fire-escape, Fire-fly, Fire-guard, Fire-irons, Fire-lighter, Fire-lock, Fire-man, Fire-pan, Fire-place, Fire-plug, Fire-policy, Fire-pot, Fire-proof, Fire-proofing, Fire-screen, Fire-side, Fire-stick, Fire-water, Fire-wood, Fire-works, Fire-worship, Fire-worshipper, New Fire festival of New Year and after plagues. Fer-vent, fiery, ardent, hot: Fer-vently, Fer-vid, Fer-vidity, Fer-vour, Per-fer-vid. Fry, to cook in a pan over the fire: Fry-ing, Fry-ing-pan, Fri-cassee, Fri-tters, Fri-tterer. Fur-nace, enclosed fire-place, oven. Parch, scorch, dry: Parch-ed, Parch-edness. Pyre, pile of firewood for cremation. War-m, hot: Warm-blooded: Warm-er, Warm-hearted, Warm-ing, Warm-ly, Warm-ness or Warmth, Warm-bath, Foot-warmer, House-warming. Brand, Bright and Burn, words, see *Bar*, Burn, bright. On the Fire-sticks for producing sacred fire for Sun-worship in Britain, etc., see WPOB. refs. in para. 1.

FIRIQ, PIRIQ

Su.—**FIRIQ, PIRIQ**, Frightful, wild beast, grief, kill, destroy. Pictured by the head of a Wolf or Lion. 9182, 9189, M.6908, 6912, 6918, 6923, B.400.
Ak.—*Umāmu*, a wild beast. 58. *Ūmu*, a beast, a lion. 54. *Labbu*, a lion. 466 (? also Wolf, *lupus*). *Nissatu*, grief. *Birqi*, lightning flash. 193. *Nēru*, strike down, kill, destroy. 720.
Eg.—*Barga, Burga*, to lighten, illumine, glow, sparkle. 204b, 215b. (Cp. Akkad, *Birqi*, lightning flash).
Sk.—*Vrikī*, a she-wolf. *Vrika*, a wolf, a dog, a thunderbolt. *Vrajyā*, march, attack, invasion. *Vrij*, to pluck, remove. (*Vājra*, a lightning bolt, the Sun, cp. Akkad, *Birqi*).
Lat.—*Ferox*, fierce. *Frig-uare*, to whine. *Briga*, strife, quarrel. I. *Brig-are*, to quarrel, fight. I. *Brigante*, robber, intriguer. I.
Goth. & Anc. Br.—*Freki*, a wolf. EI. *Freka, Frekia*, hardship. EI. *Frek*, greedy, bold. EI. *Faurhtei*, fright. U.
Nor.—*Frygt*, fright. DN. *Fruktan*, fright. S. *Fræk*, bold. DN. *Vilkas*, a wolf. L.
Ger.—*Furcht*, fright. *Frech*, bold, impudent.
Co. & Celt.—*Frehez*, vexed. Co. *Blaid*, a wolf. Co.
A-S.—*Fric*, a devourer. *Fræc*, bold, vile. *Fyrhtu*, fright.
O.E.—*Fryzt*, fright. *Fers*, fierce. *Brigander*, rob, thieve.
E.—Fright, terror: Fright-en, Fright-ful, Fright-fully, Fright-fulness, Af-fright, Af-frighted. Fierce, violent, angry: Fierce-ly, Fierce-ness, Feroc-ious, Feroc-ity, and see *Bar*, savage and *Bar*, break. Brig-and, robber, Pirate and plunderer, freebooter: Brig-andage. Prig, a thief, to filch or steal: Prig-ger, Prig-ging, Prig-gish. Lion (*Leo*), from the Akkad *Labbu*, a lion, which is probably, I think, also the source of *Lupus*, a wolf, as the Sumerians called the Lion "The great Dog," and the Wolf is the parent of the Dog or domesticated Wolf.

FIRIQ, PIRIQ

Su.—**FIRIQ, PIRIQ** (*An*-), Lady (or Lord), *Firiq* or *Piriq*; and Firiq-gi (*Gal*- or *Gulu*-), "The Maid Lady *Firiq*," defined as "The bearer of the (Magic) Drinking or Wine Jug or Bowl" i.e., *Frigg* or *Gol* or *Jörd* of the Eddas with her Magic Wine-Bowl of Urd, see *Dur*. Two male *Firiqs* or *Piriqs* are also recorded with the titles of "Lord (or god) *Firiq*" of the lightning flash and The prince of the *Gid* or Caduceus (9194, and see WPOB.239, 245 f. for representation of the latter personage on Sumerian seals). The names of these *Firiq* personages are pictured by the Wolf's or Lion's head of the previous word-sign plus the sign for Lord, Lady, god, king or queen. 9190, 9194-5. In Lady *Firiq's* title *Gi*,=maid (*Amtu*, cp. Meisn. 590).
Ak.—*Bēl* or *Šarru* (*amtu*), *šāqqu-guku*, the maid Queen of the Wine jug or bowl—a title of *Tiamat*, the she-serpent queen of the Deep. Cp. 1100 and 1097-9. *Il Nergal sa birqi*, the god of the lightning flash. 193. *Il Šamaś*, the Sun-god.
Eg.—*Berqer*, a fiend named in magic. 219b. *Parhaga* (-*khepem* or spirit), the consort of Sekhmit Baet Rā. 232a. (*Reshpiu*, the Lightning god? 433b).
Gr.—*Phryag-ma*, a wanton, insolent.
Lat.—*Virago*, a female warrior, an Amazon.
Goth. & Anc. Br.—*Frigg, Freka*, the Serpent-wolf, priestess and weird of Urd and its Magic Bowl, wife of Wodan and mother of the Fen Wolf. EI. *Friggiae stiarna*, Frigg's star or Venus. I. *Valkyr*, the virago weirds and war harpies of Wodan in E. *Frija-dag*, Friday. I.
Co. & Celt.—*Brigit*, a prehistoric goddess in Ireland. I.
A-S.—*Frig, Friga*, the Saxon Venus and wife

of Wodan (Odin). *Frigu*, love. *Frig-dæg*, Frig's day or Friday. *Walcrigge*, Saxon goddess of War.

E.—Brigit, a tutelary goddess of the Irish, and latterly (or her namesake) was canonized in the Christian calendar as St. Brigit, Brigid or Bridget. Frigg, title of *Jŏrd* or *Gol*, the matriarch Serpent-priestess or weird of the Magic Bowl or Holy Grail of Urd, wife of Wodan, and mother of the Fen Wolf who was the leader of the Wolf (cult) -tribe against King Thor with his sun-cult and Patriarchy in the Eddas. Valkyries, the virago and weird war-harpies or hounds of Wodan and maids of Frigg. This name seems to be a cognate of Frigg and Virago by the common dialectic change of *l* for *r*, rather than a derivative from *Val* or *Wal*, "slaughter" or *Val* or *Wal*, "choose," especially as the rest of the word so divided, namely *Kyr* or *Kyrra*, means "calm," which is wholly inapplicable to the Valkyries. Virago, a violent angry vixen woman, an Amazon of the Athene type. Friday, the Anglo-Saxon *Frig-dæg* or Frig's day, named after Frig or Frigg whom the Anglo-Saxons adopted as their Venus.

FIRIQ-FIRIQ, PIRIQ-PIRIQ or TIANU

Su.—FIRIQ-FIRIQ, PIRIQ-PIRIQ or TIANU (Mad-), The Western Lands or Ammuru Lands, or Land of the Muru, Marutu or Amorites. It is also defined as "The Behind" or Hinter Land (*re* the Sunrise in Mesopotamia). Pictured by the foregoing Lion or Wolf's head doubled or with the plural sign. 9220-1, B.400. N.B.—The Egyptian form of this name "*Pairqa*, foreign land," bears also the same plural sign prefixed to it, which is the equivalent of the doubling of the Wolf or Lion head-sign in the Sumerian. And the Egyptian also possesses the "*Tianu*" synonym for this *Piriq*, a name hitherto read "Tidnu." The idea of Lions and Wolves as a designation of the Western Land may have been suggested by the Lions and Wolves infesting Upper Egypt at Thinis (the early capital of Menes—Egypt being *West* of Mesopotamia) as well as infesting the coast lands of Lybia (? *Labbu*, a Lion and *Lupus*, a Wolf), Tunis (*Tann*=Wolf in Heb.) and Mauretania, which, along with the Cornish Tin mines and the British Isles with their prehistoric inscribed megaliths, and Asia-Minor and Syrio-Phœnicia-Palestine, formed, as I have shown, "The Western Land of the Morites or Amorites." See WPOB. 13, 160 f., 167-71, 183, 190, 216 f., 224-5, 257-8, 412 f., with illustrations of monuments and decipherment of inscriptions.

Ak.—*Māt Ammuru*, Land of the Muru, Martu, Murutu or Amorites. Cp. 30. *Mātaharre*, the behind or Western Land. 30. ? *Tani(t)*, the tutelary goddess of the Phœnician Punics at Carthage. (*Tann*, a wolf in Hebrew).

Eg.—*Pairqa*-smt. 982b. The *Pairqa* foreign lands—see details under *Piriq-su*. *Berg*-smt. 877b. *Barg* foreign land. *Tennu*, the district of Abydos, ? the *Ta-a-a-ni* of the Assyrians. 1057a. Tennu (*Thinis* of the Greeks) was the early settlement of Menes (who, I find, was a Sumerian) on his arrival in Upper Egypt, which, along with the rest of Egypt was a "Western Land" in relation to Sumerian Mesopotamia. *Tehnu*, Libya. 1057a. *Tanis*, ancient city of Egypt in the Delta. Str.802. *Tanis*, city of the Thebaid. Str.813. *Tanitic*, name. Str.802. *Tanitic*, mouth of the Nile. Str.800 f.

Gr.—*Thinis* (*This*), capital of the Nome of Abydos in Upper Egypt. *Tynēs*, Tunis, the province of Carthage.

Lat.—*Tynes*, Tunis and its province.

E.—*Tianu*, ancient name for "The Western Land," of the Sumerians, "The Land of the Muru, Martu Murutu or Amorites." This land of the Amorites seems to have included Egypt, Syro-Phœnicia-Palestine and the southern Asia-Minor coast-land, as well as Libya, Tunis, Mauretania or Morocco, the Cornish Tin mines and the British Isles with their prehistoric inscribed monuments from about 3000 B.C. See evidence in WPOB. references cited in para. 1. And on the Amorites in the Indus Valley, about 3100 B.C., with their inscribed Sumerian seals with translations, see WISD.8 f., 43, 51 f., 91 f.

FIRIQ-SU, PIRIQ-SU

Su.—FIRIQ-SU, PIRIQ-SU (*Su-Uku-*), The Great *Firiq* or *Piriq* nation, also designated "The Mass or Multitude of People of *Firiq* Land" (*Firiq Kurra meś*)—The Phrygians. The name is written by the duplicated Wolf or Lion head-sign with the addition of the signs for "great" and "nation." 5915, 9224, M.6921, CIWA.IV.13, 28b and CT.2, 25, 11b.

Ak.—*Nēśu* (*piriq*), The *piriq*, nation. Cp. BW. p. 209. "*Pirkhi*" in the Amarna letter of King Duśratta, the Mitani (Mede) c. 1400 B.C. appears to be probably used in the sense of "The Phrygian."

Eg.—*Pairqa* smt. 982b or The Great *Pairqa*, foreign nation—see GH.31 for *smt* as "foreign tribe"; and the plural sign prefixed, *Ii* or *Aa*, probably = *āai*, great. (In BD. it is assumed to be a land, and as with unidentified lands generally, it is described as "a district in Syria, situation unknown"). *Barg* smt. 977b. *Barg*, foreign nation or country

(also described in BD. as "a district in Syria, situation unknown").
Sk.— *Vrici-vant, Muhā Vrici-vant,* "The Great Vrici nation." *Vrika,* people of the Middle Country. *Vriji,* great ruling people in Mid-India, who patronised Buddha.
Gr.— *Phryx,* a Phrygian.
Lat.— *Phryx,* a Phrygian. *Phryges,* Phrygians. *Phrygius,* a Phrygian or "a Trojan." *Phrygia,* Phrygia or Western Asia Minor, extending formerly from Cappadocia to the Hellespont.
Goth. & Anc. Br.— *Fiorgyn* or ? "The Phrygienne," a title of the mother of King Thor in the Eddas. *Feriokar* or ? "The Phrygian," a title of Wodan, the husband of Frigg. *Feriokar-lin* or "The Feriokar (or Phrygian) Serpent (cult-man)," a title of Wodan in the Eddas.
E.—Phrygia, an ancient division of Western Asia Minor, formerly extending from Cappadocia to the Hellespont, and presumably including Troy. Phrygian, a native of Phrygia, and occasionally used for "Trojan." King Thor's mother appears to have been a Phrygian lady, and Thor or Dor himself—the first traditional king of the Goths in the British and Norse *Edda* epics—appears also to have been a Phrygian or "Trojan." and we have seen his identity with Dar-danus the first Ayran king of Troy of Greek tradition—see *Dar.* The extremely remote historicity of the Phrygians as a great ruling Aryan-Amorite people is also disclosed.

FISH, PISH, BIESH

Su.—FISH, PISH, BIESH, Fish or Great Fish, also a title of The god of the Waters, and of the Sun. Pictured by a Fish with the sign for Great. 6925, 6928, 6933, 7224, B.303. See for representations on Sumerian, Hittite, Phœnician, Babylonian and Ancient Briton seals, amulets and monuments. WPOB.247, 251, 300, etc. and WISD.86 f.
Ak.— *Mam-lu,* mighty, the great *Pish,* a title of Ia (Jah), the Sun and Marduk. 553.
Eg.— *Fettu,* fish. 262b. *Bega,* a kind of fish. 225b.
Sk.— *Visāra,* a fish. *Vish-nu,* the Sun-god as a fish, see details with representations in WISD.83 f.
Gr.— *Pos-eidon* or "The likeness (*eidon*) of *Pos* (a Fish)." The Sun-god or Neptune, represented with the body and tail of a fish. See WISD.85, for his early representation.
Lat.— *Pis-cis,* a fish.
Goth. & Anc. Br.— *Fisk,* a fish. *Fisks,* a fish. U.
Nor.— *Fisk,* fish. DNS.
Ger.— *Fisch,* fish.
Co. & Celt.— *Pisch, Pesk, Pysga,* a fish. Co. Pysg. Cy. Pesk. Br. *Iasg,* fish. Gl.
A-S.— *Fisc,* a fish.
O.E.— *Fish, Fisch,* a fish.
E.—Fish, the gill-breathing vertebrate of water: Fish-ball, Fish-course, Fish-creel, Fish-day, Fish-er, Fish-erman, Fish-ery, Fish-hook, Fish-ing, Fish-ing boat, Fish-ing fleet, Fish-ing rod, Fish-ing tackle, Fish-kettle, Fish-market, Fish-monger, Fish-plate, Fish-pond, Fish-sauce, Fish-tail, Fish-torpedo, Fish-wife, Fish-y. Fish-, in place-names: Fish-bourne, Fish-er-gill, Fish-er-row, Fish-erwick, Fish-guard, Fish-house, etc. Pisces, the Fisher, a zodiacal sign: Pisc-ine, Pisc-ator, Pisc-atorial. *Piscina* or "Fish-pond," a basin or tank on the south side of the altar in old Christian churches—possibly a survival of the Sumero-Phœnician solar cult of the sacred Sun-Fish. *Poseidon,* or Likeness (*eidon*) of Pos (or Fish), a title of the sea-god Neptune represented with the body and tail of a fish. *Vish-nu,* the Sun-god of the Indo-Aryans as a Fish. See details and representations in WISD.81 f.

END OF PART I.